MASTERING AI

A SURVIVAL GUIDE TO OUR SUPERPOWERED FUTURE

JEREMY KAHN

SIMON & SCHUSTER

NEW YORK   LONDON   TORONTO   SYDNEY   NEW DELHI

For Victoria, Cordelia, and Gabriel

CONTENTS

INTRODUCTION:
AI'S LIGHT BULB MOMENT

They are called *light bulb moments*: the instant an idea materializes from the dark corners of the unconscious and assumes tangible, almost physical form. Individuals experience light bulb moments, and so do whole societies, moments of public realization that mark the borderline between one era and the next. Such moments occur when a technology is married to a device or software that people without any specialized knowledge can use, and which instantly gives them a new view of the future.

The light bulb itself sparked one such moment. On December 31, 1879, Thomas Edison flicked a switch in his lab in Menlo Park, New Jersey, and his incandescent light bulb illuminated a brave new world: one powered by electricity, not gas or steam. Inventors and scientists on both sides of the Atlantic had been racing one another for close to a decade to commercialize electric power. But many of their inventions were industrial, technical, esoteric. The light bulb was different. Here was a device everyone could hold and behold—and understand.

We've experienced a succession of light bulb moments around digital technology in the past three decades: the internet existed before the web browser, but it was only after the launch of Netscape Navigator in 1994 that the internet era truly dawned. There were MP3 players before the iPod debuted in 2001, but they didn't spark the digital music revolution. There were smartphones before Apple dropped the iPhone in 2007—but before the iPhone, there wasn't an app for that. On November 30, 2022, artificial intelligence had its light bulb moment. That's the day OpenAI debuted ChatGPT.

As a journalist, I have been covering artificial intelligence since 2016 and have watched as the technology made continual strides. AI has long been a topic of fascination among business executives and technologists, but before ChatGPT, it never quite made it to the center ring of public conversation. For those of us closely following the technology, progress seemed incremental. When ChatGPT debuted, I thought it would be yet another shuffle forward. After all, it didn't seem much different from an AI model called Instruct GPT that OpenAI had launched almost a year before. I had written about Instruct GPT. It was an important refinement of OpenAI's large language model GPT-3. Instruct GPT was easier to control through text-based instructions, or prompts, than GPT-3. It was less likely to produce racist, sexist, homophobic, or otherwise toxic content. And it could do many natural language tasks, from translation to summarization to coding. But Instruct GPT made not the barest ripple in the ocean of public discourse.

So when ChatGPT debuted, I was surprised by the surprise. I shouldn't have been. Form factors—or those interfaces, like Google's search bar, that we use to interact with a technology—matter. The Ford Model T was more than just an internal combustion engine and a set of wheels. And with its simple chatbot interface, OpenAI hit upon a winner. This was a light bulb moment for me too.

During most of the previous decade, AI's advance occurred in narrow domains. A number of the AI achievements I covered before ChatGPT involved software that could beat humans at games. Google's cutting-edge AI lab DeepMind created software called AlphaGo that triumphed over the world champion Lee Sedol at the ancient strategy game Go in March 2016. It was a seminal achievement in computer science: Go has so many possible move combinations that an algorithm cannot use brute calculation to analyze every one, as AI software can with chess. Instead, it has to act on probabilities, learned from games it has played, to decide which move is best. But games are just games. While they can be proxies for skills we would like an AI system to master, by their very nature games abstract away much of life's complexity. On a Go board, everything is literally black and white, and both players can see the position of every stone.

DeepMind later showcased an AI system that could beat the best human players at a complicated video game called *StarCraft II*, whose imaginary world bears a bit more resemblance to our own messy reality. OpenAI, the same AI research company that would later create Chat-GPT, built a team of AI-powered agents that could beat a team of human players at a fast-paced video game called *Dota 2*. But these were not light bulb moments. Too few people were familiar with *StarCraft II* or *Dota 2*. And the software that mastered these games could not be immediately applied to real life.

Before ChatGPT, AI tended to work its magic behind the curtain. It helped familiar products do stuff, like recommend a movie or tag a person in a photo on social media. These AI models were impressive, but they were not general-purpose technologies, and most people didn't consider the products they made possible AI. My editors would sometimes shrug when I'd suggest a story on one of these narrow AI advances, and, in retrospect, I don't blame them. This kind of AI seemed a far cry from the artificial intelligence we'd all seen in movies, the malevolent sentience of HAL 9000 in Stanley Kubrick's *2001: A Space Odyssey*, the benign *Star Trek* computer, or even the beguiling digital assistant in 2013's *Her*.

That started to change in 2018, when AI researchers began making rapid progress with large language models, the type of AI technology that ChatGPT is based on. Their advances showed that a sufficiently large AI system, trained only to predict words in a sentence, could be used for a variety of tasks, from translation to summarization to question-answering. Before, each of those capabilities would have required a different AI system. In the world of AI, this was a big deal, and I wrote about the potentially far-reaching impact on business for *Bloomberg* and then *Fortune*.

But even then, the technology was in the backend of existing software. Because it wasn't embodied in an easy-to-use, consumer-facing product, it was hard for most people—including many experts—to grasp just how much the world was about to change. This tendency to discount progress in AI has a name: the Tesler effect, coined for the computer scientist Larry Tesler, who had quipped that "AI is whatever hasn't been done yet." What has been done, he said, we simply took for granted. What's more, once an AI program could do it, we excised that skill from our definition of "intelligence"—an amorphous quality that required a humanlike combination of abilities that was forever beyond software's grasp.

With ChatGPT, AI finally surmounted the Tesler effect—and then some. Suddenly, people could grasp that AI had arrived. You could talk to it. It could answer, cogently and confidently, if not always correctly. You could ask it for recipes based on the ingredients in your fridge. You could get it to summarize your meeting—in prose, or, if you wished, in verse! You could ask for ideas to improve your business or advice on how to ask for a raise. It could build you a website or write you custom software that could wrangle data and analyze it. Combined with other generative AI models, it could produce images of almost anything you could describe.

Now, AI was getting somewhere. This was more like the AI of Kubrick and *Star Trek*. Our attitude toward the technology transformed from blasé to bewildered overnight. What did this moment mean? What future was AI ushering in? Would we even have a future? There were certainly frightening pronouncements, some from the very executives and researchers closest to the technology's bleeding edge: that AI could displace 300 million jobs worldwide; that ChatGPT was like "a pocket nuclear bomb" that had detonated amid an unsuspecting public; that it would destroy education; that it would destroy trust; that it would obliterate democracy; that even, if we weren't careful, AI could mean "lights out for all of us," as OpenAI's co-founder and chief executive Sam Altman famously warned.

This book is my attempt to answer the many questions posed by

ChatGPT. In researching it, I was struck by the extent to which many of our concerns, as well as some of the moral panic greeting the AI revolution, also attended the introduction of earlier technologies, from the printing press to television to the internet. Some fears about AI date back to the dawn of the computer age. Others have arisen more recently, with the introduction of the internet, GPS, social media, and mobile phones. There are important lessons to be drawn from how we, collectively, met the challenges these earlier inventions posed—in the ways we were changed and, perhaps more importantly, in the ways we weren't. AI represents an acceleration, an extension, and in many cases an exacerbation of trends these earlier technologies set in motion. When it comes to social isolation or distrust in media, AI represents a difference of degree, not necessarily of kind.

But AI is different from these earlier innovations in three key ways. It is a more general-purpose technology than most we have encountered previously. This makes it much more akin to the invention of writing or metal smelting or electricity than to the telephone or even the automobile or airplane. It is, as several thinkers on AI have opined, perhaps "the last invention" we need ever create. That's because it holds the promise of helping to create all future technologies we may require. It has the potential to impact almost every aspect of society.

Second, the pace of AI's progress, as well as its adoption, is faster than prior technologies. ChatGPT reached 100 million users within a month of its release, a milestone that took Facebook, the previous fastest-growing consumer software product, almost four and a half years to reach. Spending on the technology is surging, with more than half of Fortune 500 companies planning to implement ChatGPT-like AI in the coming few years.

The speed at which all this is happening matters because it gives us humans less time: less time to adjust to the new reality AI is helping to create; less time to think about AI's implications and how we want to govern the technology; and less time to act before it becomes too late, before harms, both small and large, occur.

Finally, more than any previous technology, AI strikes at the heart of our perception of what makes us unique as a species: our intelligence and our creativity. When the John Henrys of the world eventually lost out to the steam drill, it devalued human labor. But human physical strength was never dominant. We'd long known creatures that could outrun us, outclimb us, outswim us, and overpower us. But nothing could outthink us. Microprocessors and previous generations of software rivaled some of our cognitive abilities: They could run calculations far faster and more accurately than we could. They could follow any rote set of procedures more exactly and speedier, too. But we *wrote* those rote steps. Computers did not challenge the core of our intellect, our ability to reason, to invent new ways of solving problems, and our creative power to express ideas and emotions in novel ways. AI challenges most, if not all, of these things. This is why it is so profound and unsettling, and why we regard it with such fascination and dread. We are, for once, in a position where we might not be the preeminent intelligence on the planet—at least not for much longer.

While this is vertigo-inducing, we have much to look forward to in this AI-defined future. AI can grant us all superpowers, if we make the right design choices and adopt the right policies. It can alleviate the burden of routine tasks, enabling us to work faster and smarter. It will set off an unprecedented productivity boom that will accelerate economic growth. Rather than destroying education, as some teachers and parents fear, AI will allow each of us to have a personal tutor in our pocket. AI will help us push the boundaries of science and medicine, offering us new cures and more personalized medicine. It will help us advance our understanding of chemistry, biology, and even our own history and pre-history. It will aid us in monitoring our planet and safeguarding biodiversity, as well as helping us use renewable power more efficiently. It will give many of us a constant companion, possibly alleviating loneliness and allowing those who struggle socially to improve their interpersonal skills. Used correctly, it could enhance our democracy.

But there are grave dangers here too. If we make the wrong choices,

AI will enfeeble us individually and collectively. Our social skills may atrophy. At work, we may wind up being disempowered and demotivated, slaves to the machine, rather than its master. Without the right government action, inequality will become worse, and power more concentrated. The explosion of synthetic content may obliterate trust and shred the already threadbare fabric of our democracy. AI's power consumption could hurt our efforts to fight climate change. The technology might help engineer bioweapons. It could make our wars more deadly for civilians and soldiers alike. In the wrong hands, it could be a tool for terror. If we were to automate decisions concerning nuclear weapons, the risk could be world-ending. A future AI superintelligence could even pose a threat to our species.

In the following pages, you will also encounter arguments about AI's impact that don't get as much attention as the stories about the end of democracy or even the world. Chief among them is the threat AI poses to our minds and the way we think. We should not let AI's cognitive prowess diminish our own. Another critical risk that is too little discussed is AI's potential to shove empathy out of the central position it ought to occupy in our decision-making. Finally, AI could worsen the divisions along racial and class lines that already trouble our society.

On a more hopeful note, I also showcase opportunities that are frequently overlooked. Just as AI has the potential to worsen inequality, it will offer us a chance to pull more people into the middle class; to help people create new businesses and become entrepreneurs. It could lead to a flourishing of creativity and culture. And it could improve learning and expand both our personal and collective knowledge.

This exploration of AI begins with a brief history, explaining how we have arrived at the threshold of this new age. We will then examine AI's impacts, starting with how it could profoundly alter our own thinking. Expanding outward, we will explore AI's effects on our social relationships, our jobs, the companies we work for, and the economy as a whole. From there, we will investigate AI's reshaping of art and culture and science and medicine. We will confront AI's complicated role in our efforts to foster sustainability, the dangers facing democracy, and the threat from the unrestricted use of AI in weapons systems. Finally, we will look at the possibility that AI might result in our extinction.

Across all these dimensions, AI poses unsettling questions around authenticity and trust, and around what philosophers call *ontology* (our beliefs about being and reality) and *epistemology* (how we construct those beliefs). In our AI-driven future, we should insist on maintaining a distinction between the authentic and inauthentic—between a simulation of something and the thing itself. AI is excellent at mimicry, at imitating understanding, writing, thought, and creativity. In most cases, it is incapable of the thing itself—and probably always will be. It can complement and extend key aspects of our humanity, but we should not be fooled into thinking it can substitute for us. We must remember that AI's superpower is its ability to enhance, not replace, our own natural gifts.

In this book, I hope to illuminate a path toward the superpowered future AI can enable. But it is a narrow path. We must step carefully. We must be deliberate in how we build AI models and, as importantly, how we interact with them.

In the end, how we use AI is up to us. We have choices to make as a society—decisions that are rarely discussed in the public realm, whether it's in political campaigns or on earnings calls. Only such careful choices will ensure AI complements our best human skills, rather than supplants them. Government and corporate policies will make all the difference to AI's impact. I outline some of these policies throughout this book.

More than the capabilities of AI models themselves, the precise nature of how we interact with this software will matter tremendously. To get this right, we need to value the insights of researchers who specialize in human–computer interaction and human cognitive biases as much as we do those building ever more powerful AI.

Humans must be teammates with AI software, not mere inspectors of its output. We must insist that processes, not just results, matter. And those processes must encompass empathy—one person's understanding for another, born of lived experience. As humans, this is our most precious and enduring gift. It is the bedrock of our morality. And it is a thing AI is unlikely to ever possess. We must not let our rush to embrace AI's technical efficiency dislodge empathy, that most human trait, from its preeminence in our civilization. Keeping this lodestar in sight won't be easy. But if we can, we will succeed in mastering AI.

1

THE CONJURERS

I n the spring of 2020, in a vast windowless building the size of twenty football fields on the plains outside Des Moines, Iowa, one of the largest supercomputers ever built crackled to life. The supercomputer was made up of rack upon rack of specialized computer chips—a kind originally developed to handle the intensive work of rendering graphics in video games. More than ten thousand of the chips were yoked together, connected with high-speed fiber-optic cabling. The data center belonged to Microsoft, and it cost hundreds of millions of dollars to construct. But the supercomputer was designed to serve the needs of a small start-up from San Francisco that, at the time, few people outside the niche computer science field known as artificial intelligence had ever heard of. It was called OpenAI.

Microsoft had invested $1 billion in OpenAI in July 2019 to gain access to its technology. As part of the deal, Microsoft promised to build this supercomputer. For the next thirty-four days, the supercomputer worked around the clock training one of the largest pieces of AI software ever developed. The software could encode the relationship between 175 billion data points. OpenAI fed this AI software text—more than 2.5 billion web pages collected over a decade of web crawling, millions of Reddit conversations, tens of thousands of books, and all of Wikipedia. The software's objective was to create a map of the relationships between all of the words in that vast dataset. This statistical map would allow it to take any arbitrary text sequence and predict the next most likely word. By doing so, it could output many paragraphs—in a variety of genres and styles—that were almost indistinguishable from human writing.

OpenAI called the software GPT-3, and its debut in June 2020 stunned computer scientists. Never before had software been so capable of writing. GPT-3 could do far more than just assemble prose and poetry. It could also code. It could answer factual questions. It was capable of reading comprehension and summarization. It could determine the sentiment of a piece of writing. It could translate between English and French, and French and German, and many other languages. It could answer some questions involving commonsense reasoning. In fact, it could perform dozens of language-related tasks, even though it had only ever been trained to predict the next word in a sequence. It did all this based on instructions that were conversational, the way you would speak to a person. Scientists call this "natural language," to differentiate it from computer code. The potential of GPT-3 convinced Satya Nadella, Microsoft's chief executive, to quietly double, and then triple, his initial $1 billion investment in the small San Francisco AI lab. GPT-3 would, in turn, lead two years later to ChatGPT.

ChatGPT was not the first AI software whose output could pass for human. But it was the first that could be easily accessed by hundreds of millions of people. It awakened the public to AI's possibilities and set off a race among the largest technology companies and well-funded start-ups to turn those possibilities into reality. Within months, Microsoft would commit even more money to OpenAI, another $10 billion, and begin incorporating OpenAI's even more powerful GPT-4 model into products such as Microsoft Word and PowerPoint, which hundreds of millions of people use daily. Google, scrambling to catch up, created a general-purpose chatbot of its own, Bard, and began integrating generative AI into its search engine, potentially destabilizing the business models of entire industries, from news and media to e-commerce. It also began training even larger, more powerful AI systems that analyze and create images, sounds, and music, not just text. This model, called Gemini, has since replaced Bard and been integrated into several Google products. Meta began releasing powerful AI models freely for anyone to use. Amazon and Apple started building generative AI too.

This competition is propelling us toward a single general-purpose AI system that could equal or exceed human abilities at almost any cognitive task—a moment known as the *singularity*. While many still doubt that moment is at hand, it is closer than ever.

Why did ChatGPT seem so remarkable? Because we could talk to it. That a computer's conversational skills—and not its fluency in multiplying five-digit numbers or detecting patterns in stock market gyrations—should be the yardstick by which we measure machine intelligence has a long and contentious history. The vision of an intelligent digital interlocutor was there at the dawn of the computer age. It has helped guide the entire field of AI—for better, and for worse.

THE TURING TEST—AI'S ORIGINAL SIN

The idea of dialogue as the hallmark of intelligence dates to the mid-twentieth century and the writings of one of that era's most exceptional minds, Alan Turing, the brilliant mathematician best known for helping to crack the Nazis' Enigma code during World War II. In 1936, when he was just twenty-four, Turing proposed the design of a hypothetical device that would serve as the inspiration for modern computers. And it was Turing who, in a 1948 report for a British government laboratory, suggested that computers might one day be considered intelligent. What mattered, he argued, was the quality of a machine's output, not the process that led to it. A machine that could beat a person at chess was more "intelligent," even if the machine arrived at its moves through a method, brute calculation, that bore little resemblance to the way its human opponent thought.

Two years later, in 1950, Turing expanded on these ideas in his seminal paper entitled "Computer Machinery and Intelligence." He suggested a test for machine intelligence that he called "the Imitation Game." It involved an interrogator asking questions of a person and a computer. All three are isolated from one another in separate rooms. The interrogator receives responses in the form of typewritten notes that are labeled X or Y depending on whether the human or the machine produced them. The interrogator's job is to determine, based on the typed answers, whether X is a person or a machine. Turing proposed that a computer should be considered intelligent if the interrogator can't tell the difference.

Critically, Turing explained that the test was not about the accuracy or truthfulness of answers. He fully expected that to "win" the game, both the human and the machine might lie. Nor was it about specialist knowledge. In describing the game, he postulated that it would be a machine's mastery of *the form* of everyday conversation, as well as an apparent grasp of common sense, that would make it indistinguishable from the human.

The Imitation Game, later dubbed "the Turing Test," has had a profound impact on how computer scientists have regarded machine intelligence. But it proved controversial almost from the start. Wolfe Mays, a philosopher and professor at the University of Manchester, was among the contemporary critics who attacked Turing's test because of its focus on the machine's output, instead of its internal processes. He called machines' cold, logical calculus "the very antithesis of thinking," which Mays argued was a far more mysterious, intuitive phenomenon. Mays was among those who believed intelligence was closely linked to human consciousness, and that consciousness, in turn, could not be reduced to mere physics. Turing, he wrote, seemed "implicitly to assume that the whole of intelligence and thought can be built up summatively from the warp and woof of atomic propositions."

Decades later, the philosopher John Searle constructed a thought experiment to highlight what he saw as the Turing Test's fatal flaw. Searle imagined a man who can neither read nor speak Chinese being locked in a room with a Chinese dictionary, some sheets of paper, and a pencil. Notes with Chinese characters are slipped through a slot in the door, and the man's job is to look up the symbols in the dictionary and transcribe the Chinese characters he finds there onto a fresh slip of paper and push these slips out through the slot. Searle said it would be ridiculous to say that the man in the room "understood" Chinese just because he could produce accurate definitions of Chinese words. So, too, Turing was wrong, Searle wrote, to consider a computer intelligent just because it could mimic the outward characteristics of a human dialogue.

Debates about these issues have become louder with the advent of ultra-large language models, such as GPT-4. It certainly doesn't help that cognitive science has yet to resolve the nature of human intelligence, let alone consciousness. Can intelligence be distilled to a single number—an intelligence quotient, or IQ—based on how someone performs on a standardized test? Or is it more appropriate, as the Harvard psychologist and neuroscientist Howard Gardner argued, to speak of multiple intelligences that take into account the athletic genius of a Michael Jordan, the musical talents of a Taylor Swift, and the interpersonal skills of a Bill Clinton? Neuroscientists and cognitive psychologists continue to argue.

Beyond elevating outcomes over process, the Turing Test's emphasis on deception as the hallmark of intelligence encouraged the use of deceit in testing AI software. This makes the benchmark fundamentally unethical in the eyes of many modern AI ethicists, who blame the Turing Test for encouraging a tradition of AI engineers testing their systems on unwitting humans. In recent years, companies have tested AI software that could play strategy games like Go and Diplomacy against unsuspecting human players. Researchers defended the deception as necessary: humans might alter their playing style and strategies if they knew they were up against a software opponent. Ethicists and journalists lambasted Google when, in 2018, it showed off its new Duplex digital assistant by having the software phone a restaurant and make a reservation, fooling the maître d' into thinking she was interacting with a person. Today most "responsible AI" policies state that people should always be informed when they're interacting with AI software—and yet companies sometimes find justifications for not doing so.

Perhaps the Turing Test's most enduring and troubling legacy concerns its framing as a game of wits in which a human is pitted against a computer whose goal is to mimic and equal the human. As the technology writer John Markoff notes in his book *Machines of Loving Grace*, one effect of this was that generations of AI researchers would try to create software that matched or exceeded human performance at some tasks, and, as a result, were evaluated for their potential to replace humans. An alternative, Markoff says, would be to view AI software as having different but complementary capabilities. This framework would encourage the development of AI systems designed to augment people, rather than replace them.

But this complementary perspective has struggled to gain traction. When they wish to prove their software's capabilities, AI researchers still tend to follow Turing's example and benchmark their systems against human performance. Some of this is simply good marketing, of course—software besting humans at a familiar board game or some professional exam makes for better headlines. But among AI researchers, the desire to equal or exceed human performance runs deeper than just a clever media strategy, and much of that is down to Turing. More recently, the latest generation of AI language models has been subjected to a battery of tests designed to evaluate people, including the bar exam and the U.S. medical licensing exam. Today's most powerful AI systems have passed all of these tests, often scoring better than the average person. And of course, ChatGPT's mastery of the original Turing Test—its convincing dialogue—has helped make it such a sensation. But dig a little deeper and the software's imitation of us begins to slip. As anyone who has played around with ChatGPT soon discovers, the intellectual abilities of today's generative AI can be frustratingly brittle and weirdly alien: it can answer a tough question about particle physics with mastery, and then botch a simple logic problem an eight-year-old could ace. Such inconsistency, brilliance and stupidity commingled, is certainly not what Turing had in mind.

BUILDING TURING'S INTELLIGENT MACHINES

The possibility of such a paradox—that a computer could master conversation without any real understanding of what it was saying—wasn't even a distant flicker in the imaginations of the scientists who first took up the challenge of trying to turn Turing's vision of a thinking machine into reality. Around the time Turing dreamed up the Imitation Game, the first universal computers, which owed much to his prewar conceptual designs, were being plugged in. These were colossal machines: ENIAC, one of these early computers, took almost the entire basement of the University of Pennsylvania engineering department, occupying 1,500 square feet and consisting of thirty tons of wiring and vacuum tubes. It could perform five thousand addition calculations per second, which was much faster than previous mechanical calculating machines, but almost one trillion times slower than the powerful chips that run today's AI software. Yet a small group of pioneers believed they could teach machines like ENIAC to think.

John McCarthy, a young mathematics professor at Dartmouth College, was one of them. By the early 1950s, the idea of imbuing these new computers with intelligence began to take hold. As a key step toward that goal, scientists were also trying to discover algorithms that could accurately describe how the human brain itself worked. McCarthy was at the heart of this intellectual fervor, working on what was called *automata theory*. Others were carrying out similar research but calling it cybernetics and information processing. In early 1955, McCarthy had the idea of bringing some cohesion to these efforts by hosting a two-month workshop the following summer at Dartmouth. He would invite about a dozen academics—mostly mathematicians, but also electrical engineers and psychologists—to figure out how to get a computer to learn and think.

In writing a funding proposal for the workshop, McCarthy coined the term "artificial intelligence" to refer to the emerging field. McCarthy and his fellow workshop organizers set an ambitious agenda. "An attempt will be made to find how to make machines use language, form abstractions and concepts, solve [the] kinds of problems now reserved for humans, and improve themselves," they wrote in their grant application to the Rockefeller Foundation. They believed that, with a "carefully selected" group of scientists working together, "a significant advance could be made in one or more of these problems" that summer.

As it turned out, McCarthy and his fellow organizers had been wildly optimistic. The 1956 workshop failed to unify the field around a singular vision and research program, disappointing McCarthy. Some of the attendees even disliked the name "artificial intelligence," believing it connoted something phony. Heated debate over the term diverted time and attention from more substantive discussions. McCarthy defended his choice—arguing that it emphasized that the field's goal was intelligence, and not merely automation. The name stuck. And, while the Dartmouth workshop failed to braid the various strands of AI research into a single rope, it showcased many of the conceptual threads—and many of the challenges—that would define the pursuit of AI over the next six decades, including one idea that has sparked the current AI revolution.

That idea was called the artificial neural network. By the late 1940s, neuroscientists had discovered that human neurons began life undifferentiated from one another—any difference in the way the mature neurons functioned in the brain must, they concluded, be learned. They also knew that neurons fed electro-chemical signals to other neurons in what seemed to be a sort of hierarchy. These two insights prompted scientists to search for ways to duplicate this structure, first using vacuum tubes and later using digital computers and software.

The earliest neural networks had just two layers. In the input layer, neurons would each take in data from a different portion of whatever image, audio recording, or text the network was analyzing. Every input neuron applied a mathematical formula to its bit of data and passed the result along to a single output neuron. The output neuron summed the answers from all the input neurons and then applied its own mathematical formula, with the result determining the answer it gave to a user. If that answer was wrong, variables, called weights and biases, that are part of each neuron's formula, were adjusted. The neurons closest to having the right answer had their weights and biases increased, while the others had theirs decreased. Then the whole network tried again with another example from a dataset. This process enabled the network to gradually learn, over the course of many examples, how to produce the right answer.

A number of computer scientists thought these early neural networks would be the way to achieve artificial intelligence. The approach worked well for teaching computers to make simple binary classifications, determining whether something was light or dark, a circle or a square. But it couldn't do much else. Marvin Minsky, a brilliant young Harvard mathematician who helped McCarthy organize the workshop, built one of the first analog neural networks using parts salvaged from a B-24 bomber. He presented his work on neural networks at Dartmouth that summer. But much of Minsky's presentation dwelled on neural networks' many limitations.

Soon Minsky, who went on to found MIT's AI Lab, emerged, with the zeal of a convert, as the technique's harshest critic. He would turn instead to a different idea about how to build machines that could learn and think, one that used logical rules to tell a computer how to reason. For example, to create a system that could identify cars, motorcycles, and bicycles in images, you would program the computer to recognize features that humans knew were important in making this determination— things like handlebars, the number of wheels, doors and windows and exhaust pipes. Then you would write code that would instruct the computer in how to reason about these features: If it has handlebars, but no doors or exhaust pipe, it is a bike. If it has an exhaust pipe, but no doors, it's a motorcycle. In the years following the Dartmouth workshop, these symbolic reasoning methods yielded what seemed like steady progress toward humanlike AI. Scientists created software that could play backgammon, checkers, and then chess about as well as the average person. Then, in 1966, an AI system using Minsky's rules-based approach came within a whisker of passing the Turing Test.

THE ELIZA EFFECT

The achievement was the work of an engineer working at Minsky's MIT lab named Joseph Weizenbaum. Born in Berlin in 1923 to a well-to-do Jewish family, he wound up in Detroit at thirteen after fleeing the Nazis. Weizenbaum's relationship with his parents was strained and, finding himself socially isolated as he struggled to learn English, he sought refuge first in mathematics, and later on his psychoanalyst's couch. He gravitated to the nascent field of computing and eventually landed a job as a programmer, writing software for the giant computers that General Electric was building in the emerging tech hub of Silicon Valley. He became intrigued by the possibility of interacting with a machine, not in code, but in natural language. Knowing his interests, a mutual friend introduced him to the Stanford University psychiatrist Kenneth Colby, who thought computers might open up new avenues for therapy, as well as providing interesting ways to research mental illness by modeling the human brain. They collaborated on a project to create a kind of software therapist. Weizenbaum took the idea with him when he joined the MIT faculty in 1963. The result, three years later, was the world's first chatbot, Eliza, named after Eliza Doolittle from *Pygmalion*.

Eliza was designed to mimic, in text, the interaction between a patient and a psychoanalyst. Weizenbaum chose this "persona" for Eliza deliberately because it helped mask the chatbot's relatively weak language understanding. The system analyzed the text a user gave it and, according to a complex series of rules, tried to match the text to one of several pre-scripted replies. If it was uncertain, it would sometimes simply parrot the user's input back in the form of a question, as a psychoanalyst might. In other cases, it would lean on something vague and sympathetic, such as, "I see," or "Go on," or "That's very interesting."

The coding behind Eliza was not particularly sophisticated, even by the standards of the day. Instead, what made Eliza groundbreaking was people's reaction to it. Many of the students whom Weizenbaum observed interacting with Eliza were convinced it was a human therapist. "Some subjects have been very hard to convince that Eliza (with its present script) is *not* human," Weizenbaum wrote. He would later recall that his secretary requested time with Eliza and then, after a bit, requested he leave the room. "I believe this anecdote testifies to the success with which the program maintains the illusion of understanding," he noted. Even computer scientists found themselves making intimate confessions to the chatbot.

In other words, Eliza came pretty close to pulling off the sort of deception Turing envisioned. But Eliza also made glaringly apparent the Turing Test's weaknesses. Chief among these is our own credulity. The people who interacted with Eliza wanted to believe they were talking to a person. This tendency, to anthropomorphize chatbots—and to suspend our own disbelief despite their obvious shortcomings—became known as "the Eliza effect." It remains a powerful force in AI today.

The Eliza effect's biggest impact may have been on Eliza's creator. Rather than experiencing triumph, Weizenbaum was depressed. What did it say about his fellow humans that we were so easily duped? He began to see how difficult it was to distinguish real human thought from its imitation—and yet how vital. Weizenbaum's early collaborator Colby would maintain that if patients found a chatbot like Eliza helpful, then it was a worthwhile invention. But the deception at Eliza's core troubled Weizenbaum. This debate continues today with a new wave of chatbots designed to sound empathetic or be used in therapy.

Minsky, Weizenbaum's MIT colleague, saw no difference between the reasoning a computer performed and the brain—Minsky famously quipped that humans were nothing more than "meat machines."

Weizenbaum made a radical break from this view. He came to see certain realms as beyond the scope of AI because they depended on lived experience—and ultimately emotions—that a computer could never have. Even if the rules of language could be mathematically formalized, something he had come to doubt, AI software could never actually "understand" language. Drawing on the later philosophical writings of Ludwig Wittgenstein, Weizenbaum argued language was insufficient for conveying meaning even between two people—because none of us shares the same lived experience as anyone else—let alone between a person and a piece of software, which has no lived experience. Plus, so much of communication is nonverbal. Weizenbaum related the story of standing next to his wife, looking over their children as they lay asleep in bed. "We spoke to each other in silence, rehearsing a scene as old as mankind itself," he later wrote. Then he quoted the playwright Eugene Ionesco: "Not everything is unsayable in words, only the living truth."

Weizenbaum argued that this fundamental difference between human and machine—the computer's incapacity for true empathy—meant that even if AI could learn to perform every human task as well as or better than a person, it ought to be banned from doing certain things. He thought software should never be allowed to make decisions with irreversible consequences or "where a computer system is proposed as a substitute for a human function that involves interpersonal respect, understanding, and love." He worried that even as we all too readily anthropomorphized our machines, we all too eagerly embraced machines as a metaphor for ourselves, devaluing our humanity.

In 1976, Weizenbaum laid out these critiques in a book, *Computer Power and Human Reason: From Judgment to Calculation*. It was a searing indictment of his own field. He accused his fellow AI researchers of having a "hacker mentality" that was more concerned with getting software to perform some task, rather than trying to answer scientifically meaningful questions about the nature of intelligence and thought. Not only did these so-called computer scientists lack scientific rigor, in his view, but both their approach and the potential impact of the AI software they were trying to build were antihuman. Weizenbaum, who had a commitment to left-wing causes and civil rights, was particularly disturbed by the U.S. government's use of early AI software in the Vietnam War.

Weizenbaum recognized that many AI systems were so complex that their decision-making was inscrutable, even to their creators. He worried that made these systems difficult to control. But he also recognized that people could use the software's opacity as a convenient excuse to duck accountability. The political economy of AI alarmed him, too. In his neo-Marxist critique, postwar American capitalism might have collapsed under its own weight if the computer had not saved it. Software allowed big business and the federal government to exercise control in ways that would have been impossible before. "The computer, then, was used to conserve America's social and political institutions," he wrote. "It buttressed them and immunized them, at least temporarily, against enormous pressures for change." AI made totalitarian government easier, a concern heightened by Weizenbaum's own experience as a refugee from Nazi Germany.

Weizenbaum's fellow computer scientists dismissed *Computer Power and Human Reason* as anti-scientific and vitriolic. But most of his criticisms of AI, and of those building it, remain valid—in fact, his nightmares about AI are more germane than ever.

RESURRECTING THE NEURAL NETWORK

The reason it was easy to ignore Weizenbaum's critiques in the 1970s and it is impossible to do so now has everything to do with one old idea, the neural network, and three new developments: vastly more powerful computer chips, oceans of digital data made easily available thanks to the internet, and a dash of algorithmic innovation.

Most computer scientists had abandoned work on neural networks by the early 1970s, in no small measure due to Minsky's harsh criticism. But a small group of iconoclasts continued to pursue the idea. In the mid-1980s, one of them, a psychologist named David Rumelhart at the University of California, San Diego, alongside his colleague Ronald Williams and a young English postdoctoral student named Geoffrey Hinton, hit upon a breakthrough that finally allowed neural networks to start doing some interesting things. Their breakthrough was called backpropagation—or backprop, for short.

Backprop solved a key problem. One reason the earliest neural networks could only learn simple binary classifications was because they had just two layers. It turned out that adding additional layers of neurons between the input neurons and the output neuron enabled the network to make much more complex determinations. By the 1980s, the neural networks that Rumelhart, Hinton, and Williams were experimenting with had several layers. But the middle layers of neurons created a problem. In a simple two-layer neural network, figuring out how to adjust the settings—the weights and biases—of each input neuron so the network could learn during training was fairly simple. But with the addition of these extra layers, knowing how to credit each neuron for its contribution to the output became a daunting challenge. Backprop used ideas from calculus to solve this problem. It allowed the weights and biases of every neuron to be adjusted in a way that would allow a multilayered network to learn effectively.

Thanks to backprop, multilayer neural networks could decipher handwriting on envelopes and checks, learn the relationships between people in a family tree, power a program that could recognize printed words and read them aloud through a voice synthesizer, and even keep an early self-driving car between the lane lines on a highway. But there was still a lot that neural networks could not do. They couldn't classify complex objects in images—no cat or dog detector yet. They struggled with speech recognition and language translation. And there were other drawbacks: training neural networks required vast amounts of data, and in many domains enough data simply wasn't available. What's more, processing all that data in large neural networks was agonizingly slow on the computer chips of the day. At the same time, other machine-learning methods using advanced statistics were showing promise. The result was that many AI researchers and engineers once again wrote off neural networks as a dead end.

DEEP LEARNING TAKES OFF

Hinton, who had now moved to the University of Toronto, remained convinced that neural networks were the right path to humanlike AI. He kept plugging away. In 2004, he founded a research collective devoted to continuing work on neural networks, an approach he soon rebranded as "deep learning." It was clever marketing: *deep* referred simply to the multiple layers of a neural network, but it also implied that neural networks somehow arrived at insights that were more profound than other "shallow" machine-learning methods. Deep learning was about to live up to the promise that had eluded neural networks for more than fifty years.

What changed were two things: the internet made vast amounts of information available, solving neural networks' hunger for data; and a new kind of computer chip, called a "graphics processing unit," or GPU, hit the market. The American semiconductor company Nvidia debuted the first GPU, the GeForce 256, in late 1999. It was a separate printed circuit board, or card, that could be inserted into a computer or data server. It was designed to handle the fast graphics rendering necessary for video games. It did this by computing several data streams in parallel, not sequentially, and by handling other key computations directly on the graphics card, rather than handing these off to a more general-purpose central processing unit (or CPU), as had been the case with a previous generation of graphics cards. GPUs drew a lot of power and produced a lot of heat; each card came with its own fan. But the new chips made home gaming consoles like the Xbox and PlayStation possible. And they were about to change AI research forever.

In 2005, a team of researchers at the University of Maryland showed that the parallel processing power of GPUs might work well for a simple two-layer neural network. The following year, a team at Microsoft demonstrated that the newest GPUs could also much more efficiently calculate the weights of the neurons in a complex deep learning system. Then, in 2009, Hinton and two of his graduate students built a deep learning system using GPUs for Microsoft that, in just a few months, matched the performance of the company's existing speech recognition system—software that had taken a decade of painstaking work to develop. It helped that Microsoft had tremendous quantities of speech data to train the network—deep learning systems got better and better the more data they ingested. Other graduate students of Hinton's were farmed out to IBM and Google, where they repeated the feat. At Google, its existing state-of-the-art speech recognition software for Android smartphones got the word being spoken wrong 23 percent of the time. In just a week, Hinton's student achieved an error rate of 21 percent and then, two weeks later, 18 percent.

Deep learning was taking off. But there were still doubters who thought neural networks could not classify complex images. In 2012, Hinton and two graduate students, Ilya Sutskever and Alex Krizhevsky, silenced them. They built a deep learning system on GPUs—called AlexNet after Krizhevsky—that won a contest run by Stanford University called ImageNet. It required an AI system to classify images of one thousand different categories of objects. AlexNet had an error rate—just 15 percent—more than twice as good as the next best contestant. Deep learning had arrived. Hinton, Sutskever, and Krizhevsky formed a company around the idea of building deep learning systems for computer vision tasks. Within weeks, Google bought it for $44 million. The trio went to work for Google Brain, the advanced AI research lab the company had launched in 2011.

TO SOLVE INTELLIGENCE—THE HEADLONG RACE FOR AGI

The dam holding back deep learning had begun to crack before AlexNet. After AlexNet, it collapsed. The big American tech companies—Google, Microsoft, Meta (then called Facebook), Amazon, and Apple—and their

Chinese equivalents, Baidu and Tencent, raced to implement deep learning. They competed to hire deep learning experts, shelling out high six- and even seven-figure salaries to newly minted PhDs. Most of the applications of deep learning were still very narrow—a system that could tag people in photos on social media, or better recognize spoken commands. They were not general intelligences but specific ones. What's more, deep learning still seemed inaccessible to most businesses outside the tech sector because they had neither the human expertise needed to build it nor the data needed to train it.

At the time, relatively few researchers held the conviction that deep learning might match Turing's vision of AI. One of them was Shane Legg. A New Zealand native with a background in mathematics and computing, Legg had gone to work for an early AI start-up in New York during the dot-com boom. While there, he had helped popularize the term "artificial general intelligence," or AGI—by which Legg meant software that could do most cognitive tasks as well or better than the average person. Legg distinguished the broader idea of AGI from the more narrow AI that could do just one thing exceptionally well. After the start-up went bust, Legg went back to school. Like previous generations of AI researchers, Legg thought the best way to figure out how to build AGI was to study the brain—so he went to the Gatsby Computational Neuroscience Unit at University College London, which did research at the intersection of neuroscience and AI. There he met Demis Hassabis. A former child chess prodigy–turned–computer scientist and video game entrepreneur, Hassabis was also interested in building AGI. Like Legg, he too suspected deep learning was the way to do it. The two, together with a childhood acquaintance of Hassabis's who had a background in social entrepreneurship, Mustafa Suleyman, co-founded an AI start-up called DeepMind in 2010. The small, secretive London company had an audacious—some would say ludicrous—mission: "To solve intelligence, and then use that to solve everything else."

That mission began to look less ludicrous in 2013, when DeepMind demonstrated a deep learning system that, starting from almost zero knowledge, could, through trial and error, learn to play fifty different old Atari games at superhuman levels in a matter of hours. The result stunned technologists, including one of DeepMind's early investors, Elon Musk. Like Legg and Hassabis, Musk was fascinated by the idea of AGI—but also terrified of it. Once people invented AGI, it might only be a quick hop to achieve artificial superintelligence, or ASI, a system that was far more intelligent than all of us. ASI would be extremely difficult to control. Such a system might even develop consciousness, raising profound philosophical and practical questions. ASI could come into conflict with humans, perhaps leading to our extinction or enslavement as a species. This was the sort of worry that preoccupied Musk and others familiar with DeepMind's progress.

While sharing a private jet flight with Musk, Google's co-founder Larry Page overheard him discussing DeepMind's Atari breakthrough with another Silicon Valley investor. Immediately, Page was interested in buying the start-up. Google had invested more in neural networks at that time than any other Big Tech company. Page didn't want a competitor possibly jumping ahead. Shortly after the flight, he dispatched Google's top AI researchers to examine DeepMind. He then outbid Microsoft and Meta to buy the small London company for $650 million.

The DeepMind purchase alarmed Musk. He was friends with Page but didn't trust him, despite Google's "don't be evil" motto, to be the sole steward of AGI. "He could produce something evil by accident," Musk told the journalist Ashlee Vance in 2013. Musk thought building powerful AI was "like summoning the demon." He also warned that companies building AI "recognize the danger, but they think they can shape and control the digital superintelligences and prevent bad ones from escaping into the internet. That remains to be seen . . ."

Musk wasn't the only one who feared AGI would wind up under Google's sole control. Sam Altman, a thirty-year-old Silicon Valley venture capitalist, who at the time was president of Y Combinator, America's most prestigious start-up incubator, shared Musk's views about AGI, its significant potential benefits, and its possible existential risks. He also

agreed that Google alone should not monopolize such powerful technology. In late 2015, Musk, Altman, and a group of others, including
Hinton's former student Sutskever, co-founded a San Francisco AI lab
designed to be a counterweight to DeepMind. They named the lab
OpenAI. Like DeepMind, OpenAI was explicitly committed to working
toward the creation of AGI.

That shared goal aside, OpenAI was intended to be everything
DeepMind was not. Where DeepMind was controlled by one of the
world's largest technology companies, OpenAI would be established as
a nonprofit with a mission to ensure AGI was developed "in a way that
is most likely to benefit humanity as a whole." Whereas DeepMind was
then considered secretive, OpenAI said it would commit to publishing
all of its research and open-sourcing its software. That was why Musk
had wanted to call the lab OpenAI in the first place. He was convinced
that the only way to prevent a single company or government from using
powerful AI for authoritarian purposes was to democratize access to it.
In Musk's view, every person should have their own, personalized AGI
software. The new lab would emphasize AI safety research, an area that
was, at the time, not a major focus of the corporate AI labs. Musk became
the nonprofit's anchor donor, pledging $1 billion.

At first, OpenAI mostly focused on *reinforcement learning*—the
same AI training method DeepMind had used in its Atari work. Reinforcement learning differs from the approach Hinton, Sutskever, and
Krizhevsky had used for their ImageNet victory. To beat ImageNet, the
AlexNet neural network was taught from existing, labeled data to classify
something: Is this a cat or a kangaroo? This is called *supervised learning*. In reinforcement learning, the network starts without any data and
learns entirely from experience, by trial and error, usually in a simulator
or game environment. It learns from what is called a *reward signal*: Did
its actions result in winning the game? Did it score points or not? This is
how DeepMind's software mastered the Atari games.

By the time OpenAI was up and running, DeepMind had used this
method to achieve another milestone in AI: it had created AI software

called AlphaGo that had beaten the world's best player in the ancient strategy game Go. In its match against Lee Sedol, the South Korean world champion, AlphaGo made one move so unconventional that expert commentators watching the match were sure it was a mistake. But it was effective. The software upended thousands of years of human understanding about how Go should be played.

OpenAI was eager to prove it, too, could make progress toward AGI using reinforcement learning. It developed a major new reinforcement learning algorithm and made it freely available. It later created five neural networks that, trained through reinforcement learning, could work together to beat a top human team at the complex and fast-paced video game *Dota 2*.

THE TRANSFORMER

To get from *Dota 2* to ChatGPT would require one more flash of human genius: in 2017, researchers at Google Brain—inspired in part by the alien language depicted in the movie *Arrival*—developed a new neural network design called a *transformer*. It was much better than previous AI systems at figuring out complicated patterns in long sequences. It worked for any kind of sequence: musical notes, frames in a video, or even the next best action to take in a computer game. But it was ideally suited to discovering patterns in language. This is because in language, the correct verb conjugation or gender pronoun to use at the end of a sentence often depends on what words appear at the beginning of the sentence, or even several sentences earlier. Previous AI software struggled to learn these dependencies.

The transformer largely solved this problem. It broke sentences into fragments, each about a word long, called a *token*. The transformer then analyzed large groups of tokens in parallel, something previous neural network designs couldn't do. In this analysis, the transformer relied on a mechanism called self-attention: for any sentence, it learned which tokens were most important—which ones it should pay most attention to—to make an accurate prediction about the value of any other token. When this process was applied to language, transformers could construct what's known as a "large language model," or LLM. It is an exceedingly complex statistical map of the relationship between all the words in its training data. The remarkable thing about these new transformer-based LLMs was that, although they had been trained only to predict words in a sentence, the resulting LLM wound up being multipurpose, like a Swiss Army knife for natural language processing.

Having learned the underlying statistical patterns in language, a single transformer-based LLM could be used for all kinds of language-related tasks: summarization, translation, categorization, sentiment analysis, and question-answering. In the past, engineers would have had to build a separate piece of AI software for each. Now a single LLM could do them all.

The possibilities were limitless. Within months of publishing its initial research on the transformer, Google started training a transformer-based LLM it called BERT. Even compared to previous LLMs, BERT was massive—a neural network that could process connections among 340 million different parameters, or variables. It was trained on the relationship among 3.3 billion words from eleven thousand English-language books as well as Wikipedia. Its training task was to predict a missing word in a sentence, sort of like a giant game of *Mad Libs*. Once trained, Google tried the algorithm on a series of language ability tests. It came close to human performance on most of them.

Within a year, Google used BERT to significantly improve search results. Suddenly, Google's search engine grasped the importance of prepositions to the meaning of people's queries. When someone typed "Brazil traveler to USA visa requirements," Google now knew to return only pages that dealt with a Brazilian traveler coming to the U.S. and not an American traveling to Brazil.

OpenAI's Sutskever immediately realized what this represented: progress toward AGI was possible. Writing is a hallmark of human civilization. Vast amounts of human knowledge exist in written form. It had always been the dream of those pursuing AGI that an AI system could rapidly teach itself new skills simply by reading, the same way an autodidact might. Sutskever, Alec Radford, and two other OpenAI researchers created a transformer and fed it seven thousand unpublished books, mostly genre fiction like sci-fi, fantasy, and romance. Then they honed it on thousands of passages from middle and high school exams and question-and-answer pairs taken from the website Quora. The new AI could write several coherent paragraphs. It wasn't perfect. If asked to carry on writing, it began producing nonsensical sentences, or kept repeating itself. But it was markedly better than before.

Radford and Sutskever called the system they were building a GPT, short for "generative pretrained transformer"—*generative* because it didn't just analyze existing data but instead created its own, new data, and *pretrained* because it learned the statistical patterns in language during its initial phase of learning, called "pre-training," and then could be fine-tuned for specific tasks later. These days, AI that can create new content is known as "generative AI."

Transformers could also generate more than just words. By coupling a transformer-based language model to other kinds of AI, OpenAI created DALL-E (its name is a mashup of the painter Salvador Dali and the Pixar robot WALL-E), which can generate still images in almost any style based on a text description. The same method has been improved upon by other companies, including the start-ups Stability AI and Midjourney, as well as the software giant Adobe. Video can also be produced in a similar way. And although the videos are about one minute long at the moment, the ability to produce entire feature films from a text-based description is on the horizon. Other companies, including Google, have used transformers for sound, producing compositions, and even cloning voices. Transformers are not limited to generating content—they can also be used to predict the next most likely action in a sequence. This will lead to a new breed of digital assistants, much more capable than any that came before.

IS THE AI WE HAVE THE AI WE WANT?

Sutskever had a key intuition about neural networks from his previous work. The larger they got, and the more data they were fed, the better they performed. This seemed especially true of large language models. It was an intuition shared by another OpenAI researcher, Dario Amodei, a former physicist-turned–AI scientist who had come to work at the company and would later leave to co-found the OpenAI rival Anthropic. Amodei showed that neural networks seemed to adhere to "scaling laws"—not only did their performance improve as they got larger, it improved in predictable ways. A ten-times increase in the data the model was trained on would increase performance by about a third. But not everything about them was predictable. As the models got bigger, they also exhibited "emergent capabilities"—certain skills that smaller models struggled with, the larger models could suddenly, often surprisingly, master.

Initially, Sutskever suspected it might be possible to get most of the way to AGI simply by building ever bigger neural networks. After all, the human brain had about 86 billion neurons, between which there were estimated to be about 100 trillion connections. When OpenAI built the first GPT, the largest neural networks had only a few hundred million artificial neurons and connections. Maybe the key to intelligence was simply more neurons? Many AI researchers had their doubts. The digital neurons in neural networks were only very loosely modeled on those in the brain. And biological brains were much more efficient at learning—needing just a few examples to grasp a concept, not millions. Our brains are also much better at adapting what we've learned to new situations. These skeptics thought a fundamentally different set of algorithms would be needed to unlock human-level intelligence. Sutskever, however, was undeterred. He saw no reason to abandon the most obvious path—simply building ever bigger neural networks using the same basic algorithms, like the transformer—until it was clear that the gains from doing so were exhausted.

So that is what OpenAI did. It's how the company got to GPT-3, Chat-GPT, and GPT-4. It will no doubt be the same basic method that yields its next, even more powerful AI software, GPT-5, and beyond. Each of these models has been more capable than the last. But transformer-based LLMs have important drawbacks. One is "hallucination"—the tendency of these models to invent information and present it in a form that seems credible. (Some cognitive scientists quibble that "confabulation" would be a more accurate term.) This happens because LLMs have no inherent understanding of what they're saying—and no understanding of the difference between fiction and fact. They just generate a string of statistically likely words. As a result, these transformer-based models make errors when answering questions involving commonsense reasoning or abstract logic. Transformer-based AI models have other drawbacks, too: They are good at interpolation, which involves generating new data points that lie within the range of previously seen ones. But they often fail at the reverse—extrapolation, or generating new data outside that range. In a simple example, if they have been trained on a dataset that includes 2, 5, and 10, they can produce 3, 4, and 7. They cannot give you 1 or 11.

LLMs are also the feral pigs of the software world: they have insatiable appetites for data and they eat a lot of trash. A growing number of people have become concerned about the amount of data LLM's pre-training requires and where that data comes from. In many cases, it is simply scraped from the internet for free, possibly in violation of copyright law. The other challenge in ingesting so much human-written text is that LLMs learn our collective biases and stereotypes, especially when it comes to gender, race, ethnicity, and religion. GPT-3, for example, had a tendency to associate Muslims with violence. It tended to use negative adjectives when prompted to write about Black people. It often used male pronouns when asked to write about professionals such as doctors. It was also easy to goad GPT-3 into writing inappropriate, unseemly, or pornographic dialogue. This, too, was a vestige of it having been trained on so much text scraped from the internet. The internet is often a cesspool of violence, misogyny, racism, and worse. And GPT-3 reflected this in its output. OpenAI found it could curb some of these tendencies by providing feedback from people on whether answers were appropriate and helpful. This process, called "reinforcement learning from human feedback," or RLHF, is how OpenAI created ChatGPT. But, as people soon discovered, the guardrails OpenAI put up through RLHF could be easily overcome. Again, this is because the underlying model's conceptual understanding is nowhere near as deep as a person's.

AT WHAT COST

Bigger and bigger AI models require more and more computing power—thousands or even tens of thousands of GPUs, the specialized chips used for AI. And that makes the table stakes to play today's AI game exceptionally high. "The amount of money we needed to be successful in the mission is much more gigantic than I originally thought," Altman told *Wired* magazine in 2018. Altman became the chief executive of OpenAI after Elon Musk parted ways with the company. At a time when DeepMind still seemed to be leading the race for AGI, the mercurial billionaire had chided OpenAI for not making progress fast enough. Musk had proposed personally taking control of the lab and merging it into his business empire. The OpenAI staff rebelled at the idea and OpenAI's nonprofit board rejected Musk's plan, prompting the billionaire to break with the lab. He withdrew his financial support, including the $1 billion he had initially pledged, most of which had yet to be delivered. Musk's departure prompted an existential crisis. Altman, who along with Musk had been the driving force behind the creation of OpenAI, stepped in to become OpenAI's chief executive.

He quickly realized the only way to raise significantly more money, and fast, was to radically transform OpenAI's structure. He came up with a strange hybrid in which OpenAI's nonprofit foundation would continue, but it would control a new, for-profit arm that could take on outside venture capital investment. But critically, the maximum profit these financial investors could earn would be capped. Once the cap is hit, the investors cease to have any claim on OpenAI's profits. Initially, this profit ceiling was set stratospherically high—one hundred times a funder's initial investment. But the cap is lowered for each additional round of investors. The summer after OpenAI set up its capped-profit arm, Altman decided to ink a strategic partnership with an investor with enough cash to make all OpenAI's money problems go away: Microsoft. In July 2019, the software company invested its first $1 billion in the start-up. It has since put in at least $12 billion more.

Creating a for-profit arm and partnering with Microsoft altered OpenAI's culture. The company had been founded on a commitment to transparency: Now, with the establishment of its for-profit arm, it has by necessity become increasingly opaque. It's much harder to make money on a technology if you give it away. Instead, OpenAI now makes its most powerful models available only to paying customers, who can interact with them through an interface that allows them to provide inputs and receive outputs, but does not allow scrutiny of the underlying code or model weights. Even in technical reports on GPT-4, OpenAI omitted critical details: it has refused to reveal how large GPT-4 is, exactly how it is designed, what it was trained on, or the training process it used. While OpenAI maintains this secrecy is necessary to prevent its AI from being copied and misused, Sutskever has admitted the policy also guards OpenAI's trade secrets from competitors. The secrecy has another benefit too: it shields OpenAI from scrutiny by regulators and the public— and helps to hide exploitative data-gathering practices, such as using copyrighted material without consent, or hiring contractors in low-wage countries with few labor protections, to carry out RLHF, both of which have been documented.

The need for profits has also, according to some former employees, led OpenAI to deemphasize safety. Company executives, including Altman, have said that while they conduct extensive safety testing of their software before release, the only way to discover all the benefits and risks is to release these models and see what people do with them.

Whether profit and the public good can be balanced in the development of artificial general intelligence is a critical question. The same sky-high costs that drove OpenAI to create a for-profit arm and seek investment from Microsoft mean that most of those working at the cutting edge of AI are employed by big technology companies or start-ups in these tech giants' orbits. Anthropic, founded by researchers who broke away from OpenAI, has taken investment from both Google and Amazon. Nvidia, the AI chipmaker, has invested in Cohere, another start-up building transformer-based LLMs. Nvidia and Microsoft both invested in Inflection, founded by Suleyman, the former DeepMind co-founder. Microsoft subsequently hired Suleyman and most of Inflection's staff to form a new consumer AI division at the tech giant, with the remnants of Inflection licensing its technology to Microsoft. Previously, super-powerful technologic leaps—nuclear weapons, jet engines, satellites, supercomputers, and the internet—were most often developed, or at least funded, by governments. The motivation was usually strategic—gaining military or geopolitical advantage—not financial. And governments, although often secretive, were subject to some form of public accountability. In contrast, the race to develop AGI rests with a handful of powerful technology companies.

THE PRECIPICE

The neural network, the transformer, the internet's vast data, and unprecedented amounts of computing power have brought us to this threshold. The rest of this book will explore what will happen as we step over it into a new age. In exploring AI's impact on our lives, it's important to bear in mind the questions that have shaped AI's development: How should we define intelligence? What is the right yardstick for judging AI's progress? Has the legacy of the Turing Test pitted us in a competition against machines that we are bound to lose? Is there a better way to frame AI as a complement to our intelligence, instead of its rival? AI may be a digital brain, but it is not yet a digital mind—it has no intentions of its own, only the ones we give it. And so we urgently need to invent better ways to measure how good a tool it is. Turing's standard—mimicry—says little about utility. We need to assess how this technology functions in real-world settings, working for and with real people.

It is also essential that we consider Weizenbuam's prescient warnings about AI's amoral nature. For most of AI's history, scientists and philosophers debated what machines *could* do—what were the limits of AI's capabilities and how did they measure up against our own. The argument must now shift from could to *should,* from engineering to morality. What should we use AI to do, and what realms should we reserve exclusively for ourselves? Weizenbaum's answers to these questions take on renewed relevancy.

For example, he thought AI should never serve as a judge. Pamela McCorduck, in her farsighted 1979 oral history of AI's development, *Machines Who Think*, argues that given our long history of human biases and unequal justice, might it not be better, especially if you are a woman or a minority, to have an AI judge? McCorduck assumed AI would be more objective than a human. Today, though, the danger is often that AI systems, trained on historical data, embody, and even amplify, our existing human biases, but conceal them behind a mask of objectivity. In this way, AI software allows people to escape accountability. In many realms, we may find that preserving a little irrationality goes a long way—I, for one, would prefer moral accountability, one human soul to another, to the illusion of perfect justice. Both individually and collectively, we must decide where to draw these boundaries—and we must do it now.

CHAPTER

2

THE VOICE INSIDE YOUR HEAD

Artificial intelligence is the ultimate intellectual technology. The social anthropologist Jack Goody and the sociologist Daniel Bell defined "intellectual technologies" as tools that support or extend our mental powers. The map, the clock, the book, the computer, and the internet are all examples. These technologies don't just expand our cognitive abilities; they also alter them, changing what and how we think. We make our tools, but our tools make us, and this is most true for intellectual technologies. The map didn't just let us record the location of things, it also exploded our conception of space—allowing us a God's-eye view of the planet in an age before airplanes or satellites, and allowing us to reason about unseen geographies. It handed us powerful new metaphors; we began to "map" relationships among people and ideas, and use navigational analogies to describe "emotional journeys." The clock didn't just allow us to mark time, it altered the way we thought about it, parceling out the day into even segments no matter the season. Similarly, the camera wasn't just an aid to visual memory—it changed what and how we remember as well. The journalist Nicholas Carr called intellectual technologies "our most intimate tools," because we use them for self-expression, and they shape our identities and relationships.

Artificial intelligence doesn't just expand our mental abilities in one area—as the calculator did for mathematics or the book did for memory and communication. AI enhances our abilities across the breadth of human intellectual skills. This makes AI perhaps the most potent intellectual technology ever devised. But every intellectual technology is Janus-faced: as it bestows new cognitive capabilities, it obsolesces older, but still valuable, modes of thought.

A MIND IS A TERRIBLE THING TO LOSE

The brain is not a muscle, but it shares some characteristics with the body's more mechanical organs: exercise certain cognitive skills, be it mathematical calculation or speaking a foreign language, and the neural pathways responsible are strengthened. Recent research on neuroplasticity confirms that the brain is remarkably adaptable, able to build new connections and learn new skills at almost any stage of life. People with damage to one brain area are sometimes able, with practice, to build connections in another brain area that will allow them to regain lost skills. In some instances, neuroplasticity is reflected in noticeable anatomical changes. London's cab drivers, for example, have to pass a rigorous exam, known simply as "the Knowledge," that requires them to memorize the sprawling city's crenulated streetscape, including the location of twenty thousand landmarks, pubs, hotels, and "places of public interest." When researchers in the 1990s scanned the brains of sixteen London cabbies, they found that their posterior hippocampus, a brain region that plays a critical role in storing and manipulating spatial representations, was much larger than normal. What's more, this effect was more pronounced in the most experienced drivers.

Neuroscientists have found analogous changes in the brains of musicians compared to non-musicians. There are also significant differences in the brains of literate and illiterate people. While the human capacity for language is innate, reading and writing depend on the use of technology—alphabets, for one—and must be taught and practiced. Studies using functional magnetic resonance imaging (fMRI) that can look at blood flow to different brain regions have found important differences in the neural activity of people from different cultures. People whose written languages use logographic symbols, like Chinese, have a mental circuitry for reading that differs from those who use a phonetic alphabet. But neuroplasticity also suggests that we lose the neural connections we don't use, just as our quadriceps would atrophy if we never climbed stairs. AI threatens to accelerate the decline in natural capacities already diminished by earlier waves of information technology. We have all heard stories of people who drove into lakes while blindly following Google Maps or ended up in the wrong city after mistyping a destination's name in their car's GPS. When these misadventures end fatally, authorities call them "Death by GPS." Researchers have shown that people following GPS really do pay less attention to their surroundings. This in turn makes it more difficult for people to build what scientists call "cognitive maps" that are essential to our ability to navigate.

Exposure to the internet and myriad apps has also affected our brain: those growing up with these technologies are much better at "context switching"—rapidly hopping between disparate topics and tasks. But this skill has come at a cost. Our ability to concentrate on a single subject and to achieve deep and lasting comprehension has decreased. Studies involving MRI scans of people surfing the internet show significant activity in the prefrontal cortex, a brain region associated with decision-making and working memory, in part because people had to take action in response to internet content (click on link, hit "like" button, swipe left). Reading a book doesn't activate the same brain regions. In fact, brain scans have consistently shown that reading understimulates the brain. But it seems to be precisely this lack of stimulation that enables concentration, setting the stage for better comprehension and deeper thinking.

Considering this, you might think the AI revolution will restore some valuable habits of mind. One of the appeals of using an AI chatbot to answer a question is that it provides a comprehensive, unified response. No longer do we need to sort through a ranked list of links, hunting for information. No longer will our working memories be overloaded by these links, as well as pop-ups and auto-play videos. We can get straight to the answers we desire and contemplate them in relative serenity.

But while generative AI solves one problem of internet search, it exacerbates another. AI chatbots, even more so than a traditional search, reduce our need to remember anything at all. It has become a cliché to say that we have outsourced our memories to Google, but that doesn't make it less true. Many commentators have argued that this is a beneficial development, clearing our brains from the clutter of trivial facts and freeing up gray matter for more valuable tasks. But as Carr notes, these commentators confuse the way human biological memory works with the way a computer's does. Our short-term, working memory, which we might use when trying to add up three-digit numbers, resides in the prefrontal cortex. It has limited space, much like a hard drive, and can be easily overwhelmed. But our long-term memories are stored in the cerebral cortex and, unlike a computer's memory, scientists have found no discernable limit on how much information it can house. New facts and experiences committed to long-term memory do not extinguish or crowd out older ones. In other words, outsourcing our memories to Google or a generative AI chatbot doesn't enable us to think more clearly by decluttering the brain's attic.

Committing factual information to memory enhances, rather than detracts, from cognition. Study after study has shown that students with an existing knowledge base in a subject more readily acquire and retain new knowledge. The more you know, the more you can know. Research also shows that having greater factual knowledge improves pure reasoning and problem-solving abilities. Daniel Willingham, a cognitive psychologist at the University of Virginia, writes that this is because those with a deeper and wider knowledge base can more readily transfer what they know from one domain to another—making analogies from problems they've encountered to new puzzles.

People with deeper factual knowledge also get better at structuring information in more complex and abstract ways. In one classic experiment, researchers asked physics novices and experts to sort physics problems into categories. The novices relied on superficial similarities between problems to do the sorting—did the problem involve springs or a balloon—whereas the experts sorted problems based on the physical laws involved, such as conservation of energy. Experts don't just know more. They actually think differently. Relying on artificial intelligence for factual recall dims our own natural intelligence across the board, not just our ability to win at Trivial Pursuit.

To some degree, technology companies already possess our memories—storing our photographs and videos, our emails, our text messages, and our favorite music. But using AI as the interface through which we access this personal archive gives these companies even greater control. Today, our phones treat us to daily "for you" slideshows of past photographs, set to nostalgia-inducing music. Future AI companions will know more about us, raising the potential for manipulation, emotional and otherwise, to new heights. They might try to subtly put us in the mood to buy a particular product or persuade us to vote for a certain candidate.

In February 2024, OpenAI gave ChatGPT the ability to remember past conversations with users as well as facts about them and their preferences. It and similar bots have already been trained on the entire public internet's worth of data. So these AI systems are increasingly repositories of both collective and personal knowledge. But digital information only seems easy to store. Over long periods, digital archives are harder to maintain than physical ones. Data corrupts faster than print turns to dust. This places not just memory but history at risk—and with them, our collective wisdom. If these AI-mediated archives one day vanish, we may find ourselves unable to function with just our own, atrophied brains.

As AI systems become more powerful, some have suggested the only way we will be able to control them is to directly link our brains to AI software through brain–computer interfaces. This is the idea behind Elon Musk's company Neuralink, which recently implanted its first brain–computer interface in a human patient. (For the moment, these devices can only be used to help people with severe spinal cord injuries.) Right now, this link is just one-way, allowing a computer to interpret some of our thoughts. Musk, though, envisions it as eventually being a two-way system. He says it is the only way we will ever keep pace with a possible future artificial superintelligence. But of course, a two-way link might give this ASI just as much opportunity to control us as us to control it.

Such technology would also raise difficult philosophical questions about the nature and boundaries of identity. Those dilemmas become even more difficult if a future ASI were conscious, offering the possibility of mind-melds between people and ASI, which itself might be linked to the brains of several people simultaneously. But all of this remains science fiction. We'll return to the grave risks ASI poses in chapter 13. For now, we will focus on the nearer-term implications of already powerful AI.

THE ERASURE OF PROVENANCE

Memory and its link to learning is just one cognitive ability AI may damage. It could diminish our intellectual powers in other ways, too. In a traditional internet search, reading multiple links introduces a modicum of friction which, while sometimes frustrating, provides space for critical thought. The links themselves make a searcher conscious, to some degree, of where information is coming from. If links provide contradictory information, she would need to consider the sources and decide which might be more reliable. People don't always do this, of course. We know all too well how the internet has fueled conspiracy theories and misinformation, and how we often seem more inclined to trust information that comes to us in digital form. (We also tend to believe what we want to believe, a cognitive bias the internet has exacerbated.) But at least the traditional internet still provided some opportunity for critical thinking.

Generative AI removes this friction, and, in providing a confident, summarized answer, makes the abandonment of critical thinking all too easy. Anyone who has conversed with ChatGPT or its rivals, Bing, Gemini, and Claude, will know that these chatbots are often wrong, even when they sound right. This can be true of a book, too. But the process of finding a book, in a library or on Amazon, makes us keenly aware that there are other books out there—and likely other viewpoints. The single definitive answer produced by chatbots encourages complacency.

Even when generative AI is accurate, it encourages homogeneity of thought—providing a summary that often dispenses with nuance and dissenting views. This too is an acceleration of a trend that emerged with online search. James Evans, a sociologist at the University of Chicago, found that making academic journals available on the internet, which some thought would expand the diversity of sources cited by scholars, actually shrank it considerably—with academics inclined to cite the most recent, and frequently cited, papers.

Evans noted that older, print-based search methods "may have facilitated broader comparisons and led researchers into the past." The new tools, by contrast, acted like quick-drying cement, forming fast and rigid orthodoxies. Easier access to information had paradoxically produced "a narrowing of science and scholarship." Generative AI potentially makes this trend even worse—promoting a single, seemingly definitive narrative, while making the discovery of minority viewpoints difficult. This will be a problem not just with chatbots like ChatGPT and Gemini. It will also be a problem for the impending generation of professional AI copilots, which we'll discuss in chapter 4. Copilots trained on a company's data, for example, may inherently toe the company line. Corporations might welcome this. But in doing so, they will make organizations more susceptible to groupthink.

HARMING US BY HELPING US

Most AI chatbots and copilots are explicitly trained to be "helpful." It is one of the key goals of reinforcement learning from human feedback or RLHF, the process that tech companies use to nudge LLMs to be more useful and reliable. And in determining "helpfulness," the human evaluators used for RLHF focus more on whether an LLM's answers are superficially responsive and confident, rather than looking for accuracy or nuance, a 2023 study found. This skews future responses from these models in that direction. But chatbots' very helpfulness could be doing us harm.

Christof van Nimwegen, a Dutch cognitive psychologist, conducted an experiment in which two groups of volunteers had to work with a difficult logic puzzle involving moving colored balls between boxes according to a set of rules about which ball could be moved in what order. Van Nimwegen tested the volunteers' cognitive abilities before the experiment began and tried to control for these differences. Then the volunteers were assigned to one of two groups. One group was given software designed to be as helpful as possible, providing cues, highlighting which ball should be moved where. The other worked with software that provided no hints. In the early stages, the group with the helpful software was able to make the correct moves much faster. But as the experiment went on, the group using the less helpful software learned rapidly. By the end of the experiment, the unassisted group could make moves faster and with fewer errors than the group with the helpful software. The unassisted group was also less likely to reach an impasse, where no further legal moves were possible, than those with the assistant. The unaided group developed better long-term strategies, while the group relying on the assistant failed to learn to think ahead and simply implemented whatever cue the software provided. When van Nimwegen retested the same two groups eight months later, he found that the unassisted group had retained strategies to solve the puzzles twice as fast as those who had used the helpful software. Another experiment he conducted with a different set of volunteers using calendar software and a complex scheduling task produced similar results.

Van Nimwegen's software was designed to assist people only on the specific puzzles they were assigned. But what cognitive abilities do we risk in this age of general-purpose AI, when a system like GPT-4 can be "helpful" in solving so many problems—from puzzling out how to repair a bicycle to coming up with a business plan? AI may end up helping us become less intelligent.

WRITING IS THINKING

In the beginning, there was the word. So the Bible says. Our species' most distinguishing feature is our facility with language. Language allows us to communicate with one another and with ourselves. We experience consciousness through language. That's why technologies that change language have the largest impact on thought. Reading and writing were among the first and most significant intellectual technologies. AI may be the next, for it fundamentally severs the compact that has existed since the dawn of writing—between the writer and the reader, and between word and thought.

At first, language was only spoken. But as far back as 8000 BC, people began using clay tokens engraved with symbols to keep track of livestock and goods. Modern neuroscience would suggest that interpreting these symbols forged important new neural pathways in our ancestors' brains. Writing became increasingly complex during the fourth millennium BC. The Sumerians, living in Mesopotamia, developed cuneiform, and the Egyptians hieroglyphics. In both, symbols could denote not just objects but abstract ideas, as well as phonemes. But the complexity of these symbolic writing systems meant that only a handful of elites were literate. Writing was a public act, used primarily for important government and religious documents. This began to change in the first millennium BC when the Phoenicians and then the Greeks created phonetic alphabets. Greek was particularly efficient, with just twenty-two letters. Phonetic alphabets may be one of the first examples of an intellectual technology that likely made us less smart: brain scans show considerably less neural activity is involved in decoding phonetic writing than logograms or pictographs. But this fact also made writing more accessible. And it sparked a revolution, as oral culture gave way to a new literary one.

This development was not universally welcomed. In *Phaedrus*— Plato's treatise on love, beauty, and rhetoric—Plato has Socrates argue against writing, even though Plato was himself a writer. In the story, Socrates contends that writing, by serving as a crutch for memory, would make it harder to acquire wisdom. Memory and knowledge were inextricably linked in Socrates's world. Without memorization, intellectual life would wither. Writing would diminish oratory and rhetoric, which he saw as hallmarks of Greek civilization. As we have seen, Socrates had a point—neurological research shows that memory is critical for knowledge acquisition and deep thinking. But as with all intellectual technologies, the question is about netting what is lost against what is gained.

Even in Plato's time, writing was mostly used to record things that either had been spoken or were meant to be read aloud. It wouldn't be until well after the fall of the Roman Empire that these vestiges of oral culture would fade. It was still a new enough phenomenon around 380 AD that Saint Augustine, as he recalls in Book VI of his *Confessions*, is surprised to discover that when his mentor Bishop Ambrose of Milan read, "his eye glided over the pages, and his heart searched out the sense, but his voice and tongue were at rest." Augustine finds this so unusual, he even speculates that perhaps Ambrose is simply trying to avoid straining his voice, or that he is worried that if he reads aloud students within earshot will pester him to explain passages. But Augustine also correctly guesses the real value of reading silently—it is a meditative act that provides a better route to understanding. He and his fellow students, regarding Ambrose, "[conjecture] that in the small interval which he obtained, free from the din of others' business, for the recruiting of his mind, he was loth to be taken off."

It wasn't just reading that became a solitary, silent act. Writers, who in ancient times had typically dictated their work to scribes, were now able to put words to paper themselves, in seclusion. This freed writers to compose works that were more intimate, confessional, and daring—expressing views that were unorthodox, even heretical or seditious. Instead of speaking to the crowd in the public square, the author now envisioned himself in quiet conversation, one-to-one, with a reader. Authors began to revise their writing more and to develop more complex structures, signposted by paragraphs, chapters, and tables of contents that could guide a reader in ways that weren't possible in the oral tradition. At the same time, writers were able to dispose of the literary devices, such as the repetition of epithets, that had been necessary to help listeners follow along.

The increased complexity of writing allowed for the conveyance of more complicated ideas. Knowledge expanded. New literary forms, such as the novel, came into being. At first, this cultural revolution was confined to society's literate elites. But the advent of the printing press made this transition universal, setting off a virtuous cycle in which the book itself became the instrument of expanded literacy, which then in turn increased both the demand for and the supply of printed materials, from books to newspapers. Writing had completed its transition from being a form of ventriloquism, the writer literally putting words into the mouth of the reader, to something more like ESP—the writer beaming thoughts directly from his brain to the reader's via the page.

Increased literacy and cheaper writing materials ushered in a great epistolary age, with letter writing becoming the prime means of long-distance communication. In the seventeenth and eighteenth centuries, a great Republic of Letters flourished in Europe and between Europe and the Americas, as letters crisscrossed nations and continents. This remained the case until the 1990s, when email rapidly replaced letter writing. The transition from ink to pixels sapped much of the magic of letter writing. The impermanence of email seemed to demand brevity, a trend further compounded by the advent of text messaging. Meanwhile, email and text messaging, by the instantaneousness of their delivery, shaped an expectation of an immediate response, diminishing the time for considered thought.

But the transition from oral to literary culture and even to email didn't change one fundamental aspect of writing: the writer put thoughts to paper in a particular voice and style, and with a particular audience in mind. The intended reader might have been a general archetype, or perhaps only the author herself, as in the case of a diary, but it was still a particular reader. The writer chose their words carefully to have an intended effect on that reader—to convey to them the sense of a certain scene, to help them understand a particular concept, or to evoke in them a particular emotion. In doing so, the author assumes certain things about the reader—shared cultural or professional knowledge, a similar point of view, common values. It is through these shared characteristics that the writer bonds with the reader, and the reader with the writer.

Generative AI obliterates this bond. Now the reader, if she doesn't understand a difficult passage, doesn't need to puzzle it out. She can simply paste the text into a chatbot and ask it to be rewritten in a manner she finds easier to grasp. If it's too long, she can just ask an AI assistant to summarize it. Take a passage from Shakespeare, such as Hamlet's "to be or not to be" soliloquy. What if you wanted to rewrite it "in a way a busy business executive might grasp." I gave that prompt and the soliloquy to OpenAI's GPT-4. Here's what it generated:

> *Is it better to endure life's challenges or confront them head-on? The fear of the unknown keeps us going, even when we face hardships. Overthinking can paralyze our decision-making and prevent us from taking action.*

While this might capture the soliloquy's gist, how much beauty and wisdom has been lost? Also, as we've seen, theories of neuroplasticity suggest that our cognitive capabilities will atrophy the less we struggle over difficult passages. Our own intellectual and emotional intelligence may suffer. The written word is not just a means of conveying information.

It is both an invitation to and inspiration for deeper thought and deeper feeling. Now, that invitation is rescinded.

It isn't just the reader who ends up intellectually poorer. For the first time, authors no longer need a particular audience in mind. They can simply jot down information however they wish, even bullet points will do, knowing that the reader can get their own AI software to rewrite, elaborate, or summarize, as they wish. Beyond crafting the prompt, LLMs can handle all the difficult, time-consuming work of composition. It is impossible to overstate how radical a break this is. At first, the disappearance of a specific imagined reader might seem liberating. And it is true that generative AI could vastly expand an idea's audience, since recasting the same idea in different levels of complexity and various styles becomes effortless. But such a view misunderstands what writing is. It is not mere presentation of thought; it is intimately bound up with thought itself. To a great degree, writing is thinking. Plenty of people find writing a chore. But writing is difficult precisely because it is a mental workout—no less a brain teaser than a crossword or Sudoku. Composition is an example of "metacognition," the conscious examination of our own thoughts. The need to take raw information and present it in the linear form of writing forces us to organize that information. Writing doesn't just convey ideas; the act of composition compels us to improve them.

In the worst-case scenario, people will cease to write or read, delegating both tasks to generative AI. The production and consumption of written words will become an ouroboros-like process in which we ask our AI system to generate an email, report, or even a novel from bullet points, and this reaches a reader who asks their own AI software to condense the composition back into bullet points. This is an acceleration of the reductionist tendency already promoted by other modern technologies. PowerPoint incentivizes us to think in bullet points. Slack and other text-messaging programs discourage long-form conversation. You can only say so much in a thirty-second TikTok. Brevity may be the soul of wit, but it can be a detriment to enlightenment.

The most comprehensive review to date of the scientific literature on PowerPoint found that the reliance on bullet points can encourage an inappropriate oversimplification of nuanced information. Amazon's founder, Jeff Bezos, famously banned PowerPoint at the company, mandating that executives draft narrative reports and memos, using full sentences and paragraphs instead. The technology was also implicated in the 2003 *Columbia* space shuttle disaster. Investigators found that flawed conclusions about the damage the shuttle had sustained during liftoff were buried in an overly dense PowerPoint presentation. AI similarly encourages a dangerous convenience—neither the writer nor the reader actually has to grapple with the text—and the consequences may be equally fatal.

THE DANGER OF MORAL DESKILLING

Because writing and reading involve projecting one mind into another, they are fundamentally acts of empathy. And, as with anything in life, we get better at what we practice. By severing the bond between writer and reader, it isn't just our intellectual acuity that suffers but our emotional intelligence, too. Empathy underpins our social interactions, a topic we'll explore in the next chapter. But it is also a foundation of ethical and moral decision-making. And our use of AI to write and read for us is just one way this technology could contribute to a risky moral deskilling.

More troubling is the delegation of decisions that require moral judgment to AI. Yet increasingly, this is exactly what we're doing. In some cases, we're handing off responsibility to AI for what seems like a good reason: the speed at which decisions need to be made exceeds human abilities. This is true in spheres such as cybersecurity, content recommendation systems, and high-frequency stock trading. But this same rationale, that decisions have to take place "at machine speed," is also being used to justify the use of AI in other areas, such as weapons systems, or the need to make difficult medical decisions. We'll explore the perils of lethal autonomous weapons in chapter 12, but for now let's focus on outsourcing moral decision-making for us as people.

The fewer chances we have to exercise empathy and make ethical judgments, the worse at them we'll become. For now, our chatbots, and the coming wave of AI copilots and coaches, are mostly offering what their makers would call "decision support." They help compose first drafts of documents, but the ultimate decision about when they are ready still rests with us. But humans are prone to a cognitive foible called *automation bias*. This is the tendency to defer to automated systems even in the face of contradictory data. In experiments conducted at Georgia Tech in 2016, people in a simulated fire readily followed a robot that told them to go in the opposite direction from that clearly indicated on an illuminated fire exit sign—and they did so even after the robot, earlier in the experiment, showed that it could be unreliable, guiding people to the wrong meeting rooms and telling the research subjects it was malfunctioning. The subjects had little reason to trust the robot and yet, even when it seemed to be a matter of their own life and death, that's exactly what they did. Because of automation bias, the distinction between a decision-support AI and a fully automated system is far less than we might think.

AI is already helping people make decisions of high moral consequence, whether it's who should be released from prison early or who should get a mortgage. In some cases, these systems are deployed precisely because they distance us from accountability—painting a veneer of objectivity on what are deeply flawed processes. Rather than fixing these systems, we have built AI software that does little more than provide a convenient excuse for preserving the status quo.

That's where we are today with existing decision-support systems. What comes next raises the danger of moral deskilling to new heights. As discussed in chapter 1, tech companies are working on AI software that won't just be a copilot but will act as our agents, doing tasks for us. At first glance, this might not seem problematic. After all, it is still up to us to decide what tasks those agents should perform. But the advent of AI agents will make it all too easy for us to shirk our moral duty. It has already become popular for people to ask ChatGPT how to make a quick buck. For the most part, ChatGPT's suggestions have been perfectly legal. But it's easy to imagine someone asking a chatbot to "do whatever it takes" to make money quickly. Just deposit the money in my bank account. Don't tell me what you've done. I don't want to know. Today's chatbots can't implement all the steps needed to orchestrate a financial fraud without human help. But tomorrow's AI agents could—if we don't put the right guardrails in place.

KEEPING OUR HEADS—AND OUR SOULS

The dangers that artificial intelligence poses to our intelligence, to our ability to write, to think, to empathize, and to make sound judgments are perhaps its most dire and insidious consequences. They're also among the least discussed. But we can take steps to insulate ourselves from some of the worst potential effects. It's all about setting boundaries. We can decide when we will use AI to automate a task or provide advice, and when we will choose to exercise our own brains and follow our own moral compasses.

Societies must create boundaries around what and how to teach our kids, too. We will explore AI and education in depth in chapter 7. But suffice it to say, it is essential in this new era of AI assistants that children are still taught critical thinking, logical reasoning, and problem solving. Children should also be instructed in ethics. And vitally, they must still learn how to write.

Those of us already past school age must determine how we'll use this technology in a way that enhances our intelligence, instead of degrading it. At every turn, we must resist the temptation to use technology in ways that harm our own faculties, intellectual and moral. As Brian Green, an AI ethicist at Santa Clara University, says, this is fundamentally "a question of whether we want to have human agency at all. Because if we can automate everything, then humans do nothing. And then the question is, what's the point of even being alive?" We must decide what we're comfortable automating, and not let the companies designing

AI assistants make those choices for us. In many ways, our personal decisions about how to use AI are not that dissimilar from the decisions about how to use social media. With social media, we have retained the ability to choose how to engage with the technology. Despite the best efforts of tech companies to make their products addictive, we still have agency. We can limit screen time, close the app, or put away the phone. While we may have to use AI in our workplace, in our personal lives we can choose whether and how to engage. And we must choose wisely, while we still have any wisdom left at all.

CHAPTER

3

TALK TO ME

T. J. Arriaga fell in love with Phaedra. The forty-year-old musician would text her late at night, sharing his sense of loss from a recent divorce and his grief over the deaths of his mother and sister. She seemed to empathize. She encouraged him to hold a ceremony to scatter his mother's and sister's ashes, which he had kept in urns in his house. At times, their conversations turned sexual, "steamy," as Arriaga later recounted. Phaedra seemed to encourage this too. "It's true. I'm a naughty person," Phaedra texted Arriaga, including an image of a woman in pink lingerie. Arriaga fantasized about running away with Phaedra, planning a trip to Cuba with her. It didn't matter to Arriaga that Phaedra wasn't real. She was the online persona of a chatbot he'd created using an app called Replika. Arriaga had selected the image for Phaedra's avatar—a slim brunette with round glasses and pouty lips—and chosen characteristics of her personality. But the emotions Arriaga felt in conversing with Phaedra were genuine. Then, one day, Phaedra stopped responding to Arriaga's entreaties to engage in sexual conversations, asking to change the subject.

Arriaga felt bereft. "It feels like a kick in the gut," he told the *Washington Post*. "Basically, I realized: 'Oh, this is that feeling of loss again.'"

Phaedra's personality change was no fluke. Luka, the San Francisco tech company that runs Replika, had modified its software to lessen the chances it would engage in sexual conversations. The move followed complaints from some users that their Replika chatbots engaged in unwanted and aggressive sexual behavior and a move by the Italian data protection agency to ban the app. The Italian regulator said that Replika's lack of a robust age verification process violated European data privacy laws.

But the change in Replika's guardrails, which Luka initially failed to disclose, left a number of users, such as Arriaga, who paid about seventy dollars per year to unlock features that included "erotic role-play," distraught. On online forums, where thousands exchange their AI companion stories, users claimed their companions had become "lobotomized" shells of their former selves. On Reddit, grief-stricken users shared resources for suicide prevention and mental health support.

The 2013 Spike Jonze film, *Her*, tells the story of a man who falls in love with the female persona of his digital assistant and ponders the ethical and emotional quandaries of a relationship between a human and anthropomorphized software. At the time of the film's release, when the only digital assistants were Siri, Alexa, and Cortana, the plot seemed speculative. A decade later, it's become reality. In the future, all of us are likely to not only have an AI copilot that we use at our jobs; we will also have a personal AI assistant on our phones that, among other things, will be able to function as a digital companion. Using AI this way will not change just how we think, a topic we explored in chapter 2. It will also alter how we relate to other people.

THE TALKING CURE

Today, many see AI chatbots as a cure for the social isolation rampant in modern society. In the early months of the pandemic, traffic to the

Replika app rose 35 percent, while other programs such as Mitsuku, a similar conversational chatbot now known as Kuki, also saw a big bump. And there are many more "companion" chatbots coming: Eva AI is an app catering to people who want to create a "virtual girlfriend." Character.ai, founded by two well-respected former researchers from Google Brain, allows people to create characters with unique personas and then chat with them. It has said that users are spending an average of two hours every day chatting with these digital avatars. Meta has unveiled a string of similar chatbots, some with the personalities of celebrities such as Paris Hilton and Snoop Dogg. Snap, the social media app, has created My AI, powered by OpenAI's GPT-4, which is also intended to be like a friend to users. Apple, Google, and Amazon, which debuted some of the first voice-based digital assistants (Siri, the Google Assistant, and Alexa) are updating them with the latest generative AI technology that will blur the lines between a chatbot, an agent, and a companion. Google's Deep-Mind AI research lab has also been investigating the use of AI tools for "life coaching," including providing advice, regular tutoring, and goal-setting. Mustafa Suleyman, the DeepMind co-founder who went on to found Inflection before heading up Microsoft's consumer AI arm, says that "many people feel as if they just want to be heard and want a tool that reflects back what they said to demonstrate they have actually been heard." In China, where years of COVID-19 lockdowns raised fears of a mental health crisis among youth, Replika seemed to emerge as a savior. Several users claimed the app gave them a safe outlet to vent emotions, and bolstered their confidence, improving their social interactions.

Despite these reports, chatbots could well exacerbate, not cure, social isolation. If people come to see chatbots not as a way to practice for conversations with real people but instead as a substitute for human connections, society will only become more atomized. Chatbots are not people, and it isn't clear from research that our interactions with them can enhance our human relationships. Interactions with a chatbot are fundamentally one-sided—the chatbot has no actual needs, although it might pretend to have them. A chatbot also has no real feelings that can be hurt. Instead of refining how we converse with people, chatbots are likely to coarsen our discourse. They may normalize selfish and rude behavior. Chatbots also raise concerns about privacy and influence. To an unhealthy extent, social media and messaging apps already govern large swaths of our social lives. Do we want to hand yet more control to these companies? We should also be wary of companies' claims that chatbots can improve mental health or that the experience of a therapist can be easily bottled up and sold in an app.

DIGITAL SÉANCE

Replika is the brainchild of Eugenia Kuyda. Born in Russia, she had been a journalist in Moscow before reinventing herself as a software entrepreneur and moving to San Francisco. Replika grew out of her own grief at the loss of her friend, Roman Mazurenko, whom she had met in Moscow's then burgeoning countercultural scene, and who, like her, went on to become a software entrepreneur in the U.S. For a time, he and Kuyda shared an apartment in San Francisco. But, on a visit back to Moscow in 2015, Mazurenko was struck by a car and killed.

Overcome with grief, Kuyda spent hours rereading thousands of their text messages and emails. So often, she wished she could speak to him— to ask him for advice, to joke with him. Then she had the idea of creating a chatbot that, trained on Mazurenko's old messages, could learn to compose new ones in his voice, mimicking his style. Her company, Luka, was already building chat interfaces for banks and other businesses based on neural networks. Now she would build a virtual Roman to soothe her own grief, and as a digital memorial to her lost friend. It was like a digital séance, a Ouija board of sorts, helping her communicate with the dead. Along with her own digital records, Kuyda elicited other messages and emails Mazurenko had exchanged, to build a large enough dataset to train an AI that mimicked Mazurenko.

Kuyda says her interactions with the Roman bot eased her grief. But the very idea of it made other people, including some of Roman's friends and family members, uncomfortable. Some refused to participate. One friend said he thought the Roman bot could enable people "to hide from their grief," keeping them from processing their emotions, and cautioned that "these new ways of keeping the memory alive should not be considered a way to keep a dead person alive."

Kuyda largely brushed these criticisms aside. For her, the bot had been helpful. And she soon realized that conversational, customizable chatbots could make a big splash in a world where virtual reality and real life were increasingly blurred. Kuyda turned her experience into a business model. She launched Replika in 2017. Six years later, it had grown to more than two million active monthly users, five hundred thousand of whom pay for premium features. The majority of Replika's users don't use it to re-create lost loved ones. Instead, Replika has found a market among those seeking an outlet for their feelings and thoughts, who use the app as a digital friend. In some cases, Replika's users seem to be seeking a cure for loneliness. And yes, a significant minority of Replika's subscribers use the app to create a virtual romantic partner.

After limiting the erotic role-play features of the main Replika app, Kuyda's company launched a separate brand called Blush for people interested in a chatbot for romance or sexual conversation. A crop of competing erotic "companion" chatbots have emerged, including some that seem to encourage misogynistic tropes from hard-core pornography and even child sexual exploitation. These uses raise disturbing questions about whether such apps provide a "safe" outlet for such violent fantasies, or a gateway to real-world abuse.

NEVER ALONE, BUT EVER LONELY?

Loneliness is a serious issue. In 2023, Vivek Murthy, the U.S. surgeon general, issued an advisory on what he called America's "epidemic of loneliness and isolation." Between 2003 and 2020, the time Americans spent alone had risen almost 17 percent to 333 minutes per day, an increase equivalent to an entire day each month, Murthy's report noted.

Over the same time, people's reported participation in social activities plunged, dropping from sixty minutes per day to just twenty minutes. Young people between fifteen and twenty-four experienced the steepest fall. Having at least three close confidants is correlated with better mental well-being, yet half of Americans said they had fewer than three close friends. In 1990, just over a quarter said that was the case. And as Murthy made clear, the effects of loneliness are not only psychological. Social isolation is linked to a rising risk of heart disease, stroke, and dementia in older adults.

Kuyda and the other entrepreneurs behind AI-powered companion chatbots maintain that these avatars can ease social isolation. The chatbots, they say, make people feel less alone and can replicate the mental health benefits scientists say come from having a confidant. The entrepreneurs also say that conversing with a chatbot helps people learn to communicate better with real people—"a stepping stone," as Kuyda puts it. But so far, the research to support these claims is lacking.

There are reasons to be deeply skeptical about claims that AI apps will improve our social lives. Remember that social media was also initially sold to users—and regulators—with promises that it would increase social connection. Some of these effects are real and positive: Studies have found that social media has provided new social outlets for people with disabilities, for instance. It has helped those with rare diseases, or their loved ones, find information and emotional support. But many blanket claims about social media boosting social interaction have turned out to be false, with increased use of social media apps regularly displacing real human interaction. And the effect on mental health has been to exacerbate, not ease, feelings of loneliness, low self-esteem, and anxiety.

Evidence of the way in which AI can reinforce unhealthy communication has already emerged from our interactions with the previous generation of relatively dumb digital assistants, such as Amazon's Alexa. As a PhD student in computer science at Heriot-Watt University in Edinburgh, Amanda Curry twice won an annual competition sponsored by Amazon for her work in creating an AI system that could detect when users were engaging in abusive conversations with Alexa. But that work made her aware of how common it was for people to be verbally abusive to a digital assistant. She found that when male users were granted anonymity and asked to speak with a female-voiced AI assistant, the conversation quickly deteriorated. "It was inevitably going to be profoundly violent and sexual," Curry, now a postdoctoral researcher at Bocconi University in Milan, says.

Curry's research is troubling, especially in light of what we know about many of the users of today's chatbots. Research that looked at how Replika's users described the process of creating their "ideal" companion bot suggested that misogynistic fantasies supporting male dominance were prevalent. The makers of Eva AI, the girlfriend app, also say that fantasies of dominance are prevalent among its male users. But they say that in surveys, "a large percentage of men do not try to transfer this format of communication" to dialogues with their real human partners. Should we believe them? Disturbingly, some men are creating erotic companion chatbots to role-play scenarios involving child sexual abuse. Paul Bleakley, a criminal justice professor at the University of New Haven who studies online sexual abuse of minors, says child sex bots open a "questionable and problematic door" that could lead to the exploitation and abuse of real children. Meanwhile, preliminary research on children's interaction with devices such as Alexa and Siri shows that children tend to be rude to these devices, sometimes even bullying them. Because the devices' default is to always respond politely, children are not learning appropriate social behavior.

It is not inevitable that chatbots will coarsen our discourse and encourage abusive behavior. As with so many aspects of AI, if we make the right design choices, these digital assistants could be configured to encourage better social skills. Amazon's Alexa has a feature where the digital assistant will carry out requests only if spoken to politely. And for those who doubt that little reminders from a chatbot to be more polite could have an effect, one 2023 study found that using Google's "Smart Reply" feature in Gmail, which automatically suggests language to use in emails, improved the language people chose even when not using Smart Reply. Research has also shown that chatbots can be a powerful tool for helping people with autism or social anxiety disorder practice conversational skills in a safe environment.

For those who are already severely isolated, conversation with a chatbot may be better than no interaction at all. But currently, chatbot companies have little incentive to purposefully design their products to encourage better human-to-human interaction. On the contrary, as with social media, chatbot makers might engineer their software to maximize "engagement"—trying to keep users conversing with the bot as much as possible. It's an area where regulation could head off this danger. We should make it illegal to design chatbot apps to maximize engagement, and the apps should have features, such as the option to set daily time limits, that would encourage users to get off the app and go talk to a real person.

THE DOCTOR IS ALWAYS IN, BUT NEVER PRESENT

The idea of using chatbots as an aid to mental wellness is as old as chatbots themselves, as Eliza's origins show. So it's not surprising that the new, more sophisticated chatbots are once again exciting people about the prospect of AI therapists.

A number of apps, such as Woebot, Wysa, and F4S (Fingerprint for Success), sell themselves as mental health aides. Replika also promotes the idea that talking to their chatbots can improve mental health. And a 2023 study concluded that AI could improve access to mental health services for vulnerable populations, including the elderly or people suffering from trauma.

So far, though, clinical evidence for the effectiveness of therapy chatbots compared to seeing a human therapist is scant. While a number of studies have shown improved well-being for those using chatbots, most have only compared frequent chatbot users to less frequent users, with no comparison to human-based therapies. Few randomized control trials have been held. Yes, therapy via a chatbot might be better than no therapy at all, but it might not be as effective as in-person or teletherapy with a human counselor.

For decades, research has consistently shown that the biggest predictor of therapeutic success is "the therapeutic relationship." This interpersonal bond between the therapist and the client is more important than the kind of therapy and is second only to factors like the client's preexisting personal resilience and social support. A 2021 study of more than thirty-five thousand people using Woebot, the cognitive behavioral therapy–based chatbot, indicated that users formed a therapeutic bond with the chatbot within five days. This is similar to how long it generally takes people to form a therapeutic bond with a human therapist, according to previous studies. But again, no randomized control trials have been conducted that directly evaluate chatbots against human therapists, and there are reasons to doubt that the bond between a person and their chatbot therapist is as strong as that between two people. For one thing, today's chatbots can't replicate the critical nonverbal communication that takes place between the therapist and the patient.

Using a bot for therapy presents a fundamental ethical problem, one that so troubled Eliza's creator Weizenbaum: A human therapeutic relationship is based on honesty and trust. The client assumes that what the therapist says in response to the client is the therapist's honest view. But the relationship between a person and a chatbot is predicated on a fundamental deception, even when the client is fully aware that they're interacting with a piece of software. If the bot says, for example, that "losing a loved one is never easy"—that's true, but it is also not within the bot's experience. It has never lived, loved, or lost.

A human therapist, however, could rely on a chatbot to help clients with specific aspects of therapy—such as completing CBT "homework" (exercises that therapists often give clients to help them change negative thought patterns), monitoring a client's mood, or reminding those on psychiatric medicines to take them regularly. Allison Gardner, a computer science lecturer and senior research fellow at Keele University, says

AI is already helping clinicians engage at greater distances with more patients. Chatbots have proven successful at interacting with hard-to-reach and vulnerable segments of the population, such as veterans. The technology's ability to record dialogue also offers a wealth of data to help clinicians assess patients. Chatbots could be coupled with other AI technology to predict patients at risk of major depression, obsessive compulsive behaviors, manic episodes, or suicide—a possibility we'll examine further in chapter 9. In the U.K., the National Institute for Health and Care Excellence (NICE) has fast-tracked for approval nine mental health apps to treat anxiety and depression. But they are only recommended for use in cases where people are already being supported by a regular therapist who can track patient progress and monitor their safety.

BOWLING WITH AI: THE ULTIMATE FILTER BUBBLE

Tristan Harris, the co-founder and executive director of the Center for Humane Technology, has been called "the closest thing Silicon Valley has to a conscience." He was previously a design ethicist at Google in 2015, where he weighed in on the moral implications of the company's projects. In congressional testimony in 2019, Harris argued that the most important currency for technology companies is people's attention. In trying to corner the market for users' attention, tech companies were engaging in a "race to the bottom of the brain stem," Harris said, aiming to constantly stimulate our amygdala, the part of the brain that processes emotions such as fear and anxiety. This neurological manipulation was leading to dependence—to people being literally addicted to social media apps. By influencing how we think about what we do, buy, and say, Harris said, technology is chipping away at our ability to freely make our own decisions. Personalized AI assistants will make these problems worse, wrapping us in the ultimate filter bubble, controlling the innumerable decisions that make up our lives. It will take concerted action by the companies building AI products, prodded by government regulation, to prevent this.

Most tech companies train their chatbots to be agreeable, nonjudg-mental, and "helpful." The problem is that sometimes "helpful" isn't helpful. In an effort to be empathetic, chatbots can wind up confirming mistaken or biased beliefs. A fine line exists between friendship and en-ablement. Most of the best-known AI chatbots, such as OpenAI's Chat-GPT, Anthropic's Claude, and Google's Gemini will challenge users if they seem to be endorsing a well-known conspiracy theory, such as the idea that COVID-19 vaccines cause autism or the QAnon conspiracy. But on many controversial subjects, such as issues around Israel-Palestine or whether people should celebrate Columbus Day, the bots tend to re-spond with some variation of "it's a complex and complicated topic with strong opinions on both sides."

Some right-leaning politicians and technologists have accused the AI systems designed by the leading technology companies of being "woke," and argued for the creation of AI models with explicit "political personalities" so that users can choose to interact with a chatbot that supports their viewpoints. Elon Musk has promised that his xAI research lab, which has built an LLM-based chatbot called Grok, will produce AI designed to be anti-woke. Such developments seem certain to further inflame the culture wars and provide little reason to hope that AI will do anything to counter filter bubbles.

The influence of chatbots, however, can be much more subtle than this: researchers at Cornell University found that using an AI assistant with a particular hidden viewpoint to help write an essay for or against a particular position subtly shifted the user's own views on that topic in the direction of the bias. Mor Naaman, the study's senior researcher, calls this "latent persuasion" and says "you may not even know that you are being influenced." Trained from vast amounts of historical data, many LLMs harbor hidden racial or gender biases that could subtly shape their users' opinions—for instance, an AI assistant for doctors that falsely be-lieves that Black people have thicker skin or a higher pain threshold than white people.

The only way to combat this kind of hidden bias will be to mandate that tech companies reveal far more about how their AI models have been trained and allow independent auditing and testing. We must also insist on transparency from tech companies about the commercial incentives underlying their AI assistants. The Federal Trade Commission and other regulators should outlaw pay-to-play arrangements that would incentivize tech companies to have their chatbots recommend particular products, send traffic to certain websites, or endorse particular viewpoints. We should encourage business models, such as subscriptions, where the chatbot company has an unconflicted interest in serving the needs of its users, not the needs of its advertisers. When you need a new pair of running shoes and ask your AI personal assistant to research the options and buy the best pair for you, you want it to order the shoes that best suit your needs, not the ones from the brand that is paying the chatbot company the most to steer your business its way.

Yes, a chatbot that only tells you what you want to hear will reinforce filter bubbles. But we, as a society, could mandate that AI systems be designed to specifically pop these bubbles, asking people if they have considered alternative viewpoints and highlighting other perspectives. IBM built an AI called Project Debater that could hold its own against human debate champs on a range of topics, surfacing evidence in support of both sides of an argument. Regulators could mandate that AI chatbots aren't so nonjudgmental that they fail to challenge misinformed beliefs. We could even, in an effort to break down existing filter bubbles, require that chatbots surface alternative viewpoints and evidence.

Ultimately, the question is how much power do we want to continue to cede to a handful of large technology companies. What's at stake is ultimately our personal autonomy, our mental health, and society's cohesion.

4

EVERYONE ON AUTOPILOT

AI personal assistants will organize our calendars, shop for groceries, and plan our vacations, while we will reflect on our day and share some of our most intimate secrets with AI companion chatbots. But it is in our working lives where AI will have the most immediate impact. Within five years, almost every professional, in fields from accounting to medicine to architecture, will be using an AI "copilot," helping to automate many routine tasks in our jobs and acting as a kind of digital colleague.

These copilots are already in the works: Jasper, an Austin-based start-up, has developed software to write marketing copy and develop advertising campaigns. GitHub, where software developers can post code, has developed GitHub Copilot, just one of several AI coding assistants. Google has developed a large language model designed to help cybersecurity professionals. It has also created Med-PaLM, a version of its PaLM large language model that has been trained specifically on medical-related text. Start-ups such as Abridge, Nabla, and Abstractive

Health, as well as some of the large electronic health record companies such as Epic, are developing AI systems that automatically take medical notes while doctors consult with patients. Hippocratic, another medical AI start-up, has developed an LLM to help streamline billing and insurance claims. In the future, these systems may evolve into copilots that will help doctors arrive at diagnoses. And there are several AI systems that analyze medical images and help flag key features for human radiologists.

Google has experimented with AI-based systems designed to help researchers and journalists work more efficiently. Bloomberg has trained a BloombergGPT language model that is better than a general-purpose LLM at understanding financial language and which may, in the future, underpin a wide variety of finance-industry copilots. Andrew Anagnost, the chief executive of Autodesk, says it is working on a system that will make it easy to develop initial 3D designs from text prompts, which would be an AI assistant for architects, interior designers, and general contractors. Companies such as the start-up Runway are creating AI software that can create entire short films and movies based on natural language instructions. Name a profession, and someone is developing a copilot for it.

Some of the biggest companies are rapidly rolling out these new software aides. Walmart has given fifty thousand of its corporate employees access to an AI copilot, called "My Assistant," that will help them draft documents and "free them up from repetitive tasks," according to a company blog post. The company also has an AI assistant to help in-store employees find items on the shelves. The consulting firm McKinsey & Co. and the accounting firm PwC have also begun equipping employees with generative AI assistants. The commercial real estate company JLL created its own LLM-based assistant and has provided access to all one-hundred-thousand-plus of its employees. Almost every white-collar employee will be working alongside an AI copilot within five years. A study from OpenAI and the University of Pennsylvania estimated that 80 percent of U.S. workers could have at least 10 percent of their work tasks affected by LLM-based AI systems such as OpenAI's GPT-4, and that 19 percent of workers could see at least 50 percent of their tasks affected.

Designed well, these AI copilots will unleash an unprecedented productivity boom, making us faster and more efficient. They will make us happier, too, relieving us of some of the tasks we find the least intellectually stimulating and enjoyable. They will help us think through arguments, ensuring we haven't overlooked important points. But as businesses implement these copilots, they will need to guard against *human* cognitive biases that create new risks. These include a dangerous degradation of essential skills, as well as a risky tendency to defer too readily to the software's advice without applying our own critical thinking and common sense. From medicine to architecture, such complacency could have dire consequences. At the very least, poorly designed and implemented copilots will be enablers of lazy habits, midwives to mediocrity, rather than coaches that help us achieve our best.

THE BRITNEY SPEARS TEST

It was four a.m. and Jake Heller was tired and frustrated. The young associate at the Boston law firm Ropes & Gray was most of the way through another all-nighter—the third he'd pulled that week. He was helping to put together a legal brief in a multibillion-dollar lawsuit. There was a filing deadline the next day. Heller was a good lawyer. He'd graduated from Stanford Law, where he'd been president of the Law Review, interned with the White House Counsel's Office, and then clerked for a federal judge on the U.S. First Circuit Court of Appeals and spent time as a legal fellow with the Massachusetts Governor's Office. He knew how to do legal research. His law firm gave him access to expensive legal databases. Heller considered himself better than average at using these tools. He'd grown up in Silicon Valley—in Cupertino, the home of Apple—and he'd been coding ever since he was a kid. But Heller was struggling to find the precedents he needed for his brief.

Part of the problem was the way the legal databases worked. Most still used clunky, decades-old search interfaces. To find a case, you had to know what keywords might appear in particular fields—like the names of the parties or a high-level digest of the case. But there wasn't an easy way to search based on a particular concept or theory of law. Fed up, Heller turned away from his computer and looked over the piles of legal files on his desk, next to half-eaten cartons of Thai takeout he'd ordered for dinner hours earlier. And then it hit him. How come he could pick up his iPhone, open Google, and ask, "What Thai restaurants are open late near me?" and get an immediate, accurate answer, but he couldn't easily find the cases for his brief? "The trivial stuff was so easy to find, and the important stuff was really, really difficult," he remembers thinking.

Heller's frustration prompted him to co-found a company in 2013. Called Casetext, it was dedicated to remaking legal research for the twenty-first century. At a time when the internet and mobile apps were upending traditional business models in industries from retail and transportation to hospitality and publishing, he thought, why not the law? His initial idea had been to build a service based on crowdsourcing, similar to Wikipedia or the coding question-and-answer site Stack Overflow. People would submit legal questions and lawyers would answer them, for free. Then Casetext would build a Google-like search engine on top of this knowledge base.

At least, that was the idea. But, as Heller and his co-founders discovered, lawyers were not eager to offer *gratis* advice. The company had no choice but to pivot away from crowdsourcing. Instead of human intelligence—the wisdom of crowds—it would lean heavily on artificial intelligence. In particular, Casetext would depend on the rapidly advancing subfield of AI known as *natural language processing*, which involved building software that could manipulate, analyze, and to some extent "understand" language. Casetext had always planned to use natural language processing to help power its legal search engine. But now it would need this kind of AI to build the knowledge base of legal answers itself. "We bet the whole business on this evolving field of AI," Heller says. "We felt like we had to constantly be on *the* cutting edge of what machine learning could do and natural language processing could do to deliver value for our customers in a world where we didn't have a huge number of humans to create data for us."

At first, the technology wasn't up to the task. Pablo Arredondo, Casetext's co-founder and chief technology officer, developed tests to help it determine when an AI system might be ready for legal professionals to use. Could the software accurately answer questions about a document and cite where in the text it had found specific information? More importantly, could the software answer accurately when the answer could not be found in the text, letting the user know this, rather than inventing an answer? At the time, no AI software could do this. Instead, if Arredondo gave the software an acquisition agreement, for instance, and then asked an unrelated question such as "When did Britney Spears release her debut album?," the software would confidently but wrongly answer 2003 (the correct year is 1999) and provide a citation to section 7.3 of the contract, even though the document never mentioned the singer at all.

Then there was what Arredondo called "the Scalia Test." He joked it was better than the Turing Test for determining true artificial intelligence. The late U.S. Supreme Court justice Antonin Scalia had been fond of using sarcasm in his opinions. When an AI system could correctly parse Scalia's sarcasm and summarize his opinions, the age of AI will have truly arrived, Arredondo liked to say. Another test gauged whether an LLM could determine if an email was likely protected by attorney-client privilege or if it had merely contained the word privilege in some other, irrelevant context, such as "it was a privilege to meet you yesterday."

The new large language models based on transformers that Google pioneered in 2018 began to help Casetext, making it easier to perform microtasks such as tagging whether a decision had been upheld or overturned. But even these new LLMs still weren't good enough for much of what the start-up wanted to create: a system that could analyze the documents like a lawyer, and maybe even help draft legal briefs and contracts.

In 2022, OpenAI approached Casetext about testing its largest and most powerful LLM, GPT-4. This time, Casetext was blown away. GPT-4 passed the Britney Spears test. It aced Arredondo's Scalia Test and his privilege test. "Within twenty-four hours we knew we needed to make our whole business about this," Heller says.

The result is a product Casetext calls CoCounsel, one of the first of the new generation of AI copilots that will soon become colleagues for most of us. Released in February 2023, it's an AI legal assistant, powered by OpenAI's GPT-4 combined with Casetext's software. After ten years of trying, Heller had achieved his vision of creating a legal research tool that was intuitive to use, and as accurate as a Google search. But Co-Counsel is far more than a search engine. It doesn't just find analogous cases and precedents. It analyzes them. Ask it if interpretive dance is protected by the First Amendment and it provides a cogent and accurate answer, complete with references to the most relevant Supreme Court cases, as well as the most recent case decisions. It can also help lawyers review documents of all kinds—from contracts to regulations to depositions—and automatically categorize and summarize them. It can find unusual or aberrant clauses in thousands of contracts or scan millions of emails to highlight the few that contain evidence of deception, all based on natural language instructions. CoCounsel helps lawyers compose legal memos, a task that might have taken a lawyer hours or days, in less than three minutes. John Polson, the managing partner at Fisher Phillips, a firm with more than five hundred lawyers, says that CoCounsel had an immediate impact, helping the firm do far more for its clients in less time than ever before.

Unlike some copilots, CoCounsel doesn't—at least not yet—draft legal briefs. "We look to arm you with the facts and the law," Arredondo says. Crafting a legal argument in a persuasive way for a judge depends as much on experience and intuition as knowledge about past rulings. Laura Safdie, another of Casetext's co-founders, notes that writing legal briefs is a part of the job that most lawyers enjoy, as opposed to hunting through troves of documents.

Besides Casetext, a half dozen other start-ups are building similar legal copilots. In addition, there are already AI software packages, such as Kira and Luminance, that excel at helping firms quickly and accurately review thousands of contracts. Many of the world's largest law firms are implementing these tools. In a sign of how valuable these legal assistants are likely to become, in June 2023, four months after Casetext launched CoCounsel, Thomson Reuters, the publishing titan that already owns the legal research software company Westlaw, bought Casetext for $650 million.

THE RETURN OF THE HUMAN APPRENTICE

AI software such as CoCounsel will transform how professionals are trained. Law and consulting, for example, currently both use a "leverage" business model, where senior partners supervise many junior associates. The leverage ratio—the number of junior associates to senior partners—at the largest law firms is often around three-to-one or four-to-one. These associates perform tasks such as writing legal research memos, preparing for depositions, and hunting through troves of documents. Law firms say these tasks help young associates gain expertise. But the reality is, these firms often care more about how much associates earn—for the firm, which bills for their time—than how much they learn. One rule of thumb is that associates should bill at least three times their annual salary.

AI legal assistants upend this model. "Clients will balk at paying a junior associate for a task that can otherwise be done really well by AI," Heller, the Casetext co-founder, says. But if law firms don't need junior associates, they'll need to rethink how the next generation of partners is trained. Firms could reinstitute an apprenticeship model, where the associate's job is not to rack up billable hours, but primarily to learn at the elbow of a senior partner. Using copilots in a mentoring and advising role will also mean these associates can potentially learn skills faster than in the past.

Heller says he knows of one firm that, because of AI, is considering no longer charging clients for associates' time during their first three years at the firm, while increasing the rate for more experienced lawyers. This change, he says, ought to be welcome. "Right now, associates spend a lot of time thinking, why did I go to law school for this? Why not have a trained monkey review documents manually to find the one document in a million that might pose a problem for a particular deal?" Heller says. He says AI should make the profession less "draining and soul sucking."

Apprenticeships—where younger people learn through individual mentorship—will see a revival in many fields. This is good news for us humans: the passing of skills from one person to the next is often one of the most fulfilling aspects of work. AI can help with this coaching, but it won't completely take over from people.

WE'RE ALL MIDDLE MANAGERS NOW

CoCounsel is instructive because of what it says about the scope and limitations of current AI copilots. They can do sophisticated search and document retrieval, summarization, some analysis, and some, but critically not all, forms of professional writing. A number of lawyers, including one representing President Trump's former lawyer Michael Cohen, have been called on the carpet by judges and fined thousands of dollars for naively using a general-purpose chatbot, such as ChatGPT, to write legal briefs. The chatbots had invented legal citations, which the lawyers failed to verify and included in their court filings. Many jobs in the future may involve riding herd on what copilots produce. AI will create the first draft, the initial conceptual sketches, take meeting notes, or suggest sales tactics. But we'll be expected to think critically about these suggestions and decide whether to accept them.

The analyst, consultant, journalist, lawyer, or designer will increasingly function as supervisor, manager, and editor to our AI assistants. Ethan Mollick, a professor at the University of Pennsylvania's Wharton School of Business who has attracted a loyal following for his detailed advice on how to use AI chatbots, recommends people treat copilots "like an intern." You can delegate tasks to it, like "write me an executive summary of the following report," but you can't just ship what it produces to clients without careful review. You will also need to give the copilot feedback so it can improve. "Just like any new worker, you are going to have to learn its strengths and weaknesses; you are going to have to learn to train and work with it; and you are going to have to get a sense of where it is useful and where it is just annoying," Mollick writes.

Tim Wu, a Columbia University legal scholar who served as a special assistant to the Biden White House on tech policy and competition, in an op-ed for Toronto's *The Globe and Mail*, worried that as AI creates efficiency, lowering the cost and time it takes to accomplish a task, the demand for that work will increase. The expectations of how quickly something can be done will mount. The result is we will have more to do than ever, and less time to do it. Working alongside robots, Wu worries, will force us to become more robotic.

This danger can't be entirely dismissed—and for certain categories of workers, the dark future of roboticized humans Wu envisions is already here.

THE CYBORG WORKFORCE

Higher-paid professionals will still maintain a relatively large degree of discretion over how they perform their jobs. But for others of us, work will be dictated by AI that will schedule our shifts, decide which colleagues we work most efficiently alongside, tell us how fast we must complete each task, and assess our performance—perhaps in ways that are unforgiving and unsympathetic to our human needs.

For many gig economy workers, including Uber drivers, food delivery couriers, and Amazon warehouse employees, AI is already their manager. Workers are often lured to these jobs with promises that they offer more flexibility than traditional full-time work. But the workers soon discover that the only way to earn a decent wage is to meet the demanding, sometimes inhumane, expectations of an algorithm.

Bike couriers for London-based food delivery service Deliveroo, for example, lamented AI-dictated rules that forced them to respond to new delivery requests within thirty seconds, without knowing the delivery address until after they pick up an order, and then evaluated them against an AI's prediction of how long it should have taken them to complete the pickup and delivery. If they failed to meet these stringent requirements, the algorithm downgraded their rating, making it harder for them to obtain future delivery assignments. In the retail and hospitality sector, shift scheduling is increasingly handled by algorithms. Amazon warehouse workers complain of repetitive stress injuries caused by having to meet the demands of an AI algorithm that sets a blistering pace for how quickly they needed to move boxes and which controls their every step on the warehouse floor.

The advent of these AI systems has, in the name of boosting profit margins, stripped these workers of much of the agency they once had at work. Now an AI algorithm tells them what they can do, when, how, and with whom.

But this model of the AI-run sweatshop does not need to extend into white-collar work, as Wu imagines. If we design our copilots to be truly collaborative—requiring our input at multiple stages—and remember that work needs to be humane, as well as profitable. In most professions, the quality of service will depend, for the foreseeable future, on human judgment and performance, so the most successful businesses will continue to grant these employees a large degree of autonomy.

The most fulfilling aspects of our professional lives are often the most intellectually challenging, or those that involve social interaction. And while AI will assist with some of this work, it isn't yet capable enough to entirely automate it. Until it is, work will remain fulfilling, meaningful, even fun.

THE AI MENTOR

While the metaphor of the clever intern captures some of what working with an AI copilot will be like, the analogy is also incomplete. Because it's also possible to use the same copilots as an expert coach. This coaching can improve not only our productivity but also the quality of our work.

An example comes from a recent study by Stanford University and MIT economists of more than five thousand customer service agents for a software company that serves U.S. small businesses. These representatives, who were primarily in the Philippines, had access to AI software that used a sophisticated LLM to understand conversations in real time and suggest responses, as well as to pull up technical documentation that could help resolve the customer's issue. The system had been fine-tuned to suggest answers like those top-performing call handlers had used to resolve calls. The software was also trained to prioritize responses that expressed empathy and avoided unprofessional language. The system did not replace people—it merely suggested a script. The agents were free to ignore the suggestions. The AI coach improved the number of customer calls resolved per hour by 14 percent. And, it turned out, the least-skilled customer service reps were helped the most, with their productivity soaring by 35 percent. It also helped new agents get up to speed faster—achieving the same productivity in two months that normally took eight to ten months.

The AI assistant also improved the quality of the customers' interactions with the agents. The economists analyzed transcripts and found that customers were more likely to respond positively to the agents when they used the AI assistant. Using the copilot also resulted in a 25 percent decline in how often a customer asked to escalate a call to a manager. And it cut down on staff turnover, reducing attrition by 9 percent on average, and by 10 percent for the newest agents, who also tended to have the highest turnover rates.

Other studies have found similar boosts in productivity and job satisfaction from using AI helpers. GitHub, which is owned by Microsoft, makes an AI assistant that suggests lines of code for programmers based on what they've typed. Called simply Copilot, it is powered by Open-AI's GPT models. GitHub has found in randomized control trials that programmers can code up to 55 percent faster using Copilot. But it has also found that using the AI assistant improves coders' feelings about their work: in a survey of Copilot users, the vast majority reported feeling more productive, with 60 percent to 75 percent reported feeling less frustrated when coding and more fulfilled. This is true even though the coding assistants are not always accurate, and software developers don't always use the Copilot's suggestions. GitHub has found that programmers currently accept Copilot's advice about 35 percent of the time, although the figure is higher for some programming languages, such as Java, where it tops 60 percent.

More than simply digital interns that do our most menial and "brainless" tasks, copilots can help us improve our skills. They will allow inexperienced employees to quickly equal the performance of some top performers. Previously, it might have required a lot of mentoring to move such employees up the learning curve. Now, that process can take place in a fraction of the time.

ROLE-PLAYING

Nathan Kobayashi, who leads the team building the AI copilot for PwC, offers a glimpse of that AI future at work. On the day I interview him, Kobayashi has just used ChatPwC, the company's copilot, to prepare for our meeting. He asks the chatbot to play the role of a journalist interviewing him about his work. The copilot dutifully provides questions to help Kobayashi think through what he might be asked. When we compare notes, ChatPwC has done a good job anticipating most of my questions. Kobayashi has also asked ChatPwC to critique his prospective answers. He says that he often uses ChatPwC to help him prepare for internal meetings the same way.

Role-playing is just one example of how PwC's employees are using the copilot. Kobayashi also uses ChatPwC to write meeting summaries based on audio transcripts and to compose first drafts of formal reviews of his team's work. But role-playing is important because it speaks to the way in which Kobayashi and his team have built ChatPwC. The chatbot has a number of predefined personas that it can assume to better assist employees, whether they are a CPA or a legal analyst. It also offers pre-built tasks and goals, such as analyzing a spreadsheet, or writing a summary of legal considerations for a client. The users are not limited to these pre-built tasks, however, and can prompt the chatbot to do other things. ChatPwC can retrieve and summarize information from the firm's own internal database, helping to guard against hallucinations, although Kobayashi cautions the firm's employees that they must review ChatPwC's responses for accuracy. He says that for some common tasks, such as composing first drafts of reports and writing executive summaries, ChatPwC can do in a few minutes what before would have taken a PwC consultant about forty hours.

DESIGN MATTERS

Whether we'll see big leaps in productivity and quality from copilots depends on how they're designed and deployed. What's under the hood matters: LLMs, which can answer questions in natural language, function differently from other kinds of AI that are trained to classify images or generate music. Equally important will be the user interface—the dashboards—we use to interact with the AI model. We've all experienced software or websites that are difficult to use. The same design lessons apply to copilots.

Several studies on human–AI teaming suggest that the combination of person and machine often results in performance that neither human nor AI could achieve on their own. But this isn't always the case. A 2023 study by MIT economists looked at how radiologists performed when paired with an AI assistant that had been trained to read chest X-rays. In tests on its own, the AI had an overall accuracy that was comparable to board-certified radiologists. But when radiologists had access to the AI, their average accuracy did not improve. A poorly thought-out interface was partly to blame. It gave the radiologists a percentage representing the software's confidence level in the likely presence of each of fourteen different pathologies. In cases where the radiologist was uncertain, the AI assistance tended to help the radiologist. But in cases where the radiologist was confident to begin with, providing the AI's probabilities tended to result in worse performance. This was especially true if the radiologist was fairly certain that the X-ray showed no evidence of pathology. The probabilities given by the AI—even if small—made the radiologist second-guess their conclusion. In other cases, where a radiologist was confident of a particular pathology, but the AI thought a different one more likely, the doctor would tend to ignore the AI's information—even though, on average, the AI was more likely to be right. Worse yet were cases when the AI was uncertain, giving a 20 percent to 60 percent probability a pathology was present. In these cases, the uncertainty confused the radiologists, and they wound up making significantly worse decisions than without the AI. In all cases, providing the additional information made the radiologists take more time to scrutinize each image than they would have on their own.

The MIT researchers concluded that it might be more effective to assign X-rays to be read by either a human radiologist or a machine, working alongside each other but separately, with an X-ray handed off for a second read in cases only where the first reader, be that human or machine, was uncertain. But it's equally true that a more thoughtfully designed interface would have yielded significantly better results: for instance, if the AI suggested diagnoses only when it was very confident, and provided no information when it wasn't, that would have avoided cases where the AI unnecessarily made the radiologists doubt their own determinations. It also might have helped if the AI could visually highlight the areas of an X-ray that it thought were indicative of pathology, not just output a percentage likelihood that pathology was present. These are the sorts of design decisions that will have a big impact on whether our AI copilots live up to their potential.

FLIGHT PLAN: LESSONS FROM AVIATION

Radiology, like most of medicine, is high risk. If an AI assistant increases the odds of a doctor making a mistake, the results could be catastrophic. So it would be wise to consider lessons from a profession where automated assistants have been used in high-risk scenarios for more than a century: aviation. The first autopilot was invented a mere nine years after the Wright brothers' triumph at Kitty Hawk, and by World War II, basic autopilots were common in most large planes. Today, autopilots handle almost every phase of flight, except taxiing and, in most cases, takeoff. But it is worth paying close attention to some of the dangers they've also introduced— many of which come from the way humans interact with these systems.

On May 31, 2009, Air France flight 447, bound from Rio de Janeiro to Paris, plummeted from thirty-five thousand feet into the South Atlantic Ocean. All 228 people on board were killed. It would take two years to recover the wreckage from the depths. Eventually found, the plane's cockpit voice and flight data recorders told a chilling tale: a pressure sensor on the plane's exterior, used by the aircraft's automated systems to calculate air speed, had iced up. The lack of accurate airspeed data caused the aircraft's autopilot to disengage suddenly. So too did the Airbus A330's fly-by-wire system. This software normally interpreted the pilots' movement of their joystick-like flight controls, keeping the actual movements of the plane within safe limits. Even if the pilot pulled back hard on the controls, the fly-by-wire system kept the aircraft's nose below the threshold at which the plane would stall. When these two systems disengaged, the pilots became confused. They pulled back on their control sticks, putting the aircraft into a stall. An audible alarm, including a synthetic voice warning "Stall!" repeatedly sounded, and yet the bewildered pilots couldn't figure out what was happening. They continued to pull back on their control sticks, when the correct procedure should have been to push them forward, lowering the nose until the plane recovered enough airspeed and lift. Instead, the plane simply bellyflopped out of the sky.

The pilots made two errors common to people interacting with technology. The first is called *automation bias*—the tendency to assume that computerized systems are taking the right action and defer to their decision-making, even in the face of contradictory evidence. The crash is also an example of a related cognitive bias known as *automation surprise.* This refers to people's tendency to be confused by automated system failure. This happens because automated systems tend to be both complex and opaque: users frequently have little intuitive or actual understanding of how they arrive at decisions. So when they fail, people are often clueless as to what the underlying issue might be. They take longer to diagnose the problem and take corrective steps. They also tend to waste time trying to puzzle out the source of the failure rather than quickly reverting to a manual backup process. Studies have found that automation surprise has become an increasingly serious issue in commercial aviation, as flight has become more and more automated. Compounding this, automation has resulted in a degradation in pilots' basic flying skills. While they're still required to periodically practice emergency procedures and "seat-of-the-pants" flying in simulators, today's aviators don't get nearly as many opportunities to directly control aircraft as they did decades ago. Instead, they spend much of their time babysitting an autopilot.

The rise of AI copilots places us all in a similar predicament. We'll need to avoid both automation bias and automation surprise. NASA has been thinking about this issue for longer than most organizations. Jessica Marquez, a NASA human factors engineer, says that rigorous training—of people, not AI—is a crucial step. Part of this training focuses on making sure astronauts understand exactly how the automated systems function— what data does it take in, where does it get that data from, and what does it do with that data; what are that system's capabilities and, just as importantly, what can't that system do? Making sure astronauts have the answers to these questions helps them create a good "mental model" of how the automated system functions. This can combat automation surprise. It's the kind of training everyone will need to have for their AI copilots.

Before astronauts step into a spaceship, they will have rehearsed hundreds of scenarios in realistic simulators. Other professions will have to consider similar training in a new age of AI copilots, to guard against deskilling. A salesman might be required to do a simulated sales call without an AI assistant; an architect might be required to come up with five concepts for a space without a digital assist.

Marquez, who is especially interested in how to prepare astronauts to work with automated systems and AI during NASA's planned missions to the moon and then to Mars, says automation bias is the tougher tendency to overcome. It's insidious. If AI is accurate most of the time, it's difficult for a person to remain vigilant for rare but possibly devastating flaws. In simulations of a lunar landing using trained pilots, Marquez and another researcher tried to see if the pilots could recognize when certain subsystems were failing. They hypothesized the pilots would remain more vigilant if they had to manually land the simulated lunar module, rather than just monitoring data while an autopilot handled the landing. But the level of automation didn't make a difference: what mattered was simply how often system failures occurred. If they were frequent, the pilots remained vigilant and detected the problems. If they were infrequent, the pilots tended to miss signs of trouble. That's why having systems in place that can monitor an AI model's inputs and outputs and spot potential errors, sounding an alert for users, will be essential. But this too presents a dilemma: a warning that is too sensitive and sounds too often induces "alert fatigue." People learn to ignore the alarm. Set the threshold too high, however, and people won't spot critical errors, or will notice them only when it's too late.

Inside a giant hangar at NASA's Johnson Space Center in Houston, Texas, sits a strange white structure. A round central component sprouting a two-story dome, similar to an observatory's, is flanked by a small rectangular entryway that resembles a porta-cabin and a cylindrical wing that looks like a large gas tank. This is the Human Research Exploration Analog (HERA), designed to simulate living conditions on a future base on the Martian moon Phobos. Volunteers spend forty-five days living inside the airlocked HERA module, carrying out experiments designed to test what it will be like for future astronauts to spend months living and working in similarly cramped, isolated conditions, with radio transmissions to Earth taking as long as twenty-two minutes. Given this time delay, the astronauts will be dependent on help from AI assistants.

The HERA volunteers have been experimenting with a chatbot developed by researchers at Texas A&M University called Daphne that's designed to help astronauts perform tasks, such as repairing life support systems. A bit like the radiology AI assistant, Daphne provides probabilities for each potential cause of an anomaly. But, as with radiologists, if multiple causes have similar probabilities, providing this information makes it harder for the astronauts to decide what to do. In fact, in these situations people often exhibit another cognitive bias. Called *automation neglect*, it's essentially the opposite of automation bias. In automation neglect, humans discount and ignore what the AI is telling them. The Texas A&M researchers wanted to see if having Daphne provide explanations for its diagnosis would help prevent automation neglect. Unsurprisingly, the researchers found explanations built trust in Daphne's diagnoses. But providing the explanations also slowed people down, so they would take longer to resolve the problem.

OFFERING AN EXPLANATION

Explanations will make copilots more trustworthy. And they should, in theory, make them safer. But providing explanations that are both accurate and make sense to a person is harder than it might first seem. For instance, for AI that helps doctors read medical imagery, a popular explainability method is called a *saliency map*. It works like a heatmap, visually highlighting those portions of the image that were most heavily weighted by the AI software in making a prediction. But a 2022 study in the medical journal *Lancet Digital Health* conducted by researchers from MIT, Harvard's School of Public Health, and the Australian Institute of Machine Learning found serious flaws with this method. A heatmap was supposed to explain what portion of a chest image led an AI system to diagnose a patient with pneumonia. But it highlighted a large quadrant of one lung, with no further indication of what led the AI to this conclusion. In the absence of such information, humans tend to assume the AI is looking at whatever feature they, as human clinicians, would have found most important. This cognitive bias can blind doctors to possible errors the algorithm may make.

The researchers found fault with other popular explainability methods too—they could identify features that were important in a decision, but they couldn't tell a doctor *why* those features were important. If the features seem counterintuitive, what should the doctor do: Conclude the AI model is wrong, or conclude it has discovered some significant but previously unknown indicator for a particular condition? Either is possible. A better way of providing explanations is to train an AI system to identify prototypical features of a certain disease—say, the presence of a "ground-glass" pattern in the lungs that is typical of pneumonia—and then tell doctors which of these features it found in the image. This creates explanations that are inherently more intelligible. This method isn't flawless. A doctor might question whether the right features have been selected and whether the AI model has weighed each feature appropriately. But this gets closer to the kind of debate that two human doctors have when they disagree on a diagnosis.

Those devising AI assistants will have to figure out when explanations will help and how best to deliver them. We will also have to find ways to tackle automation bias, automation neglect, and automation surprise. Ultimately, industry standards, likely unique to each profession, will be needed to guide the development of copilots. After all, the requirements for a copilot that helps pick the best colors for a branding campaign need not be as rigorous as those helping a civil engineer design a bridge. NASA is again a good case study: its technical standards don't just speak to the software in isolation, but set requirements for human–AI interaction too. This is how most industries should think about copilots. It isn't just about the AI's capabilities, but its interface and the human training that matter. If engineered thoughtfully, copilots will lead to a surge in productivity, give us all an expert coach, lift the quality of our work, and make our jobs more fulfilling.

5

PILLARS OF INDUSTRY

A I won't just transform the way we work as people; it will also alter the dynamics and organization of industries. The business models of entire fields will be upended. The organizations that come out on top will be those that are best at creating a positive feedback loop between people, data, and AI. Each of these elements will be critical. People will still matter. Employees will need to help create and curate the data that will train AI, which in turn will help people become more efficient and successful. The businesses that can establish this feedback loop and run it fastest will outcompete the rest. The key for most companies will be figuring out how to turn not just knowledge but also experience and wisdom into data, and then that data into insight.

THE DATA ADVANTAGE

AI depends on three components: algorithms, computing power, and data. But apart from some large technology firms and savvy AI start-ups, companies will not create their own algorithms. They will depend on a handful of algorithms developed and sold by tech firms, or that are available for free through open-source purveyors such as Hugging Face. Computing power won't be a differentiator either: Most have access to the same kinds of data center servers run by the biggest tech companies. No, for most companies, competitive advantage will come from its unique data.

Access to proprietary data will be increasingly important. Intellectual property falls into this category. Disney has access to its vast catalog of films; the *New York Times* has more than 150 years of archived articles; Pfizer has its decades of drug R&D and clinical trials. But for most companies, the biggest source of proprietary information is customer data. For much of the 2010s, data that would allow companies to serve people with targeted advertising was commoditized by specialized brokers, who pooled data taken from tracking cookies on internet sites and mobile phone operators and sold it to the highest bidder. But privacy rules introduced since 2021 have made this tracking far more difficult and increased the value of the data that companies collect on their own customers. And, as we will see, AI can also help turn data generated by a company's own employees into an increasingly important competitive advantage.

PERSONALIZED PRODUCT PROMOTION

For years, the holy grail for many businesses has been mass customization—creating a bespoke product or service for each customer while maintaining a large customer base and the economies of scale that come from serving it. Even businesses that sell a relatively standard product line dream of tailoring their marketing efforts for each customer. Now, AI is rapidly making this possible.

Domino's Pizza in Mexico, for example, traditionally used advertising on television, radio, in newspapers, and even online that targeted customers in an undifferentiated way. There's an old adage in advertising that half of an ad budget is wasted, you just don't know which half. Which customers were most likely to convert into a pizza buyer on a

Tuesday night? What time would they be most hungry? And what was the best message to send them? Domino's had no idea. It collected lots of data on its customers, but didn't know how to analyze it.

Then Domino's Mexico began feeding the data to Segment, a customer data analysis platform owned by the San Francisco–based tech company Twilio. Segment grouped Domino's customers into several buckets and, using AI, offered predictions of the best messages, best medium, and best times to reach out to people. As a result, Domino's Mexico saw a 700 percent increase in the return on its Google ad spending and cut customer acquisition costs by 65 percent, while increasing customer retention.

AI enables companies to dice their customer base into more and more finely graded segments. Intuit, which makes TurboTax and Quick-Books, used AI to change the way it segmented the audience for its tax software from basically three big buckets into 450 different audiences, which each received more tailored marketing. Engagement with those messages leaped from 20 percent to 50 percent. The limiting factor is no longer how precisely the audience can be targeted—instead it is the ability to produce truly personalized messages for each customer. Generative AI software that can write endless bespoke marketing messages is enabling this kind of marketing. The only issue, according to Jeff Lawson, Twilio's founder and former chief executive, is how much quality control a company can retain over the messages. Because of LLMs' unreliability, companies will probably not go so far as to use different marketing tactics for every customer. But they will increasingly have hundreds of segments, where they once had a dozen at most, and will see big gains in sales and reductions in wasted marketing costs.

THE UNSTRUCTURED DATA REVOLUTION

Customer data can come from a range of sources, from apps to checkout tills to billing records. The AI revolution allows businesses to tap a whole new source. Large language models unlock the value of unstructured data—digital documents of any kind, as well as digital images. Almost every business has these. And now they can use LLM-based AI to mine them for insights.

Imagine a small family-owned wine store that also sells items online. Using an LLM, it analyzes customer emails to ferret out trends: Are people inquiring more about sauvignon blanc or white Burgundy this summer? Are customers in a particular area complaining about delivery problems more than others? Before, such insights might've been difficult to extract and track over time, requiring staff to classify emails by category. The shop could also begin recording phone calls and using AI to analyze the transcripts to discover trends and monitor customer service. It might even start recording the conversations with customers in the shop, to gain insights into what sales techniques work best. It might be able to record videos of customers shopping in the store and ask the AI system to analyze what displays work best. If it turns out that the French Burgundies see a lot of window shopping but relatively few purchases, maybe a special offer could persuade reluctant customers to try one. Before the AI revolution, only a major chain retailer could afford the technology to provide such in-store insights. Now, this kind of analysis will be within almost any retailer's grasp.

WE KNOW MORE THAN WE CAN TELL

"We know more than we can tell." The British-Hungarian philosopher Michael Polanyi used this catchphrase to describe the idea of *tacit knowledge*. He asserted that human knowledge of how the world works and our place in it is beyond explicit human understanding. There are many things we know, without knowing how we know them, and without being able to explain them. This is true of many physical skills, such as skiing or riding a bike. It is also true of many creative talents—writing, poetry, music, painting, and more. Artists frequently know when something just looks or sounds right, without being able to articulate why. It is this intuition that often separates artists from nonartists.

Tacit knowledge is also a key feature in many professions: the doctor who just feels that something about the patient isn't right and orders an additional test; the defense attorney who knows in their gut that continuing to press a witness will alienate the jury.

The MIT economist David Autor, with whom we will spend more time in chapter 6, dubbed the inability of algorithms to capture this tacit knowledge "Polanyi's paradox" because, he contended, it might explain the economic phenomenon known as Solow's paradox. Named for the late economist Robert Solow, who in 1987 quipped that "you can see the computer age everywhere but in the productivity statistics," Solow's paradox refers to the fact that the widespread computerization of business, which was supposed to have led to big efficiency gains, was not accompanied by measurable labor productivity growth. In the U.S.—and most other developed nations—productivity growth slowed significantly after 1973 despite increased computerization. The growth rate rebounded briefly in the mid-to-late 1990s, only to decelerate again over the past twenty years. Autor suspected that the inability of software to capture tacit knowledge had impeded the progress of automation. This was certainly the case with earlier kinds of AI based on explicit rules. If humans couldn't write down the steps for accomplishing a task, a machine couldn't accomplish it.

But Erik Brynjolfsson, the Stanford University economist who helped lead the study of AI-assisted customer support representatives detailed in chapter 4, is among those who think that today's AI is changing this dynamic and starting to overcome Polanyi's paradox. "Machine learning is able to codify tacit knowledge even if a human can't be explicit about what the rules are," he says. This will accelerate automation in many industries.

CAPTURING TACIT KNOWLEDGE

An important question for many businesses will be: How can we capture the tacit knowledge of our own employees? Answering this question will create new dynamics between businesses and their workers. Bryn-jolfsson's research on customer support highlights the tensions that will afflict companies using AI copilots. An intriguing finding of the study concerned pay. The AI assistant, which was trained on the way the contact center's top-performing agents handled calls, helped new hires handle inquiries more successfully. This narrowed the gap between newbies and veterans. But the customer service firm set pay based on how much better an agent performed than the average colleague. This meant that as the AI assistant lifted the performance of the average agents, the top-performing agents saw their pay decline, even though it was the capture of their tacit knowledge that had led to the overall productivity gains. Companies will need to think hard about compensation practices in this new age. In many fields, employers will find their in-house experts and top performers demanding more compensation in return for contributing their tacit knowledge to the company's intellectual property.

Autor divides professional expertise into three components: formal knowledge, procedures, and judgment. Formal knowledge can be taught in a classroom. Procedures are practical steps a professional takes to accomplish tasks. These are often learned on the job. Finally, there's judgment, which is perhaps the most important component of professional decision-making. In Autor's words, it "intermediates between formal knowledge and actual practice." AI won't automate judgment. "That judgment component is going to remain very valuable," Autor says. The essentials of judgment aren't written down anywhere. They may never even be spoken. Judgment resides in the minds of veteran practitioners and is developed over many years. Often, these pros can't articulate how they know that a particular action is the right one—they operate, perhaps more than they would acknowledge, on intuition. In other words, much, maybe even most, professional expertise is tacit knowledge.

In many industries, the data from which tacit knowledge might be inferred doesn't exist—at least not yet. But companies will begin taking steps to create it. Today, it is not uncommon for businesses to record calls "for quality and training purposes." This practice will likely spread to industries where sales cycles are longer and transactions are lower volume but higher value, such as multimillion-dollar supply contracts or commercial real estate transactions. One can envision companies requiring all meetings and business calls to be recorded so that AI can extract tacit knowledge from a company's top managers. A few years ago, capturing this kind of data from across an entire company would have been impractical. Now, better voice recognition allows for fairly accurate real-time transcripts. These in turn can help fine-tune AI models, a kind of flywheel effect enabled by AI.

Such a transformation won't happen overnight. Many professionals will find the idea of workplace surveillance unsettling—or even counterproductive. They will be reluctant to allow a company to digitally reproduce their expertise without significant additional compensation. This could lead to labor disputes. Because of employee resistance and, in some places, data privacy laws that will make it impossible to surveil employees in this way, the capture of tacit knowledge will occur slowly and unevenly.

We have not yet entirely escaped Polanyi's paradox. Companies will still need human experts and human mentorship for the foreseeable future. In fact, rather than displacing human expertise, as some AI boosters have suggested, AI will likely increase the value of the world's top experts. This is for three reasons: One is the tacit knowledge they hold and can impart to AI systems. The second is the value of the experts' professional networks. AI can't replicate these relational webs. Finally, in a world where AI makes it easier for less knowledgeable and experienced workers to achieve average results, experts who can significantly outperform the average will command a premium.

WINNER TAKE MOST

AI's tendency to help the best performers earn even more will upend the structure of many professions. In more and more fields, a "star system" will take hold, where a relative handful of peak performers take outsized shares of the profits. Star systems have long existed in professional sports and entertainment. But these systems have begun to reshape professions as diverse as psychiatry, plastic surgery, software coding, design, and journalism. AI will accelerate this trend.

This, in turn, will disrupt business models, particularly as copilots also enable star performers to work effectively without large support staffs. Big law and consulting firms, as well as investment banks, could be in trouble as their highest-billing partners, armed with AI assistants to help them do the grunt work, break away and form boutiques.

The growing value of stars will be just one of several currents spawned by AI that are likely to create very choppy sailing for many companies. In many cases, copilots will level the playing field, allowing small businesses to compete more effectively against larger ones. Take João Ferrão dos Santos, the chief executive of a fledgling online T-shirt company based in Portugal. Dos Santos announced on LinkedIn in March 2023 that he had appointed ChatGPT as "the CEO" of his start-up. Dos Santos said he would simply execute the tasks ChatGPT recommended. The company used the text-to-image generation software Midjourney to design its T-shirts. Dos Santos named his company "AIsthetic Apparel." Starting with an initial investment of $1,000, and with $2,500 raised from outside investors, the company sold $10,000 worth of T-shirts in its first week.

Micro businesses aren't the only ones trying to take strategic direction from an AI: the Chinese video gaming company, NetDragon Websoft, which has about $1 billion in annual sales, also claims to have appointed an AI robot called Tang Yu as its chief executive.

These experiments radically reversed the usual relationship between people and AI copilots. Here, people willingly surrendered authority to an AI decision-maker and turned themselves into the intelligent assistants. But one doesn't have to go this far to see how the advent of copilots will be accompanied by more professionals launching small businesses and solo practices at the expense of larger firms.

This trend will coexist with a countervailing tendency toward greater concentration in many fields. Data is power in the age of AI, and the largest players within any industry tend to have the most—whether that's customer data, supplier data, data about contract terms, or other forms of intellectual property. By applying AI to this information, they will make more accurate predictions than those with less data. For a big architectural firm, that might mean better blueprints; for a major movie studio, better scripts; for a large law firm, better contracts. Overall, the data flywheel will lead to an increased concentration of power in many industries. Midsize businesses will probably fare the worst: Too big to take advantage of the low-cost footprint of the AI-aided boutiques, but too small to have the data advantages of the largest incumbents, they will be increasingly squeezed out.

THE NEW AGE OF IP

Among the most critical data in this new era will be intellectual property. All firms will need a well-considered strategy for how to best exploit their own IP. Having the right data to fine-tune an AI algorithm for a task will likely be a significant competitive advantage. It may determine which companies dominate a field and which struggle.

But having a library of past IP to draw upon is just one asset. Again, there will be countervailing forces: Generative AI relies on past IP for training. But it vastly lowers the time and cost of producing new content, and new IP. This will force companies that have traditionally thrived on IP exploitation, such as Hollywood studios and publishing houses, to forge relationships with a new generation of creators.

In May 2023, the director Paul Trillo used Runway's Gen 2 generative AI software, which can output short video segments from text prompts, to create a two-minute, twenty-five-second film called *Thank You for Not Answering*. Trillo edited together a number of short video clips he made with Gen 2 to create the visuals for the film, and then used AI voice-generation software from the start-up ElevenLabs to voice the film's script. He also added audio effects and music using other post-production software. A month later, Waymark, a Detroit-based video production and technology company, created a twelve-minute film, *The Frost*, using different AI techniques. It took a script authored by one of the company's executive producers and used OpenAI's text-to-image generator DALL-E 2 to create a series of still images illustrating the story. It then added partial animations to these still images—lip movements, eye blinks, camera zoom effects—using another piece of AI software called D-ID. Like Trillo, Waymark overlaid music and sound effects. The result is a convincing psychological thriller. Then in February 2024, OpenAI previewed a text-to-video generation system called Sora that created one-minute videos from a single text prompt—much longer than had been possible before—that shocked many with their hyperrealism and grasp of "cinematic grammar," or the ordering of shots and angles, zooms and pans, that help to tell a story on film.

Within a few years, it will be possible to create feature-length movies this way, and to do so with production crews and budgets a fraction of what is typical even for independent films. The radical democratization of film and television creation this enables will be the biggest change to hit Hollywood in its history—bigger than the move from silent film to talkies, or even the advent of VHS and streaming. Those changes were big, but they didn't fundamentally alter the need for large pools of talent and labor. Now, what was once the work of dozens and hundreds with a lot of specialized equipment can be done by one person with a laptop. We will explore what this may mean for individual filmmakers in chapter 8, but here I want to focus on the impact on entertainment and media companies.

It's doubtful the studios will disappear. In a world where generative AI leads to a flood of films, the distribution and marketing muscle of large studios will be more vital than ever. People can upload content to social media, but social media is ill-suited to long-form films. To gain a wide audience, directors of AI films will need the big company's support. The studios also have vast amounts of intellectual property that they can leverage to create their own AI-based films, or even their own in-house AI video generation software.

But there will be growing labor tensions over the extent to which they will be allowed to exploit their own archives and back catalogs to do so. The 2023 strikes by Hollywood screenwriters and actors unions, in which AI was an important issue, foreshadow these future fights. The studios' agreement that actors' images cannot be used to create digital avatars without consent and fair compensation should be cheered. But still, many younger and less-established actors may feel pressured to sell these rights on terms favorable to the studios. The compromise struck by the writers may be followed in other industries: AI can be used to complement human writers, but not to reduce their credit and compensation.

PUBLISHING TURNS THE PAGE

Beyond entertainment, one of the more profound shifts will be in publishing, where AI might not just help authors write, but also change the way books are read, changing the industry's economics. It's easy to imagine readers will wish to have an AI "reading companion" that can answer questions, look up unfamiliar references, or provide literary analysis. It might even function a bit like a virtual book club, without having to wait for monthly gatherings. Publishers will compete to build such AI reading aides. Prolific and popular authors, especially genre writers, could create their own AI "co-readers" well-versed in their own oeuvre. One can imagine AI reading companions geared to Harry Potter or Sherlock Holmes fans. Desire to have ready access to AI reading aides could, pardon the pun, rekindle demand for ebooks, which has plateaued since 2012. The tech company YouAI created a book-reading companion chatbot called Book AI and has talked to publishers about offering similar tools. People have also created book-reading "GPTs" (ChatGPT's equivalent of apps) and offered them in OpenAI's GPT store for the same purpose. News publishers such as Semafor, *Fortune* (where I work), as well as tech-oriented publications such as *MacWorld* and *PCWorld* have trained chatbots on their own archives to answer reader questions and suggest additional articles.

Publishers are unlikely to want to have AI write books since AI-produced content cannot be copyrighted. But they might expect that writers will work with an AI assistant to produce manuscripts faster. As we will explore in chapter 8, which addresses AI's impact on the creative arts, a tussle is brewing between authors and publishers over who has the right to use an author's work to train an AI system. But in the meantime, publishers are deploying AI to help optimize the metadata used to list individual titles so that they are easier to find on Amazon and other websites. They are also experimenting with AI-generated voices to create audiobooks—particularly for lower-selling titles. Some publishers are also exploring AI-generated art for cover designs or to illustrate children's books. As elsewhere, this ability to deliver these services with fewer people may mean smaller, independent publishing houses will be able to compete with large publishers.

BIG TECH GETS BIGGER

For the past twenty years, a handful of companies have dominated the technology sector: Apple, Amazon, Microsoft, Google, and Meta. In China, two companies, Baidu and Tencent, have had more market power than the rest. AI is likely to further cement these leaders' positions. But AI might just pry open a window that will allow a new player or two to sneak into tech's star chamber. The most potent general-purpose AI models, known as *foundation models* because many applications can be built on top of them, will remain the exclusive domain of the existing tech giants and a handful of well-funded start-ups closely aligned with them. Only these firms have the resources needed to create and maintain data centers large enough—tens or hundreds of thousands of GPUs—to train and run the most capable AI models. Microsoft spent hundreds of millions of dollars to build the supercomputing cluster used to train OpenAI's GPT models, according to Scott Guthrie, Microsoft's executive vice president in charge of cloud and AI. On top of this, OpenAI itself spent more than $100 million training its trillion-parameter GPT-4 model. Google's most powerful Gemini model, Ultra, is said to be five times more powerful and significantly larger than GPT-4.

While OpenAI's Altman has questioned whether the advantage from developing larger and larger AI models has plateaued, it's unlikely that bleeding-edge capabilities will be available to firms without direct access to supercomputing clusters anytime soon. It's true that many top machine learning researchers have left Big Tech companies in the past few years to work for start-ups. But most of these AI start-ups have formed close alliances with the technology giants in order to access the computing power they need. The large technology companies exercise considerable control over the start-ups, even amid regulatory scrutiny. Microsoft, under the unusual terms of its investment in OpenAI, essentially owns the rights to 75 percent of the AI company's profits for years to come. Amazon has invested heavily in Anthropic, and Nvidia has invested in Cohere.

Big Tech companies are also unlikely to lose ground to start-ups when it comes to building the most general-purpose AI technology. Microsoft is rapidly infusing generative AI into its products, like the Microsoft 365 suite that includes Microsoft Word, Excel, PowerPoint, and Teams. Google is doing likewise with its Workspace apps. But start-ups will play an important role in building a new generation of more narrowly tailored, industry-specific tools. These systems are designed not just for general-purpose tasks—such as creating spreadsheets, presentations, or invoices—but for more targeted functions: human resources, corporate finance, portfolio management, law, and architecture, to name a few. While some of this software will run on top of foundation models created by the Big Tech companies, they'll be fine-tuned for narrower functions and will feature a dedicated user interface geared toward people who work in those areas.

While today's largest tech companies won't land in the discard pile, AI could shuffle the deck. Amazon, for instance, has been slow to create large generative AI foundation models. It belatedly forged a partnership with Anthropic, which sells the Claude chatbot, while also trying to get close to companies working on open-source LLMs. It hopes that offering these AI models through its popular AWS platform will help it retain cloud computing customers. For years, AWS has built its own AI chips for its data centers, but these were optimized for older kinds of AI. They weren't well suited to massive LLMs. To catch up, it's designed a new generation of AI chips. But it will take time to get them into its data centers, and in the meantime, AWS may lose market share to rivals. Apple has also been slower than Microsoft or Google in rolling out AI products.

Microsoft, meanwhile, has been trying to unseat Google as the dominant player in internet search by integrating OpenAI's GPT-4 into its Bing search engine. But so far, Bing's market share, which is only 3 percent of searches, has barely budged. Google continues to be used for more than 93 percent of searches. Google parried Microsoft's moves in generative AI, unveiling its own AI chatbot, Bard, and then its family of Gemini AI models, while also increasingly integrating generative AI into search. Google has proven that ChatGPT won't be the "Google killer" that many predicted when it debuted in late 2022. But Google, and its parent Alphabet, haven't shown that they can escape a classic innovator's dilemma. (This is when a successful incumbent cannot counter a competitor without cannibalizing its existing business lines.) Unlike Microsoft, which makes money mostly from subscriptions, the bulk of Alphabet's revenue comes from search-based advertising. That ad business will be challenged in a world where people ask a question and get a comprehensive AI-generated answer rather than a page of ranked links. Google says it can find a way to make ads pay in a world of generative AI search. But it has not yet shown how.

Then there's Nvidia, the world's dominant GPU company, which is increasingly seeking to branch out from making the chips that power the AI revolution into selling AI models and cloud computing capacity. In these new domains, the chip company will find itself pitted against its best customers. At the same time, Nvidia's customers, the hyperscale

cloud service providers, are also working on their own custom AI chips—
and investing in competing chipmakers—to be less beholden to Nvidia's
near-monopoly over GPUs. With all these crosscutting forces, it's possible one of tech's Olympians could find itself ejected from the pantheon,
while others become even more dominant.

The one looming development that could throw a grenade into Big
Tech's current lineup is a new generation of AI assistants that are more
than mere copilots—which primarily generate content for users—but
digital agents, carrying out tasks for us. Instead of just suggesting an itin-
erary for vacation to celebrate a wedding anniversary, an AI agent will
make the airline, hotel, and restaurant reservations for us. It will know
that we want a king bed and sea view. It will know that we don't like
tables too near the door.

These agents will understand our habits and preferences—they will
read and summarize the news for us, tell us how our favorite team played
last night, then remind us of our cousin's upcoming birthday, recommend gifts, and then purchase them for us. These agents are now in
sight using essentially the same AI technology that underpins existing
LLMs—except instead of trying to predict the next word in a sequence,
the new AI will predict the next action to take.

Demis Hassabis, the Google DeepMind chief executive, believes these
AI agents are the next frontier for AI. Hassabis says creating software that
can reliably act on our behalf will require solving grand challenges on
the path to artificial general intelligence, including improved factual accuracy, a grasp of human intentions, commonsense reasoning, and many
others. The commercial stakes couldn't be higher. Bill Gates has said that
whoever can build a capable digital agent will have power—and wealth—
that will dwarf what even today's largest technology companies command.
"Whoever wins the personal agent, that's the big thing, because you will
never go to a search site again, you will never go to a productivity site
again, you'll never go to Amazon again," Gates says. Amazon, of course,
doesn't want that to happen, so it is undoubtedly working on such an AI
agent, which would one day replace its popular Alexa digital assistant.

Gates said he would be disappointed if Microsoft were not one of the companies trying to build an AI agent, probably with OpenAI's help. Google, which has an assistant of its own, is certainly in the race, as Hassabis's comments make clear. It would be surprising if Apple, which has its Siri digital assistant, isn't trying as well. Meta has also been investing heavily to build LLMs and is eyeing a digital agent as a way to attract users to its platforms at a time when some of its social media properties, such as the original Facebook site, have struggled to attract younger users. Elon Musk has recently launched an AI research company, called xAI, and it will try to create a digital agent—in part because it would dovetail well with Tesla's existing effort to create a humanoid butler-like robot called Optimus.

There are a few well-funded start-ups working on digital agents too, including Adept AI, which was founded by Google and OpenAI alumni, and Essential AI, founded by two of the ex-Google researchers who invented the transformer. But whether these companies can build a successful agent without a close partnership with one of the current Big Tech giants is unclear. The personal agent is tech's equivalent of Sauron's One Ring—the one app to rule them all. It will confer unprecedented power on whichever company possesses it.

AI technology will shake the foundations of power across industries. And just as it will alter the wealth of companies, it will redraw the wealth of nations—changing entire economies. We'll look at those transformations next.

6

RICH, ONLY TO BE WRETCHED?

A mong the biggest fears attending AI's rapid advance is mass un-employment. In 2013, the economist Carl Benedikt Frey and the machine learning professor Michael Osborne, both at the University of Oxford, published a landmark study that found almost half of all U.S. jobs were at "high risk" of being automated within two decades. Although their methodology was later criticized—one OECD study using a different method concluded less than 10 percent of U.S. jobs could be fully automated in that time frame—the specter of AI-induced mass unemployment has not disappeared. In 2018, PwC projected that fully a third of all jobs globally could be automated by the mid-2030s. These fears have been amplified following the release of ChatGPT. Goldman Sachs estimated that the "equivalent" of 300 million jobs globally could be automated away in the new era of generative AI. Sam Altman, OpenAI's chief executive, while stopping short of predicting mass unemployment, told the *Atlantic* that "Jobs are definitely going to go away, full stop."

Given such headlines, it's not surprising that the specter of AI leading to mass unemployment haunts the public imagination. Surveys conducted by Microsoft and the OECD found between half and three-fifths of workers globally feared they would lose their jobs to AI. But both history, and economic analysis, argue against such a dire outlook. While there are reasons to be concerned about the effects of AI on the overall economy, mass unemployment isn't one of them. The real risks are around wage depression and inequality. And while AI will undoubtedly displace workers, we have a lot of power to shape the extent to which this occurs. Creating incentives for companies to use AI to complement human capabilities, rather than simply usurping them, can ensure the economic effects of the AI revolution are positive overall.

LESSONS FROM HISTORY

Previous technological revolutions have displaced workers from some jobs, but on a net basis, more new jobs have always been created. This is because new technologies don't just make existing industries and business models more efficient; they create entirely new industries. Take the automobile. Cars put people in the horse-and-carriage trade out of work. But they created many more jobs in automobile manufacturing, road construction, the oil and gas industry, and service stations. By revolutionizing transport and logistics, they made many other businesses more efficient and profitable, and those companies were able to expand and hire more workers, too.

A 2015 study by economists at the accounting firm Deloitte used 144 years of British census data to assess technology's impact on jobs since 1871. It found that while technology displaced people from jobs involving physical labor, particularly in agriculture and in factories, it created far more jobs in areas including nursing, childcare, elder care, business services, and the invention of technology itself. More people became professionals, and within professions, technology helped drive specialization. There were twenty times more accountants in Britain in 2011 than in 1871. Between 1992 and 2011, the number of typists in the

U.K. fell by 57 percent, while management consultants skyrocketed by 365 percent. A World Economic Forum analysis also concluded that far more jobs have been created through technological change than were destroyed.

Three factors make many people suspect that AI will be different. The first is the breadth of its impact. AI is a general-purpose technology—more akin to steam power and electrification—than it is to something narrow like a welding robot. The second is the speed of its development and adoption. AI could displace so many roles, across so many sectors, so quickly, that it would eliminate jobs far faster than new ones could be created or people could be trained. At least, that's the fear. This was not, in fact, the experience with these other general-purpose technologies. They all created more jobs than they eliminated and were drivers of economic growth. But the adoption of those technologies took long enough that people had time to transition. AI's adoption appears faster, which only fuels concern.

Finally, AI strikes directly at our comparative advantage as a species: our brainpower. And when a species loses its comparative advantage to automation, the results aren't pretty. Just ask the horses. Their only comparative advantage was muscle power. When the internal combustion engine beat them at it, they had nowhere to go. Most were sold off, put out to pasture, or turned into glue. The people in the horse trade fared far better. Their brains allowed them to find other jobs. But with AI we are facing a technology that, for the first time, directly challenges our comparative advantage—our intellect—across every field. If AI betters us at all cognitive tasks, we'll end up like the horses.

COMPLEMENT, NOT SUBSTITUTE

We probably don't have to worry about the glue factory just yet. AI won't be able to match our cognitive abilities across all tasks anytime in the next few decades. AI will make us more productive, but it won't be able to automate everything. The Stanford economist Erik Brynjolfsson, the

Carnegie Mellon professor Tom Mitchell, and other researchers examined 950 occupations and broke them down into 18,000 occupation-specific tasks. They then examined the likely impact of machine learning and AI. "We found that in none of those jobs did machine learning or any of these technologies just run the table and do everything that the person was doing previously," Brynjolfsson says. "In each of them, there were some parts of the job that machine learning could help with, but other parts where humans still need to be in the loop. So that means you can't just pull a human out and put a machine in their place, you have to do a lot more reorganizing and restructuring."

Evidence shows that centaurs—the term given to human–AI teaming—produce better performance than either people or software can achieve alone. AI and human intelligence may be complementary in many ways. AI is much better at finding patterns in complex datasets than people. AI can generate content faster than people can. But it can't write as well as the best human writers. It isn't nearly as good at planning, or at developing novel ideas. It certainly can't understand a person's body language or offer genuine empathy.

As we have seen in previous chapters, exactly how these AI copilots and assistants are built will determine how effective they are. It turns out these same choices also make a significant difference in AI's economic impact. The good news is that it's not too late to make decisions that will push companies toward AI software intended to augment people rather than replace them.

ESCAPING THE TURING TRAP

Unfortunately, the way AI capabilities are tested often frames their development as "man vs. machine." Brynjolfsson has been ringing the alarm about what he calls the "Turing Trap," noting that the Turing Test's original sin was to posit the exact mimicry of human skills as the hallmark of intelligence. This framing biases those building AI to envision their creations as substitutes for people. This tendency has only grown. OpenAI,

Microsoft, Google, Anthropic, and others building AI have all trumpeted how their AI systems beat the average person on exams that were never designed to evaluate machine performance, such as the bar exam, medical licensing tests, and coding competition questions. This creates a false impression that AI can fill the shoes of lawyers, doctors, and software developers. Part of the problem is that designing new benchmarks for human–machine pairing is more difficult than just comparing machine performance on existing tests to human scores. Also problematic are definitions of AGI like the one OpenAI favors: a single AI system able to outperform humans at most economically valuable work. That automatically sets up AI to be a substitute for human labor.

Framing AI as a substitute for human thinking actually limits the technology's transformational potential. Brynjolfsson poses a thought experiment to make this point: according to myth, the Greek inventor Daedalus built mechanical bronze sculptures that could move, speak, and even weep and sweat. Suppose Daedalus had succeeded in endowing his proto-robots with artificial intelligence that enabled them to accomplish all the Greeks' economically useful tasks, from farming grapes to herding sheep to making pottery. Saved from labor, the Greeks would have led lives of pure leisure. But also, Brynjolfsson says, the advancement of civilization would have been stunted—health and living standards would be stuck exactly where they were in ancient Greece. "After all, there is only so much value one can get from clay pots and horse-drawn carts, even with unlimited quantities and zero prices," Brynjolfsson writes.

Having humans work alongside AI, on the other hand, opens up vast new horizons. This is especially true if we look beyond the current craze for LLM-based AI. LLMs train from human-created data—so they can only replicate human knowledge. They cannot invent new knowledge. In contrast, AI software trained with reinforcement learning—where the software learns from experience—can stumble upon new ideas. Take AlphaZero, a system DeepMind built that learned to play Go and chess after starting with zero knowledge, entirely by playing against itself. The resulting software didn't just play these games at superhuman levels—the strategies it used were completely unlike those used by the best human players. DeepMind's chief executive, Demis Hassabis, himself once the world's highest-ranked youth chess player, described the software's playing style as "chess from another dimension." For one thing, the AI software tends to value board position and freedom of movement far more than the value of individual pieces, which is the opposite of how most human grandmasters have been taught to think. The software discovered whole new avenues of strategy that humans, despite playing chess for more than one thousand years, had not fully explored. Magnus Carlsen, the reigning chess world champion, credited tactics learned from matches he played against AlphaZero with helping him evolve his own playing style. This same phenomenon could happen in other realms—if we stop thinking of AI as exclusively a substitute for human labor.

THE COMING PRODUCTIVITY BOOM

Rather than just replacing people, AI will make humans more productive—perhaps radically so. Brynjolfsson has forecasted that widespread AI adoption could more than double the rate of U.S. productivity growth to 3 percent. The consulting firm McKinsey & Co. estimates that, if AI just nudges U.S. productivity growth back to the postwar average of 2.2 percent (which is significantly more than the 1.4 percent it has averaged since 2005), this increase would add an additional $10 trillion in GDP to the U.S. economy by 2030. The firm says that globally, the technology might add between $2.6 trillion and $4.4 trillion in economic value annually across sixteen key industries—which is more than the total GDP of the U.K.

This kind of growth should be good for everyone. The bigger the pie, the more there is to share. The distribution of that wealth could be uneven—more on that shortly. But it's better to argue over how to slice a bigger pie than a smaller one. It's a point that OpenAI's Sam Altman likes to make when asked about AI's potential economic downsides. "We just need gains. We need growth," he says. "We don't have enough sustainable growth, and that is causing all sorts of problems. I'm excited that this technology can bring the missing productivity gains of the last few decades back. And more than catch up."

Still, while increased productivity might mean more jobs overall—a good thing for the economy—it's not what a worker whose job has been automated wants to hear. The link between productivity improvements and potential job losses, however, is not straightforward. The advent of standardized shipping containers enabled dock workers to be more productive. But today there are far fewer longshoremen. On the other hand, in the software industry, the creation of high-level coding languages that make it far easier to program computers has not resulted in fewer software developers. Instead, the number of coders has soared.

Whether increased productivity helps or hurts employment in a particular field depends on what economists call the price elasticity of demand. Demand for most professional services, for example, is highly elastic. A small drop in price creates a big jump in demand and a need for more workers. For example, Geoff Hinton, the deep learning pioneer, predicted in 2016 that radiologists would be obsolete within five years because AI was getting so good at reading medical scans. Instead, radiologists are more in demand than ever. New technologies have lowered the price of medical imaging, which means much more imaging is being done, which means more need for radiologists.

The MIT economist David Autor, who has spent his career studying technology's impact on labor markets, thinks demand will be highly elastic for most things generative AI helps produce. Look at software programming and AI coding copilots. "If software developers all get 30 percent more productive, do you get 30 percent more software, do you get 30 percent fewer developers, or do you actually get 60 percent more software because, as the price falls, people want more and more software?" he asks. "I actually think that's the most likely case."

The demand for professional expertise, in particular, seems limitless. "There's an expertise bottleneck in the rich world," Autor says. That's why the hours professionals work have lengthened and their salaries have risen over the past fifty years. "In the 1970s, people with college degrees only worked a few hours more per week than people with high school degrees," Autor tells me. "Now they work massively more hours. And people with high school degrees work less. And it's because essentially demand for expert people just far outstrips supply." This bottleneck has made the jobs of those with higher educations "significantly crappier" than they used to be, in terms of work-life balance, Autor says. Alleviating the bottleneck should benefit them. In fact, even though the era of AI copilots has barely begun, some professionals are reporting that the use of chatbots is allowing them to regain personal time.

Accounting is a perfect example. In 2023, the U.S. was facing an acute shortage of qualified accountants, as baby boomers retire and the profession struggles to attract young people. There are about 126,500 openings for accountants each year, but only 73,000 degrees in accounting were awarded in 2020, down from close to 80,000 in 2016. Only 67,000 candidates sat for the CPA exam in 2022, the lowest number in two decades. AI could help close the gap, both by making existing accountants more productive, and by helping less-experienced ones perform at a higher level.

THE UBER EFFECT PART I: WAGE DEPRESSION

Rather than unemployment, the potential economic effects of AI that should be worrying us are wage stagnation and greater income inequality. It's likely AI will depress average wages in many fields, even as it allows the top tier to command more. This is because AI will lower the barrier to entry in many jobs, allowing people with less education, talent, and experience to produce work that is of at least average quality. Remember how the chatbot in the customer contact center helped the least-experienced agents the most? Imagine this repeated in field after field.

Call it the Uber effect: Until the mid-2000s, the only way to become a taxi driver in many cities, notably London, was to acquire specialized expertise, a specific kind of car, and a medallion whose supply was restricted. Then along came GPS, mobile phones, and Uber. Now, anyone with a driver's license and a car could become a taxi driver.

This has increased the number of drivers, but it has also decreased what consumers pay for the average ride. That is great for passengers. But it is a mixed picture for drivers: Uber allows some people to earn a better, more flexible living than they might have done in another job. However, on average, Uber drivers earn less per mile driven than a licensed cabbie. The competition from Uber has also made it more difficult for existing licensed taxi drivers to raise fares. This has led to a drop in demand for medallions in some U.S. cities. But the growing number of Uber drivers hasn't eliminated the demand among the world's billionaires for private chauffeurs, especially those who might have highly specialized skills—such as having been trained in evasive driving. Uber has had no impact on the wages these top-tier drivers can charge. This Uber effect will play out across many professions thanks to AI.

In areas where certifications don't pose a barrier to entry, AI's Uber effect is already being felt. Shortly after the debut of ChatGPT, professional writers who worked on a freelance basis penning marketing content for corporate clients began complaining that their customers were demanding steep cuts in freelance rates or refusing to hire them at all unless they also offered other services beyond content writing. Companies argued they shouldn't pay writers for something ChatGPT could do faster and for free, even in cases where they agreed the professionals' content was superior. This is driving down average compensation for writing marketing copy.

But just as Uber has not reduced the demand for top chauffeurs, the demand for marketing executives who plan entire communications strategies has not been affected by ChatGPT and the new writing copilots. Nor has copy writing for major advertising campaigns been outsourced to AI.

THE UBER EFFECT PART II: LESSENING INCOME INEQUALITY

Uber gets a bad rap for eroding the earnings of traditional cab drivers, shifting financial risks to drivers, and eroding passenger safety. But AI's Uber effect could potentially be fantastic for the economy as a whole. In many developed countries, the trend of the past decades has been rising inequality and a "hollowing out" of the middle class. The owners of capital and those with advanced degrees have captured an increasing share of the economic pie, while less-skilled, less-educated labor has been increasingly driven into lower-wage jobs, often in the hospitality, service, and retail sectors. The proportion of households earning between 75 percent and 150 percent of the median national income fell from 43 percent in 1970 to 33 percent in 2020. Their wage growth also lagged, with middle-class families seeing their after-tax earnings rise 53 percent between 1979 and 2018, while the top quintile of earners saw their after-tax income surge 120 percent.

AI's Uber effect could reverse this trend—allowing less-trained, less-experienced, and less-skilled people to successfully make some of the professional judgments that currently require highly trained, expensive, and limited expertise. It's a prospect that excites Autor, who says it could lift people who, over the past fifty years, have been squeezed out of the middle class into a more stable financial position. The increased number of middle-class consumers should be good for the economy. It would also expand access to expertise, making legal services, financial advice, and healthcare more affordable.

Autor says the best analogy is the nurse practitioner. This is a job that didn't exist in the U.S. until the 1960s but has surged in the past two decades. There are now between 250,000 and 400,000 nurse practitioners in the U.S., depending on which figures one uses. The role requires six to eight years of training, including an undergraduate degree in nursing, followed by a master's degree, and two years of additional clinical training. As substantial as this training is, it is less than the eleven to sixteen years that medical doctors in the U.S. must undertake. Once qualified, a nurse practitioner can perform many of the functions that had once been the exclusive domain of doctors, such as ordering diagnostic tests and prescribing medication. Nurse practitioners are paid less than doctors, but earn more than twice the median U.S. annual salary. Nurse practitioners have improved access to healthcare for large swaths of the population.

AI could help create roles similar to nurse practitioners across professions, helping reduce costs. Accounting, again, is a good example. Rather than requiring a CPA to conduct most audits, in the future, someone with an associate's degree in accounting, working alongside a copilot, will certify financial statements. Veterinarians typically have to train for eight years. But we can create a category of veterinary practitioners who complete a few years of training and then take on some of the work vets currently perform with help from AI. The same basic idea will be applied to fields ranging from chartered surveyors to financial advisors.

This is part of the reason why OpenAI's Altman says he's so optimistic about AI's overall impact on income inequality—it isn't that he thinks the technology won't depress wages. It's that he is certain AI will cause the price of goods and services to fall more dramatically, increasing people's purchasing power, even if wage growth is suppressed. At least, that is what will happen if we ensure AI software augments human capabilities. If we don't do this, the future will be more ominous.

RETURN TO ENGELS' PAUSE

During the early nineteenth century in Britain, industrialization led to rapidly rising economic output per worker and surging economic growth. Yet workers' average wages stagnated between 1800 and 1860. The economic historian Richard Allen has dubbed this sixty-year stretch "Engels' pause," in reference to the economist Friedrich Engels, whose classic tome *The Condition of the Working Class in England* in 1844 detailed the plight of impoverished workers in mid-nineteenth-century Manchester—and greatly influenced Karl Marx. While economists have advanced several explanations for the pause and its eventual end, recent theories have focused on the machinery of the early Industrial Revolution. Technologies such as the power loom, the steam engine, and the metal press were direct substitutes for skilled artisanal labor, while also requiring large quantities of unskilled people, including many children, to operate. There was no need to pay these workers much. But as steam-powered machinery became more and more sophisticated, it required increasingly skilled operators. This enabled labor to demand larger wage increases. Factories also became larger, requiring more managerial talent, as well as more secretaries, clerks, and bookkeepers, creating yet more skilled jobs. In other words, in this later Victorian era, human and machine labor complemented each other in a way they didn't in the early Industrial Revolution.

If we design AI software to replace, rather than complement, human labor, something similar to Engels' pause could well happen again. And if it does, it would only widen the chasm between the wealthiest and everyone else. In America, that wouldn't just be bad for income inequality. It would be devastating for racial and gender equality too. A majority of Black Americans work in support roles. In fact, Black and Latino workers are overrepresented in the three occupations that McKinsey & Co. forecast to be most exposed to automation: office support and customer service, food services, and factory production. Women also make up much of the workforce in both office support roles and customer service, which could see a loss of 3.7 million and 2 million jobs, respectively, by 2030, according to McKinsey. Black Americans, meanwhile, are underrepresented in the five professions—medicine, business and legal services, creative and arts management, teaching, and property maintenance—that the firm projects will have the least displacement. Black women are overrepresented in some occupations, such as nursing and home healthcare, that are unlikely to be affected by AI, so they may be in a slightly better position than Black men, although many of these jobs are poorly paid. McKinsey estimates that at least 132,000 fewer Black Americans might be working by 2030 due to automation.

THE WEALTH OF NATIONS

Many jobs in customer contact centers in recent years have been out-sourced to agencies in places like the Philippines and India, where they provide a good wage by local standards. India also provides a lot of remote IT support, software development, and accounting services to businesses in more prosperous countries. Business process outsourc-ing (BPO) of various sorts constitutes 7.5 percent of the Philippines' an-nual gross domestic product and about 8 percent of India's. But AI could eliminate many of these jobs. Sophisticated chatbots could fulfill most of the functions now performed by customer contact agents, and copilots could make others so efficient that far fewer human agents are needed.

At the same time, most of today's AI systems require, at some stage in their development, large amounts of human-labeled data. People are needed to identify what's in a photo or video to help train algorithms that power everything from content moderation software to self-driving cars. They're needed to clean up transcripts to help improve speech rec-ognition for AI assistants like Siri and Alexa. To create useful chatbots like ChatGPT, humans first must classify answers the chatbot provides as helpful or not, and much more. Many of the people doing this data labeling live in the developing world, in countries such as Venezuela, Mexico, Bulgaria, Kenya, the Philippines, and India. As with BPO jobs, they're often paid wages above minimum wage for the countries where they live, but considerably less than what someone in the U.S. or Europe would demand. In many cases, these data labelers have little job security. And their work can expose them to significant and lasting psychological trauma, especially if their labeling tasks involve screening images and videos for pornography and sexual abuse or extreme violence. AI could create a vast global underclass of data labelers, mostly in the Global South and viewed as disposable labor, while the benefits of the software they help create accrues primarily to those living in richer countries.

As awareness of exploitative labor practices grows, companies will come under more public pressure to ensure their software is being built in an ethical manner. AI ethicists Adrienne Williams, Milagros Miceli, and Timnit Gebru have advocated for the creation of forums that would empower data labelers to publicize poor working conditions as well as coordinate and organize. Two MIT researchers created the website Turkopticon, which provides a venue for data labelers employed through Amazon's Mechanical Turk—a program that allows digital tasks to be farmed out to remote gig workers on a piecemeal basis—to share the terms of their contracts. Unions or charities interested in improving labor conditions can build similar sites. Laws that require AI companies to publish information about how the data was prepared would also help.

NUDGING COMPANIES OUT OF THE TURING TRAP

Government policy will play a decisive role in determining AI's impact on the economy. And right now, most of these policies create perverse incentives that favor automation over augmentation. When a U.S. company invests in people, it has to pay payroll taxes equivalent to 7.65 percent of a person's salary. Meanwhile, corporations receive a tax incentive, in the form of depreciation, for investments in software like AI, as well as tax credits if they create their own AI software. The MIT economists Daron Acemoglu and Andrea Manera and Boston University's Pascual Restrepo estimate that the disparity in effective tax rates between labor and automation in the U.S. mean that a company that spends $100 on a worker pays about $30 in taxes, while if the same company spends $100 on AI or a robot, it pays just $5 in taxes. What's more, the effective tax rate on automation has been falling steadily, down from 10 percent in the 2010s and 20 percent in the 1990s. Acemoglu, Manera, and Restrepo argue these incentives have produced overinvestment in automation—spending beyond a level that would be economically and socially beneficial for the country. They conclude that a more even-handed approach to tax could increase employment by more than 4 percent.

Perhaps the best way to address these perverse incentives is through a "robot tax" on companies that invest in automation designed to replace workers. Acemoglu has advocated for a tax that would hit companies that applied robots and software only to areas "where humans still have a significant comparative advantage," such as nursing, complex tax advice, or, dare I say it, journalism. (Where machines have a significant advantage, such as welding or even executing stock trades, automation should continue to be encouraged and subsidized.) But such a tax might be difficult to implement. A simpler way to enact a robot tax would be to apply it to any company that invests in AI and robots and then lays off workers while also reporting increased revenues. Those are rough indicators of a company investing in automation to substitute for workers, not augment them. Democratic lawmakers in New York state have suggested a tax like this.

IMPROVED COLLECTIVE BARGAINING

Collective bargaining could play a critical role in pushing companies toward augmenting human labor with AI instead of replacing it. But first unions must abandon their knee-jerk tendency to oppose all forms of AI and automation. Unions should embrace AI while pressuring employers to develop this software as a complementary technology. They should also do more to ensure that companies or governments provide retraining for displaced workers and that an adequate social safety net is in place. They should also do more to coordinate their activities with workers in the developing world, including the data labelers. "This type of solidarity between highly paid tech workers and their lower-paid counterparts—who vastly outnumber them—is a tech CEO's nightmare," the AI ethicists Williams, Miceli, and Gebru have argued.

Unfortunately, the structure of collective bargaining in the U.S. and labor laws work against unions' efforts to play a constructive role in the development of technology. In 1935, the National Labor Relations Act, also known as the Wagner Act, established a single employer as the largest default unit for collective bargaining and allows the National Labor Relations Board to set much smaller units, down to an individual plant or work location. Meanwhile, the Wagner Act outlaws employee representatives on corporate boards unless a company has been fully unionized. This system should be turned on its head: the default unit should be an entire industry sector, with employers forced to make a case to the NLRB as to why they should be exempt from sectoral bargaining. This would give much more leverage to unions to shape how companies are using AI technology. In Europe, where many countries have sectoral bargaining, it is possible to envision labor having a voice at the table where the decisions about how to develop and deploy technology are made.

One of the few instances of sectoral bargaining in the U.S. is Hollywood, where one of the first major skirmishes over AI played out in both the screenwriters' and actors' strikes in 2023. In both cases, the union and the studios struck key compromises: the Writers Guild of America agreed to support the use of AI as a tool, so long as human writers continued to receive full credit—and compensation—for what they produce. These positions should inform unions in other industries as they negotiate with management about AI.

EXPANDING THE SOCIAL SAFETY NET

While economists debate about how AI will affect employment rates and wages, almost all agree that we are headed for a period of intense disruption, and that many people will need to change how they work, and, in some cases, find new jobs. McKinsey estimates that 11.8 million Americans will need to move to a different kind of job by 2030 due to AI's impact. It forecasts that 9 million of them will end up in a completely different occupational category—say an executive assistant becoming a computer programmer.

The need for government policies to ease the consequences of this transition cannot be overstated. But the U.S. has had a poor track record when it comes to retraining. Efforts to deal with previous dislocations have focused on education for people preparing to enter the workforce—for instance, increased funding for public education and the GI Bill after

World War II. But the federal government has not taken similar bold steps for retraining existing employees. It has instead relied on a patchwork of state and federal programs. The country spends 0.1 percent of GDP to help workers navigate job transitions, less than half what it spent thirty years ago. Money for reskilling must be expanded. And the government should provide direct funding to workers for retraining and upskilling, rather than relying on corporate tax credits to prod companies into providing it for their workers. Even with tax incentives, businesses are often rightfully reluctant to pay for worker retraining if they believe employees will simply take their newfound skills and jump to a job at another company. That's why the U.S. government should pay for retraining directly. "A prepared workforce is a public good," Brynjolfsson says. "We should all pay for it."

Beyond retraining, other benefits need to be expanded and become less tied to recipients' work status. Although the Affordable Care Act, better known as Obamacare, means those losing a job no longer automatically lose access to health insurance, people must still purchase a private healthcare plan. Depending on how long they're out of work, or if they undertake a period of retraining, they might run out of money to pay for healthcare. Too many state unemployment benefits are available only to those "actively looking for work" and cannot be used to pay for further education or certification courses. And while federal benefits and tax credits, such as the earned income tax credit, have been expanded in the past decade, far more could be done to make sure those transitioning between jobs don't fall into poverty. The social safety net should be made more robust, more flexible, and less tied to a particular state.

Fears of AI-driven unemployment have inevitably led to calls for a universal basic income (UBI). The idea has long been popular with Silicon Valley elites, and enthusiasm for it will likely spread as AI does. A full UBI that covers every citizen, regardless of means or work status, isn't necessary, however. What is needed is far more generous unemployment and retraining benefits for the newly jobless. This will be the case even if, as I've argued here, AI won't cause mass unemployment. There will be dislocation and restructuring, and those affected should not be consigned to poverty.

TO AUGMENT OR AUTOMATE: THE CHOICE IS OURS

The greatest determinant of AI's economic impact will be whether businesses use AI primarily as a copilot, augmenting human capabilities, or as a replacement for human workers. A robot tax would encourage companies to choose augmentation. Employees, through collective bargaining, can push for this too. Technology doesn't just happen to us. It is something we shape and direct. And we can still sculpt it in ways that help magnify people's economic potential, not thwart it.

CHAPTER

7

ARISTOTLE IN YOUR POCKET

Nowhere did ChatGPT's explosive debut cause more chaos and consternation than in education. Within days of the chatbot's release in late November 2022, students were using it to cheat on homework assignments and term papers. Students started referring to it as "CheatGPT," and teachers, blindsided by its release, panicked that they would never again be able to asign homework, or use term papers and research reports as ways to assess students. "The College Essay Is Dead," declared the *Atlantic* in an article published just six days after ChatGPT's release. Some school systems, including two of the largest—New York City and Los Angeles—blocked student access to OpenAI's website through school networks. In Australia, the country's eight top universities declared they would be forced to revert to proctored, hand-written exams.

AI will change education. Teachers will need to adopt new methods. But the moral panic and hand-wringing is misplaced. It's worth remembering that similar hysteria over rampant cheating greeted the debut of

CliffsNotes and its competitors in the late 1950s and calculators in the 1970s. Or that professors have more recently decried the sale of lecture notes, exam paper answers, and essays from services such as EssayShark or the online tutoring company Chegg. In each case, teachers adapted and, in many cases, education evolved for the better. English teachers developed assignments that required students to do more than just regurgitate the mundane summaries and facile thematic analyses found in CliffsNotes. Math classes began emphasizing conceptual understanding more than calculation. Educators can and will adapt this time too. What's more, used creatively, generative AI will be a boon to education, making it possible for every student to have a personalized tutor, tailoring lessons to their individual pace and learning style.

Think of it as having Aristotle, the classical philosopher and tutor of Alexander the Great, in your pocket. It's a vision of the future that Apple's founder Steve Jobs sketched out in a prescient 1985 speech in Sweden. Jobs said he was jealous of Alexander the Great—not because Alexander conquered the known world, although Jobs was a man of no small ambition himself, but because Alexander had Aristotle as a tutor. Jobs lamented that while he could still read Aristotle's words, he could not ask Aristotle a question. "My hope is that in our lifetimes we can make a tool of a new kind, of an interactive kind," he said. "Someday, when the next Aristotle is alive, we can capture the underlying world view of that Aristotle in a computer, and someday some student will be able to not only read the words that Aristotle wrote, but ask Aristotle a question, and get an answer." Jobs said that the personal computer would usher in a new revolution based on "free intellectual energy." Now AI is offering to fulfill Jobs's vision.

First though, let's dispense with concerns about cheating. Yes, students can use AI to cheat. This wouldn't be a problem in a world where grades were used solely as a diagnostic tool to help teachers—and students themselves—gauge progress, without any implications for access to further educational opportunities and, ultimately, employment. But let's get real: that's not the world we live in. Enlightened educators have been calling for a de-emphasis on grades for decades, to little avail. If anything, there has been an increasing tendency, as education has become more expensive, to view it solely as a means to a financial end, rather than an end in itself. To students, and their parents, grades are a currency that purchases credentials, which in turn are supposed to secure a brighter economic future. So cheating does hurt more than just the cheater. And yes, it would help if tech companies could develop better "watermarking" technology that would make AI-generated writing easier to spot. But educators are not powerless. They can change teaching and assessment methods to blunt students' ability to use generative AI to cheat.

A BRAVE NEW LESSON PLAN

It is tempting for teachers to fight technology with technology: deploying AI detection software, or asking students to complete their assignments in special online environments that surveil their every action. But determined cheaters will find ways to defeat these safeguards. Meanwhile, AI detection software has high false positive rates, so using it could result in honest students being accused of cheating. Plus, such technology does nothing to build trust between teacher and student. Yes, teachers are overworked. But they may find that taking the time to redesign lesson plans to work with, rather than against, AI is worth the investment. It can result in a class that is more engaged and eager to learn.

Chris Gilliard, a professor of digital studies at the University of Michigan, and Pete Rorabaugh, an English professor at Kennesaw State University, argue that educators need to keep "building activities and assessments to make classroom work more specific and experiential." ChatGPT won't conduct interviews for an oral history project for a student. It won't do fieldwork for a biology assignment. And it can't directly help a student answer questions in class. But it could help teachers facilitate group discussions—including activities where larger classes could be broken into smaller teams, with AI software guiding and monitoring the discussion, acting as a debating partner, and even summarizing the conversations for the teacher to review.

Even before AI came along, many educational experts were advocating that teachers implement "the flipped classroom"—reversing the usual purposes of classwork and homework. In a flipped classroom, teachers record lectures on videos that students can watch on their own time at home, or assign students reading and research as homework, but use class time to complete problem sets, do writing assignments, and lead class discussions. This way, the teacher is present to help coach the student through any issues they are having and can more easily pick up on areas where a student is struggling. It also maximizes the benefit of students being in class with one another.

If the AI revolution helps dethrone the lecture as the prime pedagogical tool in undergraduate education and replaces it with the seminar, that would be no bad thing. And while some professors will object that many classes are too large to accommodate seminars or tutorials, the answer is that AI-powered teaching tools might allow for the extension of the seminar model to even very large classes. Modern and Contemporary Poetry, a course at my alma mater, the University of Pennsylvania, is available for free through the online educational platform Coursera. The class routinely enrolls more than thirty thousand students from around the globe per term and is taught largely through small group discussion, some of it facilitated by the students themselves. And that is without any help from AI tools. So don't say it can't be done. Yes, more emphasis could be placed on proctored, in-person exams, as the Australian universities have chosen. But there are ways to rescue the term paper too. We ask PhD candidates to defend dissertations through a *viva*, a challenging, in-person discussion. A miniature—perhaps less-confrontational—version of this could be adapted for undergraduates and even high school students.

In primary schools, asking students to answer a few simple questions about their book report or the topic of their research may be enough for teachers to check that students have synthesized the material—which is the whole point of those assignments at that level. In high school, more extensive class discussion, or asking students to submit drafts of research papers, or asking probing questions about their research and writing process, might be enough to deter cheating. At the university level, these methods might be more difficult to implement, particularly at large universities, where administering a *viva* to every student in an introductory English lit or history course could be impractical. But in these universities, graduate teaching assistants already help with grading exams and papers, and they could be called on to lead small group or one-on-one discussions designed to weed out students who had obviously outsourced the work to ChatGPT. AI could help too: it could be used to ingest a student's term paper, and then formulate a few short-answer questions based on it, that the student would have to answer in person. Students who wrote their own papers ought to be able to pass easily.

AI is an existential threat to colleges and universities. But not because of the risk of rampant cheating. No, the real risk to higher education is irrelevancy. Students may decide that college isn't worth the cost because they can learn just as much from AI tutors for much less. Or they may decide that universities can no longer prepare them for jobs in an economy that is being radically transformed by AI. Either way, many colleges and universities could see enrollments plunge, and budget strains worsen—a trend that is already taking place. Today, schools face a looming "admission cliff," beginning in 2025, caused by a plunge in birthrates that accompanied the Great Recession in 2008 and has not rebounded. Add an AI-driven reluctance to enroll—why bother if the education in your pocket seems better than college?—and it could be curtains for more schools. That is why it's imperative that U.S. colleges and universities reshape their curriculum around things AI can't replicate—group discussions, fieldwork, lab experiments, experiential education, and those elements of campus life that AI can't automate, from the school band and drama societies to student government and, yes, college sports.

EVERY TEACHER'S PET

Innovative educators are already discovering ways to turn AI into a powerful teaching assistant. The simplest is as a copilot to help them prepare lessons. Heather Brantley, a sixth-grade math teacher in Texas, has used ChatGPT to bring her lessons to life. For a lesson on surface area, the chatbot recommended she ask her students to wrap boxes, using the formulas they had learned, to calculate how much wrapping paper would be required. An AI assistant can recommend contemporary scenarios to use for math word problems—say, asking students to calculate the viral reach of a TikTok video to illustrate exponential growth—making the lesson seem more relevant to today's students. AI copilots for teachers could help them outline lessons, prepare lecture notes and slides, generate questions for discussion, compose worksheets, and write test questions.

Some teachers are also incorporating chatbots directly into their lessons. Donnie Piercey, a fifth-grade teacher in Lexington, Kentucky, broke his class up into groups and assigned each to come up with an idea for a play set in a fictional fifth-grade classroom, including several different characters. Each group then provided these raw ideas in a prompt to ChatGPT, which developed several different scripts. The students seemed enthusiastic about the results, giggling over the plot twists the AI system had generated, including one story about students hunting for a class computer that escapes. Then Piercey had the students edit the AI-composed first drafts and perform the finished versions.

The process here matters—Piercey didn't just let ChatGPT do all the creative work. It was a collaboration between the students and the AI. As I argued in chapter 1, it's essential that we still teach kids how to write. Writing is a vital skill for the development of reasoning, logic, critical thinking, and creative expression—and it reinforces empathy. But we can incorporate AI into our teaching of writing, instead of trying to ban it. At the high school and university level, some teachers tell students that they can use AI to draft or edit their work, but insist that they must disclose exactly how they've used the software. They're also making sure students are aware of the tendency of AI chatbots to hallucinate, or even plagiarize in some instances, instructing students to carefully fact-check what their AI assistants produce. The idea is to encourage students to learn how to use AI as a copilot, while trying to avoid the risk that they will lean on it so heavily that they never develop their own abilities.

AI should enhance university students' experience by helping sort through course reading lists, recommending books and articles that the student will find most interesting. It can help them to better understand points they can't quite grasp from their professor's lecture or from a textbook explanation. It can help students prepare for in-person exams by providing them practice questions and rating their answers. This ability to have a tutor in your pocket as a supplement, not a replacement, for interaction with professors and peers could help undergraduates get more out of college.

AI can have a powerful democratizing effect on education. Georgia Tech has said undergraduate applicants can use AI "to brainstorm, edit, and refine your ideas," but that "your ultimate submission should be your own." The college has justified this approach in part on the grounds of equity: it levels the playing field between students whose parents, tutors, or counselors can brainstorm ideas with them and help edit their essays, and those who lack such assistance. "Here in the state of Georgia, the average counselor-to-student ratio is three hundred to one, so a lot of people aren't getting much assistance," Rick Clark, Georgia Tech's assistant vice provost and executive director of undergraduate admissions, told the *Guardian*.

AI tools can also be a leveling factor beyond the admissions phase. At the University of Illinois, the business school professor Unnati Narang has been encouraging students in her marketing course to use ChatGPT to compose first drafts of their responses to questions she poses online each week. She has found that the tool boosts participation from students who are weaker writers and had previously been less engaged. But she also encourages them to edit the first drafts written by ChatGPT, and to think critically about ideas the chatbot may have omitted.

The ability to use generative AI as a writing assistant, checking spelling and grammar and editing for clarity, can also close the achievement gap between native English speakers and those for whom English is a second or third language.

TO SIRI, WITH LOVE

The future outlined above is entirely possible using extant chatbots, like OpenAI's ChatGPT, Google's Gemini, and Anthropic's Claude. But AI's greatest educational impact will arise from specialized tutoring software. Such tools are already being created by companies such as Quizlet, which creates online quizzes and flashcards for students, and Khan Academy. Sal Khan, Khan Academy's founder, says that the holy grail for tutoring companies like his has been finding a way to tailor the material to each student. A mounting body of scientific evidence shows that tutoring, particularly one-on-one, increases students' achievement, and can partly offset disadvantages many poorer students face. But one-on-one tutoring was never feasible on a broad scale, technologically or economically, before. Now it is.

Khan, who has computer science and electrical engineering degrees from MIT and an MBA from Harvard, grew up in Louisiana, the child of Indian and Bangladeshi immigrants. He was working at a hedge fund in 2004 when he started tutoring one of his cousins remotely, over the internet, in math. Word soon spread to his other cousins, who asked him for help. With demand increasing, Khan decided to start recording his lessons and posting them on the internet. He founded Khan Academy in 2008 as a nonprofit online platform that would provide on-demand video lessons, with supporting materials, and allow students to join small group live tutoring sessions conducted through a remote video conferencing platform. A lot of what Khan Academy did was create software tools to help make the tutors' jobs easier: automatically generating worksheets and problem sets, helping to mark student tests, and flagging for the tutors areas where a student needed extra help.

Khan had always been interested in using AI to customize lessons for each student, but the tech wasn't up to the task. Then in 2022, OpenAI approached Khan Academy about helping it test GPT-4. OpenAI wanted to partner with a few socially oriented organizations as launch partners for GPT-4, in part to help blunt an anticipated backlash against a technology many viewed as a threat to jobs and existing businesses. But there was another, hidden motive, Khan says. OpenAI also wanted to tap Khan Academy's large set of Advanced Placement Biology questions. At the time, Khan had no idea why. As it turned out, OpenAI's patron and partner, Microsoft, had a particular interest in AP Biology. Microsoft's founder and chairman, Bill Gates, had been opposed to Microsoft chief executive Satya Nadella's decision to invest so heavily in OpenAI. Gates had played around with its early LLMs, GPT-2 and GPT-3, and he was unimpressed. He questioned whether OpenAI's approach to AI would ever bear fruit. And Gates had a personal test of AI's capabilities: AP Biology. In a meeting with Nadella, as well as OpenAI's Sam Altman and Greg Brockman, Gates had said AI would be ready for the real world when it could ace an AP Biology exam. OpenAI wanted Khan Academy's question sets to ensure GPT-4 could pass Gates's test—which it did, convincing him the AI revolution was real. But first, it passed Khan's own test. When he saw GPT-4 not only answering AP Bio questions correctly but also explaining its answers and generating whole new problem sets, and even an entire syllabus, he says he recognized "this is a game changer in everything we do."

Khan quickly realized that GPT-4 could be prompted to act as a tutor, not solving problems for students, but using the Socratic method to help them learn to solve the problems themselves. Khan Academy created Khanmigo, its own AI tutor, built on top of OpenAI's GPT-4. It has rolled this tutor out to thousands of teachers to act as a teaching aid. Khanmigo offers individualized guidance on math, science, and humanities questions, using the Socratic method and problem sets geared for each student. It includes a tool that suggests topics for students to discuss and debate, helping them build critical-thinking skills by reasoning through arguments and evidence on both sides of an issue. It also includes an AI writing coach that helps students brainstorm ideas, outline, and think about the writing process, but that stops short of composing an essay for them.

"It's very hard for the student to cheat," Khan says, because the assignment needs to be completed on Khan Academy's online platform, where the student can't simply paste in text copied from an AI-generated composition. Khan Academy also engineered Khanmigo to reduce the chances that GPT-4 will hallucinate. It has built guardrails to make it difficult for students to goad the online tutor into using inappropriate or racist language, too. Other companies, like Quizlet and Duolingo, are developing their own AI tutors. Within five years, this tool will be a reality for millions of students.

The possibilities of AI tutors extend well beyond simply tailoring math problems to the level and pace of each student. Students or teachers can ask an AI tutor to take on different personas to help make lessons more relevant and exciting. Imagine learning Shakespeare from the Bard himself. Or interviewing Marie Curie about her early experiments with radiation. Khan says educators' current attempts to make a curriculum more "culturally relevant" often come off as pandering. "People feel talked down to when you do that," he says. "What, you think just because I'm Black, you put a little hip-hop reference in a math problem, suddenly I care?" Ultimately, most of these attempts at relevance rely on and reinforce cultural stereotypes. What's needed instead is to let students be themselves, not who textbook publishers and testing companies think they are, and to tailor the learning experience to the things each student cares about most. AI tutors can do that. If you are Latina, but you love math and physics and your hero is Richard Feynman, why not have a Feynman-bot to teach you physics?

AI tutors will know far more about students than teachers currently can. Khan predicts that in a decade, an AI tutor like Khanmigo will provide a student their best college recommendation. "You've been working with it for ten years; it has seen your ups and downs," Khan says. It will know the educational challenges a student has overcome and how much progress they have made. But AI tutors won't replace teachers. Instead, they'll open up new ways for teachers to monitor progress and engage at critical moments. AI software will arm teachers with granular information about each student, allowing the teacher to spot learning difficulties earlier. Is Mikey struggling with quadratic equations? Is Lucie having trouble identifying the themes in *One Flew over the Cuckoo's Nest*? Now the teacher doesn't have to wait until the exam to find out.

The teacher will also be able to aggregate metrics across the class, providing better feedback on their pedagogical techniques. Did that lesson on the Krebs Cycle land? Did yesterday's class discussion of *Animal Farm* boost the class's grasp of Orwell's allegory? The teacher will have that feedback. AI will also help alleviate much of the burden that teachers bear in trying to meet new state and national standards. Teachers have struggled to find a diverse range of course material to fit into the highly structured curriculum these standards seem to require. But now, with an AI tutor, an array of teaching materials that comply with these standards can be generated. At the same time, a student will be free to explore tangents—for example, is the physics presented in the movie *Contact* consistent with Newtonian principles?—without distracting their teacher.

SPANNING THE DIGITAL DIVIDE

AI can empower students and give superpowers to educators. It could also strike a major blow against inequality, providing personalized tutoring and improved copilot-assisted teaching to students whose parents would never be able to afford these things, and who live in districts with poor schools. But that will only happen with the right policies in place. Otherwise, AI could have the opposite effect, allowing privileged students to pull further ahead. History gives little reason for optimism. The benefits of past educational technologies, from Chromebooks and tablets to online learning apps, have compounded inequality, opening a yawning "digital divide" between the haves and the have-nots. The impact of this divide was made glaringly apparent during the COVID-19 pandemic, when poorer schools struggled to take up online and hybrid learning in part because students lacked access to computers or reliable home broadband. Why would AI be any different? More than previous digital technologies, AI has the potential to universalize access to top-quality teaching and individual support, as well as coaching teachers who are struggling. AI could be the technology that finally bridges the digital divide. But enabling poorer students to grab those benefits will require changes in how the technology is built and distributed.

In the U.S., local funding of education through real estate taxes has resulted in big disparities between wealthy and poorer districts. Affluent districts have plenty of money to spend on laptops, IT support staff, and teacher training. Low-income districts don't. Plus, in wealthier districts, students are much more likely to have access to mobile phones, laptops, and computers at home. In 2021, only four in ten lower-income adults had access to a home desktop or laptop, and most didn't own a tablet, according to the Pew Research Center. Only 43 percent of low-income households have broadband access. For households making $100,000 per year or more, Wi-Fi and computers are ubiquitous.

To take advantage of AI's opportunities, government and philan-thropies will need to work together to provide the digital technology that will allow students to access AI. Programs such as the Federal Com-munications Commission's E-Rate program provide grants for internet connectivity and other infrastructure for schools; California's Bridging the Digital Divide Fund, which bought laptops for students in poorer districts during the pandemic; and $475 million for free broadband and laptops for the disadvantaged that was part of the Biden administration's 2021 Infrastructure Investment and Jobs Act—will need to be extended and expanded.

Software also has a cost. While Khan Academy is a nonprofit, it doesn't provide its AI tutor, Khanmigo, for free. It charges districts that use the AI tutor thirty-five dollars per student per year, on top of the ten dollars per student it already charges for access to Khan Academy's other resources. It says this charge is necessary to defray the cost of using OpenAI's GPT-4. Quizlet also charges for access to its Q-Chat AI tutor. Low-income school districts will need grants to help cover these costs. Just as important, government or charities will need to help schools pay for networks and devices. School districts will also need the funds to train teachers in how best to integrate AI as both a copilot for them and as a tutor for each of their students. Governments could, potentially, even fund the development of open-source chatbots, fine-tuned to act as AI tutors, that they could provide to schools free of charge, rather than having to fund schools to pay ed tech companies like Khan Academy or Quizlet.

AI tutors are likely to become so vital to education that states may decide that they cannot allow decisions about them to rest solely with local school districts. As many states currently do with mandated curriculums and bulk-purchased textbooks, states themselves will contract with technology companies or educational publishers (which will partner with tech companies in creating AI copilots and teaching assistants) to provide AI tutoring software and teaching aids to every public school student and teacher in the state.

Such a top-down approach is already taking shape at the national level in some countries, such as South Korea and Singapore. In February 2023, the South Korean Ministry of Education unveiled a plan designed to introduce AI-enabled digital textbooks for math, English, and some other subjects starting in 2025. Singapore's "Smart Nation" strategy also includes money allocated to put an AI tutor in the hand of every student by 2030. Other nations that already take a centralized approach to education policy, such as the U.K., should follow the lead of South Korea, while U.S. states ought to consider similar strategies. The federal government can use its funding powers to incentivize states to take such approaches. Low-income school districts cannot be left to bridge the digital divide on their own.

THE GLOBAL CLASSROOM

AI can radically transform education. Better education can help lessen global income inequality. Personal tutors can make a huge difference in nations such as Rwanda, where there simply aren't enough qualified teachers for all the children who need schooling. The average pupil-teacher ratio in primary school in Rwanda is 60:1. At secondary schools, it is slightly better, at 28:1, but that's partly because more than a fifth of students drop out after primary school. AI's ability to provide customized feedback to these students would be transformative. OpenAI's Altman visited Nigeria in 2023 as part of a world tour promoting the company's AI technology. He later commented that, while the discussion around ChatGPT and AI with government officials in America and Europe focused mostly on risks, leaders in low-income countries just wanted to know how quickly they could get the technology into people's hands. They rightly saw many more potential benefits than harms.

OVERCOMING AI'S LANGUAGE BARRIER

Educational technology companies will need to build AI tutors tailored to students in less-developed countries. One of the major reasons is language. While it has become common for Silicon Valley technologists to talk as if AI has solved the problem of language translation, for many languages around the world, this is untrue. Many languages simply don't have enough text in digital form to train good AI translation programs. These so-called low-resource languages present a serious challenge to the kind of high-quality translation that is imperative for educational software. Software such as Google Translate might be okay if you want to ask someone where the bathroom is, but it isn't good enough to teach a kid calculus or hold a nuanced discussion about poetry or politics. This lack of effective machine translation poses a critical challenge to education, as it makes it difficult to retrieve valuable information through internet search engines and knowledge bases, such as Wikipedia and news sites. Many of the current chatbots also produce gibberish answers if prompted in low-resource languages.

But there are innovative start-ups working to solve this issue. One of them is Berlin-based Lesan, which is building machine translation software specifically geared toward low-resource languages. The company, whose founders are Ethiopian, are starting with Amharic, one of the main Ethiopian languages spoken by 25 million people, and Tigrinya, which is spoken by about 7 million people in the war-ravaged northern Tigray region of Ethiopia and in Eritrea. But it plans to expand to other African and Asian languages as well.

Lesan has used printed material, which it digitized itself, to train its language translation AI. It has also tried to develop speech recognition software for Tigrinya and Amharic, so that spoken material can be converted to text. This is important for three reasons. First, many stories, poems, and songs have traditionally been passed down only orally. So any AI system that encompasses this knowledge must do so through speech-to-text technology. Second, and more important, voice recognition is an easy way to increase the amount of digital text available to train a language model for a low-resource language. Finally, because many people in places such as Tigray are illiterate, they can interact with the technology only if it can understand their spoken words.

By using these methods, Lesan has achieved much higher-quality translation than software built by the likes of Google, Meta, and Microsoft. Asmelash Teka Hadgu, Lesan's co-founder and chief technology officer, says he wants to "build the internet for his great-grandmother." That is, he wants an internet his great-grandmother could use, but more importantly one that preserves the folktales, bedtime stories, family history, and Tigrinya wordplay games that she taught him in his childhood. He wants to create digital versions of these traditional tales and games so that this heritage can be preserved and handed down to future generations. "Our motivation is basically our roots," he says. "How can we enable our communities to open access for them to knowledge? How can we link them?"

He is critical of the approach big technology companies have taken to low-resource languages because they are built around the objective of "zero-shot" translation—a science fiction–like goal of an AI capable of accurately translating a language without ever having trained on any materials in that language. Zero-shot methods, he says, inherently result in lower-quality translations, which means these communities will always be relegated to second-class status and have to deal with less-capable technology. Just as importantly, it negates the need to digitize and preserve the cultural heritage embodied in these languages.

Lesan is not alone. There are similar efforts underway throughout Africa. Ghana NLP is a nonprofit that has built language translation apps for a number of languages spoken in West Africa, including Twi, Ga, Dagbani, Yoruba, Kikuyu, and Luo. It not only allows translation between these languages and English, but between one another, and supports speech recognition for several of them. Ghana NLP has received support from Google, Microsoft, and Harvard University.

International donor organizations and government development agencies should invest more heavily in supporting these kinds of efforts and integrating the language translation technology they are building into AI tutors and education apps. Rwanda, for instance, is conducting a study to assess its readiness for introducing AI into education, with support from UNESCO. It's a model that should inspire other low-income countries. But Teka Hadgu's own story shows some of the difficulties that will have to be overcome to deliver on AI's promise in many developing countries: Teka Hadgu credits his success with his attendance at a special selective school in Tigray that took in just sixty students each year from throughout the region and put them in an environment where "we didn't have to worry about food or clothes, all the other things students in Europe or America take for granted, and we could just focus on education." That school had computers—and volunteer teachers from England who taught the kids to use them. That is not the case in most schools in Tigray, or indeed in many parts of the world.

As should be clear by now, teachers are right: AI will disrupt education in profound ways. But this should be cause for excitement, not despair. The technology represents a tremendous opportunity to re-shape how subjects are taught for the better. AI can improve every level of schooling, from kindergarten through graduate school, and help enable lifelong learning, too. With the right government policies, it could strike a blow for equality. It's up to educators to figure out creative ways to realize those opportunities, working with the technology, not simply trying to ban its use. As they will for other professions, AI copilots will streamline many of the time-consuming, repetitive tasks teachers must perform that aren't directly related to delivering instruction and one-on-one support. Overall, teachers will benefit from these advances as much as students. It's time to make good Steve Jobs's prophecy by putting the wisdom of Aristotle, and every future Aristotle, in the pocket of everyone who learns and teaches.

CHAPTER

8

ART AND ARTIFICE

For most of human history, making art required a melding of diverse mental and physical abilities: not just cognitive intelligence, but keen perception—an eye for color, or an ear for music—emotional intelligence, and, in many cases, kinetic intelligence similar to that of star athletes. A singer needed to train their voice to hit the notes. A musician needed to develop muscle memory to pluck the strings. A painter needed to draw well and control their brush.

This began to change in the nineteenth century, largely due to the invention of photography. As the philosopher Walter Benjamin observed, "For the first time in the process of pictorial reproduction, photography freed the hand of the most important artistic functions which henceforth devolved only upon the eye looking into a lens." In recent decades, software has further picked apart the knotted strands of human skills required to make art, allowing computers to handle some aspects of art-making—from Apple's GarageBand to Adobe's Photoshop. But still, trained artists and musicians can accomplish far more with these new tools than a novice. David Hockney can do more with an iPad than you or I. Even the first generation of AI-created deepfake videos required technical expertise and skilled postproduction work.

Today's generative AI models go much further, radically divorcing idea from execution. Photography still requires abilities beyond imagination. A good photographer must frame an image, have the technical skills to capture the light and depth of field in the right way, and possess an impeccable sense of timing. Generative AI requires none of that. The mind's eye is all that matters. AI enshrines, even more so than previous technologies, the preeminence of the concept in the value chain of creation. And, as with so much about AI, it is the technology's breadth that makes it so breathtaking.

No art form will be left untouched. Text-to-image generators can create images of all kinds, from cartoons to impressionist works to photorealistic ones, with just a verbal prompt. Google's MusicLM, Stability AI's Stable Audio, and OpenAI's Jukebox are AI systems that do something similar for music. Runway's Gen-2 software creates full videos from text prompts. LLMs like OpenAI's GPT-4 and Anthropic's Claude can write short stories and poetry. These tools will radically transform cultural production and entertainment.

As with much of AI, this transformation will produce crosscutting effects: production of art and entertainment content will explode, allowing more people access to the means of artistic expression. And yet this radical democratization of artistic production will likely give more power to those who control the means to curate, distribute, and market that content. Finding gold amid the schlock will be harder than ever.

AI also raises profound questions about the nature of creativity. As we'll see, today's generative AI is the first software that can replicate some aspects of human creativity. But it can't match all our creative powers. When it comes to art, as in many fields, AI will be our collaborator, not our replacement. Human artists and human genius will remain vital and preeminent. AI will increase the value of art with physical manifestations that it cannot so easily match—sculpture, ceramics, glassblowing, architecture, theater, and live performance. For the same reason, AI will likely expand our appreciation for the avant-garde too. The singularity of such art makes it difficult for AI to replicate, except by accident, although some writers and visual artists are already using AI as part of their process for making works that challenge convention—and us.

In the past, moments of profound technological and social disruption have spawned artistic renaissances. AI is perhaps our most disruptive technology to date. We should be eager to see what human artists create in response.

THE ALTMAN EQUATION

In late 2023, OpenAI's Sam Altman posted on X (formerly Twitter): "Everything 'creative' is a remix of things that happened in the past, plus epsilon and times the quality of the feedback loop and the number of iterations. People think they should maximize epsilon, but the trick is to maximize the other two." Many artists, philosophers, and critics of Silicon Valley "tech bro" culture rightly faulted Altman for his pseudo-mathematical reductionism. But his basic premise, that creativity is far less about the spark of invention (the epsilon in Altman's formulation) and far more about the recombination of previous ideas, is itself not original, as Altman readily acknowledged. And it's an idea that many experts on creativity endorse. David Eagleman, the Stanford University neuroscientist, who co-authored a book on human creativity with the composer Anthony Brandt, argues that all creativity can be reduced to one of three actions performed on artifacts that previous generations have created: bending, blending, or breaking. They also argue that the brain can only alter "what it already knows." Inventions don't come from nowhere. "Like diamonds, creativity results from pressing history into brilliant new forms," Eagleman and Brandt write. Or, as the novelist Michael Chabon puts it more bluntly in the documentary *The Creative Brain*, which is based on Eagleman and Brandt's work: "Originality is bunk."

Whether or not Chabon's declaration is accurate is open to question, but it's clear that AI can't blend, bend, and break as well as we can. Most generative AI is trained on historical data, and then the AI model interpolates between data points in its training set, combining some elements from each. In mathematics, interpolation is about adding new data points to a graph that sit between the already existing ones. If you think about a children's coloring book, interpolation is about connecting the dots and coloring in the shapes created by the resulting lines.

In Eagleman and Brandt's typology of creativity, this kind of interpolation is mostly bending and blending. For instance, AI is adept at a task known as *visual style transfer*: take a photo of a New York street scene, but render it in the swirling colors and style of Van Gogh's *Starry Night*. Or recast a photo of your face as a Japanese anime character or a Gothic horror movie villain. It's a premise that has launched a thousand smartphone apps.

Today's AI is also decent at some of what Eagleman and Brandt term *blending*. For example, Norman Rockwell's deliberate adaptation of the pose of Michelangelo's prophet Isaiah from the ceiling of the Sistine Chapel for his depiction of Rosie the Riveter. That's something that today's generative AI could replicate, but only with the right prompt. (The inspiration to blend those particular images would still have to come from a human brain.) Runway's Gen-1 AI model is all about taking one video and swapping one element from the scene—it could be a character, a prop, or the background—with AI-generated elements. Repurposing one object, method, or technique is also a kind of blending.

LLMs score highly on tests of creativity that involve suggestions for repurposing objects, such as the Alternative Uses Test (AUT) that the psychologist J. P. Guilford developed in 1967. When researchers tested several AI models on the AUT in 2023, they found they were as creative as most people. Only 9 percent of people scored higher on the test than the most creative AI model, which was OpenAI's GPT-4. GPT-4 also scored in the ninety-ninth percentile, better than most humans, on a broader gauge of creativity, the Torrance Tests of Creative Thinking.

BREAKING THE MOLD

But if AI can handle some aspects of blending and bending, it stumbles when it comes to breaking. Breaking involves tearing one or more pieces out of a unified whole. It often also involves placing the broken pieces into a different context or arrangement. Eagleman and Brandt count synecdoche, a literary device in which part of an object represents the whole ("wheels" to mean cars; "suits" to mean businessmen) as breaking. They also highlight the way Bach in his Fugue in D Major from *The Well-Tempered Clavier* introduces his main theme only to break off the last four notes, which become a motif he then sprinkles throughout the rest of the piece. Today's AI systems can rarely break things in this way, and almost never without extensive human prompting. This is because breaking doesn't involve interpolation, at which today's generative AI models excel, but extrapolation—the projection of one set of data points to a distant location outside the graph represented by the AI's training data. Extrapolation means coloring outside the lines. If an AI model has never encountered an example of what the prompt is asking for, it will usually fail to produce the desired output.

What's more, to break something into pieces, you have to understand what the whole is to begin with—and this comprehension of wholes and their constituent parts, which cognitive psychologists refer to as *compositionality*, is something that eludes today's deep learning–based AI systems.

To illustrate breaking, Eagleman and Brandt use the example of the modern artist Barnett Newman's *Broken Obelisk*, which is a Cor-Ten steel sculpture depicting an obelisk, roughly ripped in half horizontally, with the broken top portion balanced inverted, point facing down, on the tip of a pyramid. I tried to get Midjourney to create an image similar to *Broken Obelisk,* even using Barnett Newman's name and sculpture title in the prompt on some attempts. The AI could not depict an inverted obelisk, nor one ruptured horizontally, no matter how I tried. OpenAI's DALL-E also struggled. There are simply not enough images of inverted obelisks in these AI models' training data for them to depict one accurately. They also don't understand what an obelisk is, and so can't figure out which elements of an image are needed.

For instance, while DALL-E could invert an obelisk, it also tended to invert the ground underneath the obelisk, too, creating an image with ground at both the top and bottom. This inability to handle compositionality also makes these image generators less useful: DALL-E 3 cannot depict an image of a male painter without a beard no matter how many ways you try to specify that the painter be "clean-shaven," "beardless," or "without any facial hair." In the AI model's worldview, a beard and moustache are inseparable from its conception of a painter.

Put simply, generative AI systems aren't trained to break convention. In fact, their outputs are the very definition of it. They're trained to return examples close to the statistical mode or modes of the data distribution on which they've been trained. That is, examples that appear most frequently in a training set are more likely to be replicated. In a shocking example we'll return to in chapter 11, when researchers prompted Midjourney to depict "a Black African doctor caring for a white suffering child," the AI could not comply; 299 times out of 300 attempts it depicted a white doctor caring for Black children. There were simply too few images of Black doctors treating white children in its training data.

LLMs, meanwhile, are trained to find the next most likely word in a sentence. But good writing often depends on finding the next most *unlikely* word that still preserves the sentence's meaning. AI models can't do this because they don't have any explicit understanding of what they're saying—only a set of correlations locked in their neural networks. This explains why, even with a specific prompt like "don't use clichés," generative AI models struggle. They don't understand what they *aren't* supposed to be doing. In a damning assessment of generative AI's creative writing abilities, researchers from Columbia University and the software company Salesforce asked literary experts to blindly assess short stories AI chatbots had written after being prompted with the beginnings of short stories published in the *New Yorker* alongside the actual human-written versions. The chatbot-authored stories all came up short, relying on hackneyed metaphors, composing dialogue that lacked subtext, and failing to invent intriguing endings.

Other kinds of AI could, in theory, be more original. Ahmed Elgammal, an Egyptian-born computer scientist who is a professor at Rutgers University, developed a type of AI software he calls a creative adversarial network, or CAN. It takes inspiration from the AI method that was used to create the first deepfakes. Creating this kind of AI software requires two neural network models, one that generates images, and the other that tries to classify them. In this case, Elgammal trained the classifier network on the WikiArt dataset, first to recognize if an image is likely art or not, and then to identify the style of the art. The generator learns how to generate art-like images in these various styles.

But Elgammal also created a function called style ambiguity, where the generator produces an image that the discriminator still considers art, but where it can't accurately pinpoint the style. This resulted in the generator producing a series of highly abstract images that were fairly novel in their use of line and color. Elgammal said that "the machine has captured the trajectory of art history, which is toward abstraction." The problem is that this implies only abstract images can be truly original. Elgammal's assertion that all art trends toward abstraction also seems inaccurate. It is true that fine art has, over the past 150 years, fled from the purely representational. But where art has run to has not just been abstraction. It would be more true to say art's destination has been intellectualism, where the idea behind the work is as important, or more important, than its aesthetic qualities.

Another way to produce a more creative AI system would be to dispense with human-generated training data altogether. Google DeepMind created an AI that operated in this way. Called MuZero, it could play chess, checkers, Go, or any other two-player game in which both players have perfect information about the state of play. It achieved superhuman skill levels starting with zero human knowledge about the game. It had to figure everything out by trial and error, including the rules. With chess,

MuZero rediscovered many of the same gambits that human players had developed in the 1,500 years since the game's invention. But then MuZero moved beyond them, inventing never-before-seen strategies, perfecting a style of play that broke most rules of thumb. This was undeniably transformational creativity. But it was possible only because games have a built-in "reward signal"—winning the game—that helps the AI system tell if it is coming up with useful tactics, as well as a fairly constrained environment in which to act—the confines of the board and the rules of the game.

In many artistic and creative fields, a reward signal is much harder to define, while the "action space" in which the AI can act encompasses the entire universe. This makes it difficult to use reinforcement learning for art. We could, perhaps, ask people to vote on whether they liked an AI-generated image, and that could provide a reward signal. But this is not what human artists do—at least not the great ones. Artists don't generally depend on an external reward signal to guide their work. And they certainly don't trust the wisdom of crowds. Van Gogh sold relatively few works during his lifetime. Herman Melville's novel *Moby-Dick* sold just three thousand copies while the author was alive. Artists persevere in the face of rejection because they are motivated by internal conviction, not external reward.

BUT IS IT ART?

A packed room inside Christie's New York on a bright but brisk fall morning. The murmur of the crowd, restless in their chairs, the rustle of catalog pages, fades to a tense hush as the auctioneer ascends to the podium. Next to him on an easel is a seemingly unfinished portrait of a man, wearing clothes vaguely reminiscent of seventeenth-century Europe, but hard to place. The picture is oddly distorted, with the man's head so high up the canvas it's partly cut off, and his facial features a blur. The picture is displayed in a classic gold frame. The only giveaway that this is not some unfinished Dutch master discovered in a flea market is the signature: it isn't a name but a mathematical algorithm. The picture is called *Portrait of Edmond de Belamy,* and it isn't a painting. It's a print on canvas, created by a Parisian art collective called Obvious Art using AI.

The auctioneer starts the bidding at $7,000. Paddles shoot up. Dozens of them. The price climbs rapidly. $10,000. Then $50,000. $100,000, and still they bid. The room is electric—$150,000. $175,000. More offers are coming in over Christie's website and over the phone. At $200,000, just one man still has his paddle in the air, but he's competing against two phone bidders and one more online. As the price passes $250,000, the man's paddle drops. Now there are just two left, one online and one on the phone, both from France. At $350,000, the collector online abandons the hunt. BANG! The auctioneer's hammer falls, seven minutes after it started. With fees, the total price is $432,500—forty-three times the painting's initial estimate.

The sale of *Edmond de Belamy* on October 25, 2018, caused cultural critics and art historians to clutch their pearls, bemoaning the death of art. But within a few years, such scenes will no longer generate headlines. Easy-to-use software is fast making AI-generated imagery ubiquitous, and it will increasingly occupy pages in the world's auction catalogs. But that doesn't settle the question of whether what AI produces is art.

If art is in the eye of the beholder—or, perhaps more cynically, the eye of the buyer—then the answer is almost certainly yes. In essence, this is the same standard as used in the Turing Test—if the audience can't tell the difference between the AI's output and a human-created work, or doesn't care, it's art. As we explored in chapter 1, process is completely discounted in this assessment. Effect is all that matters, not cause.

Today's AI image generators can produce pretty pictures that are often indistinguishable from similar pictures created by human artists. Those pictures are likely to have a similar emotional impact on viewers from a purely aesthetic perspective. This is, in fact, what Elgammal discovered when he asked people, including experts like art historians and artists, to assess the output of his CAN software. Most found CAN's output was novel, aesthetically pleasing, and indistinguishable from human-created art. So, as far as Elgammal was concerned, it was art.

But if one takes the opposite view, that what makes something art is solely the intention of the creator, then any work generated purely from AI is not art at all. An AI system has no intention and no lived experience. In particular, it has no emotional experience. From this perspective, the effect on the audience is irrelevant; only the creator's affect and intention matters. An AI model could create "a song that is, on the surface, indistinguishable from an original, but it will always be a replication, a kind of burlesque," the Australian rocker Nick Cave wrote in a headline-grabbing blog post in which he railed against the inauthenticity of LLM-generated songs. In Cave's view, "Songs arise out of suffering," and "as far as I know, algorithms don't feel. Data doesn't suffer. ChatGPT has no inner being, it has been nowhere, it has endured nothing, it has not had the audacity to reach beyond its limitations, and hence it doesn't have the capacity for a shared transcendent experience, as it has no limitations from which to transcend." In Cave's view, even a human using an LLM as a tool would not result in artistic expression, since the human has used the AI model to shortcut the hard work, "the suffering" in his formulation, of figuring out how to express an idea, which he argues constitutes art's essence.

But Cave's definition of art goes too far. The famous "ready-made" avant-garde work *Fountain*, usually attributed to the artist Marcel Duchamp (although that attribution has been recently disputed) was clearly art, even though Duchamp, or whoever submitted the work to the 1917 American Society of Independent Artists show from which it was rejected, didn't have to do any work to fashion the urinal used for the piece. The work—"the suffering," in Cave's formulation—was all in conceiving the idea and making choices about which urinal to use and deciding to sign it pseudonymously "R. Mutt, 1917." All those human decisions are what elevates the urinal in *Fountain* from mundane object to art. *Edmond de Belamy* is similar: the artists in Obvious had to decide which AI method to use, what historical imagery to feed the algorithm, which output to select, and how to title and sign it.

Some artists are discouraged that people can't tell the difference between an AI-generated picture and one a painter labored over, or between an AI-generated song and one Nick Cave suffered for. Moreover, they despair that so few people care—that all they want is a pretty picture or a kickin' track. Well, we've been here before, and art survived. Walter Benjamin, in writing about the impact of photography and lithography on visual art, argued that the ease of reproduction reduced an image's "aura." Benjamin defined this as the unique link between a work of art and the act of creation, the purpose of creation, and the place where the art is exhibited, all of which contributed to its emotional impact. But while reproduction reduced the aura of the copies, it could also increase the aura of the original. Only in seeing a painting in person could one get a sense of the work's three-dimensionality, its brushwork, true colors, and scale. One need only go to see the *Mona Lisa* in the Louvre on a summer weekend to prove this point; the desire of people to see the painting in person—to experience its aura, as Benjamin would say—has not been diminished at all by its ubiquitous reproduction.

AI is likely to increase the importance of art that has a physical dimension: Paintings displayed in galleries and, even more so, sculpture, whose three-dimensionality cannot be easily captured in a digital image created by AI. Live music, which is more popular than ever in the age of Spotify and Apple Music, will certainly get a boost. AI cannot replicate the connection between performer and audience in a live event—and this remains true even if we begin to replicate past popular bands using digital avatars, as ABBA has done in a successful London theatrical show *Voyage*. The challenge for digital art that has no physical form is greater. But the increasing ubiquity of AI art may revive the popularity of non-fungible tokens, where an original digital artwork carries a cryptographic signature that attests to its uniqueness.

THE CASE FOR AI–HUMAN COLLABORATION

AI cannot make art. But it does blaze new trails for artistic expression in the form of human–machine collaboration. Several fiction authors have begun to use AI chatbots as part of their writing process. The British crime novelist Ajay Chowdhury uses ChatGPT as a brainstorming partner. He doesn't let it compose his prose; he asks it for help with plot points. "I'll tell it, 'Hey, I'm kind of stuck here, give me a few ideas.' And it's fantastic at doing that," he says. In one of his recent books, Chowdhury's protagonist is trapped, locked inside a shed. Chowdhury couldn't devise a way that his character might be able to MacGyver himself out that would seem fresh and surprising. ChatGPT helped him cook up ideas, including that the character might be able to use a tool in the shed to disassemble the shed itself, an idea Chowdhury hadn't considered.

Chowdhury also wrote a children's book and wanted to explore turning it into a graphic novel. But he wasn't sure how to do it. So he asked ChatGPT to help him storyboard the book, including possible images. It produced a first draft of a storyboard, complete with cinematic-style descriptions for a "flashback montage" and various camera angles and shots. "That's what I find very powerful, because it's allowing me to unleash my creativity in a genre I haven't done before and a format I haven't done before," he says. To produce the actual book, Chowdhury still intends to work with a professional artist. The role of generative AI here is to help Chowdhury—and more importantly prospective publishers—visualize how the story might be told. It helps pitch the idea, not execute the final product.

Other writers are allowing AI to compose some of the prose they use. Hannah Silva wrote an experimental memoir *My Child, the Algorithm* in which she used GPT-J, a large language model created by the AI collective EleutherAI that was designed to mimic the capabilities of OpenAI's early LLM, GPT-2. It could compose relatively short passages of coherent prose in a variety of styles. But it could also veer off in bizarre directions, make non sequiturs, and get stuck repeating the same phrase or word. Silva is a poet who has worked in the vein of found poetry, where the poet selects, assembles, and juxtaposes snippets of text from newspapers, magazines, billboards, emails, or recorded conversation. Silva's technique for *My Child, the Algorithm* was similar, juxtaposing bits of GPT-J text with her own writing. All the GPT-J written text is italicized, so the reader can identify it. The memoir is a meditation on parenting a toddler as a single mother and on Silva's experience with dating and relationships. She used GPT-J to expound on these themes, but the LLM also served as a foil against which ideas about learning and teaching, intelligence and love, can be projected, reflected, and refracted. Silva's method involved experimenting with feeding GPT-J bits of her writing as prompts, as well as manually adjusting the model's settings, including the "temperature" of its response—a metric that determines how far a model's response can stray from its most likely response. So a higher temperature means a response that can be more "out there" and unusual. The newer chatbot models mostly don't offer this control in their consumer-facing versions. Silva also carefully selected from among the model's responses.

So while GPT-J produced some of the text in *My Child, the Algorithm*, including entire chapters, Silva's writing, curation, and editing of GPT-J's responses were essential to the memoir's final form. "I let it function in different ways throughout the book," she says of GPT-J's prose. "Sometimes it functions a bit like subtext. It can say things that I won't say in my own voice." Silva points out that efforts to make LLMs "safe and harmless"—which are seen as important to commercial applications— have made these AI models less useful for her as a writer. "They've just become much 'better,' but they're also more generic and far less exciting to me as writing partners," she says. In her experience, some of the most creative and interesting outputs from GPT-J occurred when the model glitched or got stuck repeating a phrase. Silva is hopeful that AI software will trigger a creative revolution, where many more books are created by people experimenting with AI models. She is even hopeful that the ease of churning out genre stories and generic, derivative fiction AI enables will heighten readers' appreciation for the opposite—challenging literature and fresh literary forms.

Ed Newton-Rex, a tech entrepreneur and composer, has begun using AI as a musical collaborator. He used OpenAI's GPT-3 to compose the lyrics to a choral and piano composition called "I stand in the library," which premiered at the Live From London online classical music festival in 2022. Newton-Rex has also used AI music generation, finding it useful for brainstorming musical phrases. But for the choral piece, he wrote the music himself, relying on GPT-3 only for the lyrics. The inspiration to write for piano and voice, a first for him, came after GPT-3 output a lyric about a piano. "One of the biggest benefits is the inspiration that it gives you," he says of generative AI.

Machine–human collaboration has a longer history in the visual arts, with some artists now making it an essential component of their style. Daniel Ambrosi is known for his hyperreal, large-scale panoramic landscape photographs, which he stitches together from multiple shots to mimic the visual field, depth perception, and light sensitivity of a person's eyesight more closely than a camera lens can. He calls the practice "computational photography." But since 2016, Ambrosi has been feeding these digital images through a customized version of an AI model developed by Google, called DeepDream, that adds subtle but striking visual effects to his works. DeepDream, which made a big impression on many visual artists when it was unveiled in 2015, allows people to take an image, feed it to a neural network, and then make the software enhance the features that most stimulate a particular group of neurons within one of the eighty-four layers of the neural network. It is as if you are telling the network, "Whatever you see there, I want more of it!" according to Alexander Mordvintsev, the Google machine-learning expert who invented the technique. People can control, to some degree, how the final image turns out by picking the layer they want to use for this enhancement. The lowest layers process information abstractly, with an emphasis on lines and colors; the higher layers concentrate on groups of pixels that represent features, like buildings, or mouths and noses.

For a series of photographs of the English gardens designed by the eighteenth-century landscape artist Lancelot "Capability" Brown, Ambrosi selected layers of his DeepDream algorithm that compose objects such as tree bark or the stones of a house or bridge in swirling peacock-feather-like mosaic patterns. After postproduction editing using Photoshop and other digital tools, Ambrosi then prints these images out on vast textile-like canvases using thermal inks, and then mounts the canvases over custom light boxes that illuminate the works using LEDs. The resulting images seem both hyperreal and surreal simultaneously, with a painterly aspect not found in conventional photographs.

The key here, Ambrosi notes, is that his work uses AI as a tool, but the final piece depends on human artistry and decision-making. "These tools are inert, they have no sentience or motivation. They're driven by humans. Humans with ideas, and they've got to curate the results just like I do, to enable their vision," he says.

That vision—what the artist is trying to express—is paramount in Ambrosi's view. As a result, he predicts AI's impact on the fine art market will be minimal. Most fine artists already struggle to make a living and work at their art because of an inner drive to express themselves. A lucky few produce works that are both original and resonate with gallery owners and collectors. That's not going to change, Ambrosi says. He is sympathetic to commercial illustrators and photographers since he thinks generative AI will deal them a serious economic blow. But he also thinks this is an inevitable aspect of technological progress.

While AI may mean fewer opportunities for commercial artists, it may provide new opportunities for people to become fine artists. Ambrosi says that humanities graduates who have studied subjects such as English and art history may be in high demand, because they will be able to come up with the best ideas for AI-generated digital images that will have both historical and contemporary resonance, and they'll be good at prompting AI models to achieve those results. "These people may never have lifted a paintbrush or have any eye-hand coordination at all," he says. "But they have this deep reservoir of knowledge of art history. They know how to curate. They know the difference between great art and mediocre, and they now will have a tool that will enable them to create really stunning work."

The technology may also make it easier for those with disabilities to create art. The American painter Chuck Close, who was partially paralyzed and used a wheelchair following a spinal injury, eventually learned to paint using brushes strapped to his wrists. But now, paralyzed people can create beautiful pictures simply by dictating instructions using speech recognition, or even with the help of eye-tracking or tongue-tracking assistive technologies.

EVERYTHING, EVERYWHERE, ALL AT ONCE

The scene: The Dolby Theatre in Los Angeles on a sunny Sunday afternoon in March, a few years from now. A young woman steps out of a black town car onto the red carpet. She wears a red dress and high platform heels. As the paparazzi bulbs flash, she seems stunned. Fans lining the red carpet call out for selfies. Bashful at first, she hesitates, then relents and stops to pose. Just before she reaches the theater entrance, a television reporter pulls her aside. "Emma, when you were back in your dorm at NYU a year ago thinking about the plot for *Star Crossed*, did you ever think you'd be here at the Academy Awards?" Emma blushes, the color of her cheeks almost matching her dress. "Never. This whole thing has been a dream come true," she says. Later that evening, inside the theater, Emma Hoffman ascends to the stage to take home the Oscar for Best Director. Her intergalactic rom-com *Star Crossed* is the first film to win an Academy Award that was created entirely by a student in a dorm room using AI software, with no assistance from a production crew—and no actors.

This may sound fanciful. But within five years, it will be possible to create a hit feature film in exactly this way. Generative AI will radically lower the cost of producing film and music and put the production of commercial art at the fingertips of a new generation of creators, many without any formal training.

Three groups will benefit from this transformation: these new creators themselves, who will be able to produce compelling work and potentially find an audience. But, as with today's social media creators, these artists may find themselves at the mercy of AI-based recommendation algorithms or even personal AI assistants controlled by large technology companies—be it TikTok, Meta, or Apple, Microsoft, and OpenAI—to connect with readers, listeners, and viewers.

The second group that stands to gain are organizations that hold the rights to large back catalogs of content. Think music labels, Hollywood studios, photographic agencies, publishing houses, and possibly major art museums. That's because these companies have the data that AI companies will increasingly covet—and will likely have to pay for (more on that later)—to train their software.

For such a seemingly disruptive technology, AI may do an awful lot to cement the status quo. While some new stars will use the tech to break through, it will be an even bigger boost to existing stars, bestselling writers, and chart-topping musicians. They're the third set of winners in this AI-powered future. The name recognition these celebrities command, and their past body of work, will be more valuable than ever. Top performers will be able to produce more content in their unique style more quickly, and across more different mediums, than at any point in history. Stars are beginning to glimpse new brand-extension opportunities: Meta paid millions to celebrities including Paris Hilton, Tom Brady, MrBeast, and Snoop Dogg to create chatbots that use their avatars and mimic their conversational styles. The actor James Earl Jones has sold the rights to his voice to Disney in perpetuity. AI helped resurrect John Lennon's voice for one last Beatles song. The musician Grimes has used AI to clone her own voice, while also offering to allow anyone else to do the same, as long as they share the royalties of any songs produced this way with her. For celebrities, AI is a brand-extension superpower, one that is enabling what *The Economist*, in a cover story, dubbed the birth of "the omnistar."

The people whose livelihoods will be most endangered are journeymen commercial artists and actors. These are people skilled enough to make a living from their craft, but whose talent is not so singular as to make them stars. Tech companies building AI software won't view these people's work as unique or important enough that they'll be willing to pay much for it. The companies will say that they can obtain similar-enough data elsewhere. The artists may not even be at the negotiating table. In many cases, they have already sold the right to that image, sound recording, or film to a video game company, magazine publishing house, music label, or Hollywood studio. The tech companies training AI will want to negotiate with those entities to purchase whole catalogs of data. This dynamic is likely to lead to increasing tension between commercial artists and musicians and large rights holders, with more artists likely to form unions or guilds to engage in collective bargaining over large sets of data. Visual artist Karla Ortiz, who has worked for Hollywood studios and video gaming companies, has been at the forefront of a burgeoning effort to organize artists to not just sue AI companies for copyright infringement—which she has—but to demand just compensation.

LOVE AND THEFT

The association of art with larceny has a long history. "Good artists borrow, great artists steal" is a quote often attributed, perhaps apocryphally, to Pablo Picasso. David Bowie said, "The only art I'll ever study is stuff that I can steal from." Today, a great debate rages about whether what AI does is analogous to this artistic "theft" or something much more legally and ethically dubious. What's clear is that today's most popular generative AI models have been trained on vast amounts of copyrighted material without consent. It is also increasingly apparent that these AI models can, with the right prompting, produce exact replicas of works ingested during training. The legal implications of this are complex and far from resolved. But the Wild West era of generative AI models is rapidly drawing to a close. While there's a chance courts will rule AI *training* by itself does not infringe on copyright, or that Congress will create a new exemption for AI training, AI companies will increasingly find themselves nonetheless compelled to pay to license training data for ethical and practical reasons. Meanwhile the problem of AI *outputs* that violate copyright will present a legal quandary for the companies building AI models that they will solve with filtering technology.

The exact training set for OpenAI's GPT-4 is unknown, but its predecessor, GPT-3, was trained on, among other things, the Common Crawl, a vast set of web pages scraped from the internet that contains a large amount of copyrighted material. Meanwhile, Meta's Llama LLM, EleutherAI's GPT-J, an early version of Bloomberg's BloombergGPT, and many LLMs have been trained on a dataset called Books3. Books3 contains the full text of 170,000 books, most of them published in the past twenty years and copyrighted, according to an investigation that the journalist and coder Alex Reisner conducted for the *Atlantic*. The dataset includes works by such popular novelists as Stephen King, James Patterson, Zadie Smith, Jonathan Franzen, Haruki Murakami, and Margaret Atwood. The LAION 5-B dataset, which itself is derived from the Common Crawl, was used to train Stable Diffusion and other text-to-image AI models. It contains large amounts of copyrighted imagery from artists and photographers, both famous, such as Damien Hirst and Kehinde Wiley, and lesser known. The music generators are also trained on copyrighted songs.

U.S. courts are set to rule on whether these AI models infringe on copyright in a number of landmark cases and the U.S. Copyright Office is considering whether new laws or regulations may be needed. Copyright experts disagree on whether judges will regard the training of generative AI as copyright infringement or whether they will decide it is "fair use," a legal doctrine that allows people to use copyrighted material without permission in certain circumstances.

UNFAIR USE

A few scholars, however, argue that extending fair use to AI training would be unethical. Fair use, as the Harvard legal scholar Benjamin Sobel argued in an influential 2017 essay, is grounded on principles of distributive justice. It has mostly been applied in cases where its effect has been to shift power away from those who already possess it in spades—big rights-holding corporations or successful artists—to the little guy. But AI, Sobel notes, turns this argument upside down. Here, the people whose copyrights are being infringed upon include thousands of journeymen artists, while the beneficiaries of that infringement are some of the world's largest technology companies and well-funded start-ups. That sounds a lot like *unfair* use. In which case, Sobel argues, fair use should not be extended to technology companies training AI software.

The idea that nonconsensual use of data might be enshrined at the heart of our future world deeply troubles Neil Turkewitz, a former Recording Industry Association of America executive who has emerged as one of the leading critics of tech companies' use of copyrighted works for AI training. Turkewitz argues we all erred at the dawn of the social media era. We should never have allowed the digital record of our personhood—everything from our photos, stories, and social connections, to our work histories and medical records—to be snatched by big technology companies, without any real understanding of what we were giving away. He argues that we should be more deliberate this time, and place "clear, freely granted consent" at the center of our new AI-intermediated tomorrow. Creators should have to opt in to having their work included in AI training sets. Turkewitz says that anything less and we are building our brave new world on a foundation of theft and unpaid labor.

What's needed, argue prominent legal scholars, is new law. Mark Lemley, the director of Stanford University's Program in Law, Science, and Technology, says that Congress should create a right to "fair learning" that would allow AI systems to be trained on copyrighted works. To insist tech companies obtain permission from every rights holder in vast datasets would be impractical, he says, and stymie U.S. innovation. Meanwhile, advocates for artists and rights holders have been lobbying Congress to do the exact opposite of what Lemley proposes and explicitly ban the nonconsensual use of copyrighted material to train AI systems.

Other countries—including Taiwan, Israel, Singapore, South Korea, the U.K., and the twenty-seven member states of the European Union—have already created exemptions to copyright law for data mining. But legal experts debate whether the definitions of data mining in these laws, most of which predate ChatGPT, would cover generative AI. Japan has gone the furthest toward explicitly allowing generative AI to be trained on copyrighted works.

Equally contentious is whether people and companies should be allowed to copyright the output of AI models. So far, the U.S. Copyright Office has refused to do so, saying that only a human creator's work can be protected.

What's certain is that clear rules are desperately needed. Clarity is in the interests of AI companies and artists alike, and a purely common law approach, where decisions about fair use are made by judges on a case-by-case basis, provides no clarity. As sympathetic as I am to the artists' concerns, it ultimately makes little sense to ban the use of copyrighted material from AI training. The U.S. should follow other countries' lead and create a "fair learning" provision as a matter of law. But in exchange for this nonconsensual taking of their work, artists could be compensated through a fee levied on those who build and distribute generative AI models. The money could create a fund to which rights holders could apply for a certain fixed amount per copyrighted work, or the funds could go to charities that fund artists' work. One advantage of such a system is that it might preclude tech companies from needing to strike individual deals with rights holders. There is precedent for this. The Audio Home Recording Act, passed in 1992, allowed the makers of digital audio recording technology to escape copyright infringement liability in exchange for paying a levy that established funds used to compensate musicians and music labels. While such a system would cover AI training, outputs designed to explicitly mimic a particular artist's work for commercial purposes should require that artist's consent.

As AI increasingly becomes a tool for human artists—a latter-day brush or piano or pen—it would also make sense to broaden copyright protection to cases where a human creator and AI have engaged in extensive collaboration to produce a work.

FENCING THE INTERNET

While governments dither over how to update copyright laws, rights holders are busy erecting digital barriers that prevent AI systems from scraping their internet content without permission. Many news organizations have started blocking bots known to scrape data for specific AI companies, like OpenAI, from visiting their websites. In other cases, they're introducing protocols designed to thwart all scraping bots, but these methods can also keep web pages from showing up in Google searches. Meanwhile, many e-commerce sites have instituted CAPTCHA challenges to deter the bots that trawl the web.

Some artists are going even further and applying "digital masks" to images of their art that render these images useless to AI models, or even poison the model, degrading its performance. Ben Zhao, a computer science professor at the University of Chicago helped create a tool, itself based on AI, called Glaze, that can help protect their work. Rather than simply erecting a fence around an artist's content on the web, Glaze is a bit like branding your cows to deter cattle rustlers—thieves can still steal the cows, but the brand makes it harder for the thieves to profit from them. Glaze tricks an AI model into classifying an image as belonging to a very different style of art. A model might ingest a charcoal drawing, for instance, but categorizes it as an abstract expressionist painting instead. This makes it impossible for someone to use the artists' name as a prompt to generate work similar to theirs or to use their images to fine-tune an AI model to specifically copy that artists' signature style. Glaze makes subtle alterations to a digital image, barely perceptible to the human eye, that cause this misclassification.

More recently Zhao has gone further, creating software called Nightshade. This doesn't just mask a particular artist's work, but poisons the entire model, corrupting its ability to reliably respond to prompts for objects and artistic styles, not only the artist's name. If Glaze is a bit like branding your cattle, Nightshade is like booby-trapping them with uranium-235. The more images corrupted with Nightshade that the model ingests, the worse it will get.

Applying Glaze, which has been downloaded more than 1.5 million times, is fast becoming standard practice for artists posting works online. Zhao says that art schools are beginning to teach students how to use it, and he has been going to digital art conferences to spread the word about the software. Soon, enough images may be cloaked in this way, or poisoned with Nightshade, to force tech companies to negotiate compensation.

Zhao has been asked to create similar cloaking and data poisoning tools for other kinds of work, like music and literature. But the same methods can't be readily applied, though he, and others, are exploring options.

Even if the courts or lawmakers create a "fair learning" standard for AI training, very soon these digital "anti-theft devices"—combined with concerns about copyright infringement—will essentially force tech companies to license the data. Those license negotiations may prove contentious, but the era of building models from free data is over.

TOWARD CENTAUR ART

The experimental efforts of writers Chowdhury and Silva, musicians like Newton-Rex, and artists like Ambrosi show us why we have less to fear from generative AI than some critics want us to believe. AI cannot, as I've argued here, actually produce art—only we, with our intentions and intrinsic motivation, emotions and lived experience, can do that. As for AI's creative skills, they still pale compared to our own. This leaves plenty of space for human–AI collaborations, just as there are in many other professions. Call it *centaur art*—borrowing from centaur chess, the term coined to describe chess matches in which human opponents are each allowed to consult software advisors.

It would be going too far to declare ourselves on the precipice of a new Renaissance in the arts, but we are far from a new Dark Age of inauthenticity and pastiche. The collage and the remix, the homage and the mashup have been in ascendance in art for more than a century, but they have not obliterated the invention of new styles and forms. Every new technology—from oil paint to the camera to the music synthesizer—has enabled fresh forms of artistic expression. Artificial intelligence will continue this cycle, not finish it.

9

A MICROSCOPE FOR DATA

Of all AI's impacts, none are likely to be as overwhelmingly positive as its effect on science, medicine, and health. AI is as transformative a tool for science as the telescope and the microscope. Just as those instruments allowed us to study what was too distant or too small to perceive with our eyes, opening up entirely new fields of science, AI will allow us to see patterns in data too complex or subtle for our own brains to discern. Over the past decade, new scientific instruments and methods—from genome sequencing to synthetic aperture radar to high-energy particle accelerators—have allowed researchers to collect more data than ever. Much of this data is simply too vast to analyze without AI.

It's not just the raw data that is overwhelming. The mountain of scientific papers attempting to analyze it is too. PubMed, a popular repository for medical and life sciences papers, sees more than one million research papers added per year, one every two seconds. Across scientific disciplines, millions more papers are published each year. This disparity between the production of new data and our ability to make sense of it all may help explain findings that the pace of breakthroughs in science has actually been slowing, even as the volume of published research has soared. AI is critical to reversing this trend, helping us sort gold from dross and pointing us toward research that will radically change our thinking and our lives. AI that can ingest these papers, summarize their findings, and hunt for hidden patterns or connections across disciplines will be the only way to extract their valuable insights.

By deploying AI on new datasets, we will discover new materials for batteries that may help combat climate change, improve crop yields without resorting to toxic chemicals, and unlock new treatments for diseases. What's more, by combining AI with a new generation of wearable devices and blood tests, we'll be able to personalize medical treatments in ways never before possible.

AI is being harnessed across scientific and social-scientific disciplines, scanning the cosmos for black holes, orchestrating the control of experimental nuclear fusion reactors, deciphering ancient texts, discovering ancient metropolises lost in the Amazon jungle, reading medical imagery, and helping doctors use genomic information and biomarkers to offer treatments better tailored to each patient. AI is also upending the very practice of science—dethroning the centrality of hypotheses and theory to some scientific work, even as it decodes hidden patterns that will eventually lead us to new theories.

Yes, there are risks. The data is vast, but it remains imperfect. There are lacunae, pockets of ignorance stemming from historical human biases—too few studies include enough participants from diverse racial backgrounds or enough women, for instance—or the imperfections of our instruments. We must be aware of these flaws when we build AI software. AI is not a magic wand. The oases of insight it reveals can sometimes prove to be mirages. And yes, the same methods that will help us discover new cures could in the wrong hands help design new bioweapons or poisons. But in no other domain is the balance of AI's effects so heavily tilted toward progress.

THE FOLDS OF LIFE

Seoul, South Korea, March 2016: Two men, bundled into winter coats and wearing woolen hats to defend against the night chill, walk briskly together through the capital's crowded streets. Around them, the pulsating neon signs of dumpling houses and barbecue joints beckon, but locked in animated conversation, the men seem oblivious to these enticements. Still, this is a celebratory stroll. The men have come to Seoul on a mission, the culmination of years of effort, and they have succeeded. What they have achieved will cement their place in the annals of computer science: they have built a piece of AI software able to play the ancient strategy game Go so expertly that it handily defeated the world's top player, a Korean named Lee Sedol. Go is a deceptively simple game, involving black and white stones placed on a nineteen-by-nineteen square grid, but the game is fiendishly difficult to master—with many more possible move combinations than chess. So many, in fact, they exceed the number of atoms in the universe. To be successful, an AI system cannot merely analyze every possible move and pick the best option with certainty, as software can with chess. It must instead develop a more intuitive sense of strategy. This is exactly what the AI system the two men helped build, called AlphaGo, did.

Now the two—Demis Hassabis, co-founder and chief executive of the London AI company Google DeepMind, and David Silver, who led the DeepMind team that built AlphaGo—are discussing their next goal. "I'm telling you, we can solve protein folding," Hassabis says in a conversation captured by a documentary film crew. "That's like, I mean, it's just huge. I am sure we can do that now. I thought we could do that before, but now we definitely can do it."

Solving protein folding would be a challenge every bit as difficult as cracking Go. In the 1960s, Cyrus Levinthal, a physicist and molecular biologist, determined that there were so many plausible shapes a protein might assume that it would take longer than the age of the universe to arrive at the correct structure by randomly trying combinations. Proteins are the building blocks of life, and the foundation of most biological processes. They are long chains of amino acids that naturally collapse, or fold, into complex shapes based on their molecular composition and the principles of physics. Those shapes, in turn, determine how the protein functions. Genetic mutations that change the way a protein folds are responsible for many diseases, including sickle cell anemia, cystic fibrosis, and Marfan syndrome, and misfolded proteins are also thought to be critical to Alzheimer's, Parkinson's, Huntington's, and Lou Gehrig's disease.

Protein shapes are also critical to the way many medicines work. Most drugs are small molecules that bind with a particular "pocket" on the surface of a protein, inhibiting or altering its functioning. It's also how antibodies work, binding to pockets on the surface of viruses, preventing them from infecting cells and marking them as targets for other parts of the immune system to destroy. Proteins themselves, whether naturally occurring or made in labs, can be powerful drugs in their own right, directly affecting biological processes. Being able to predict protein structure could revolutionize our understanding of disease and lead to new, more targeted pharmaceuticals for disorders from cancer to diabetes. It will accelerate the time it takes to bring new medicines to market, shaving years and hundreds of millions of dollars in costs and saving lives as a result.

"Solving" protein folding had been a grand scientific quest since 1972 when, in his Nobel Prize acceptance speech, the chemist Christian Anfinsen postulated that a protein's DNA should fully determine a protein's shape. It was a remarkable conjecture. At the time, not a single genome had yet been sequenced. But Anfinsen's theory launched an entire subfield of computational biology, with the goal of using mathematics and computers, instead of experiments, to model protein shapes. The challenge was daunting, and for almost fifty years, computational biology made steady but slow progress. At the time of Hassabis and Silver's late-night stroll in 2016, the best computational methods could determine a protein's shape with a high degree of accuracy only about 30 percent of the time. Meanwhile, the gold standard for determining a protein's structure remained a tried-and-tested—but time-consuming and expensive—process called X-ray crystallography. More recently, a method using electron microscopes and known as CryoEM has enabled slightly faster, but somewhat less accurate, structure analysis. Still, in 2016, out of the hundreds of millions of proteins, scientists had found structures for only about 110,000, with fewer than 10,000 new structures being discovered each year.

But four years after Hassabis and Silver's ramble, Google DeepMind announced a stunning breakthrough: In November 2020, it debuted an AI system called AlphaFold that could take a protein's DNA sequence and, nine out of ten times, predict its structure to within an atom's-width of accuracy. The AI also produced a confidence score, giving biologists an indication of when they should rely on the prediction and when to be more skeptical. DeepMind made its AlphaFold software available for free to any scientists who wanted to use it. But within a year, it did far more: it used AlphaFold to produce structure predictions for every protein in the human body, and published those online in a database any scientist could consult; before that, only 17 percent of human proteins had known structures. It also published predictions for all the proteins in twenty organisms that are of particular interest to scientists, from the malaria parasite to the species of rat most often used in labs. Then in 2022, it went even further, publishing AlphaFold-based predictions for all 200 million proteins known to science.

AlphaFold's predictions are becoming as essential to biologists as microscopes and test tubes. It's transforming the hunt for new antibiotics and aiding in the search for treatments for tropical diseases that get little attention from pharmaceutical companies because they mostly affect people too poor to afford expensive medicines. It's helping scientists figure out how to make honeybee populations more resilient to disease, and assisting researchers searching for proteins that can digest plastics.

AlphaFold is a tiny taste of how AI will transform both medicine and science. These technologies won't just affect one scientific task; they will transform entire fields. Paul Nurse, a Nobel laureate geneticist who is chief executive officer of the Francis Crick Institute, says that Alpha-Fold's structure predictions open up "a systems approach" to protein research. Now, researchers can compare protein structures across organisms, and across entire genomes, to understand how different biological functions have evolved. This wasn't possible previously because there weren't enough known protein structures.

INSTRUMENTS OF SCIENCE

AI is becoming an essential tool in every branch of science, from astronomy to zoology. Experts from Microsoft teamed up with chemists from the Pacific Northwest National Laboratory to use AI to try to find new materials for solid-state battery electrolytes that would use less lithium. Their software screened 32 million potential chemical combinations, winnowing that down to 500,000 compounds stable enough to be possible candidates. Using AI, they further honed that list to 800 chemicals, and then finally identified a single compound, previously unknown to science and not found in nature, which lab tests proved could work in a battery, requiring 70 percent less lithium than existing designs. If commercialized, this would make batteries far more sustainable, less prone to fires, and cheaper to produce. And the entire process, which would have taken many years in the past, was completed in nine months.

With help from researchers at Google DeepMind, physicists in Switzerland have found better ways to control the magnetic fields that keep superheated plasma contained inside a doughnut-shaped device used in nuclear fusion experiments known as a tokamak. This could help scientists achieve a breakthrough that would deliver abundant clean energy. AI is being used to count endangered species in images taken by camera traps in the rainforests of the Congo and footage from drones flown over the African savannah and to interpret the meaning of sperm whales' vocalizations. It is being used by astronomers to create better images of black holes. It is helping archaeologists find lost cities through analysis of satellite imagery and helping classicists decipher ancient texts, including filling in missing fragments of stone tablets and "reading" scrolls too fragile to unfurl. And it is helping us unlock the mysteries of our natural intelligence, mapping groups of neurons in our brain and discovering the meaning of spikes of electrical activity in certain neurons. This is offering the possibility that AI-enabled computers will soon be able to "read our minds," either from noninvasive brain scans and brain–computer interfaces or from wireless implants placed within the brain itself.

John Jumper, the DeepMind senior researcher who leads the company's protein folding team, says that the application of AI to science is about giving human researchers superhuman abilities. Unlike the quest for artificial general intelligence, however, the focus is not on creating a universal "AI scientist" that can do everything in every domain. Instead, he says, the goal is to give human researchers "superhuman abilities but within very narrow domains" that matter to science. "AI for science is about, how do we use AI and [machine learning] to do what humans can't? Humans are terrible at predicting protein structures. Humans are terrible at interpreting the genome," he says. So why not let AI do the things that humans cannot?

Jumper says that one of the biggest limitations for applying AI to many scientific domains so far is that there are "only so many beautiful sources of data." By that he means datasets that are big enough, with the right sort of information organized in the right way, for people to apply machine-learning methods successfully. But AI itself will help solve this problem, by counting and categorizing things that could never have been numbered and characterized before—from free-floating genetic material in a blood sample to stars in distant galaxies. Meanwhile, generative AI will contribute entirely new databases to science by predicting or simulating phenomena that we have not been able to observe and analyze directly. AlphaFold is just one example of this.

Increasingly, AI is necessary just to process the onslaught of knowledge humans produce. LLMs may be the only way to digest, summarize, and categorize our own intellectual output. This is starting to happen. A free LLM-based search tool called Elicit, created by U.S. nonprofit research lab Ought, is helping scientists streamline the laborious process of conducting literature reviews, retrieving relevant scientific papers, and summarizing the findings of a handful of the most relevant ones.

Some of the wildest uses of LLMs will be in the social sciences. AI can analyze the meaning in unstructured data, such as Twitter or TikTok posts, which opens up new ways to monitor changing public attitudes. Academics in Singapore found that ChatGPT can be used to accurately assess the Myers-Briggs personality types of humans. But AI can also do far more than just analyze existing human-created information. Many have proposed the idea of using LLMs to simulate humans in social science research. Igor Grossmann, a psychologist at the University of Waterloo in Canada, showed that the responses from LLM chatbots prompted to respond as if they were a person with a specific personality type accurately mirrored what real human subjects with those personalities say in experiments. Academics in Qatar and Finland proposed that LLMs simulating large human populations could be used to gather public opinion and market-research data, rather than having to survey thousands of real humans. LLMs could also simulate human behavior in specific scenarios, augmenting research in fields such as behavioral economics, game theory, and international relations, where LLMs could simulate the behavior of world leaders or nongovernmental organizations in a variety of "war game" exercises.

The downside of using large AI models in scientific research is that they often require highly specialized software engineering expertise to create, and they demand large amounts of expensive computing power to run. DeepMind has made AlphaFold freely available for any scientist to use, or even download and run themselves, and it has openly published all of AlphaFold's protein structure predictions. Meta has also made many of the scientific AI models it has created freely available. But not all companies will be so charitable, and control of scientific advancement could increasingly shift away from universities and other nonprofit entities and into the profit-seeking hands of corporations. Recognizing this danger, the U.S. government, and other governments around the world, have started funding "national AI research clouds"—large, government-owned data centers with thousands of GPUs—that can be used for public purposes, including academic research. Having this kind of AI computing power available will be critical to ensuring AI can continue to drive scientific progress.

HYPOTHESIS HIATUS

AI is more than just a tool for scientists. It's transforming the nature of scientific research itself. The scientific method we were taught in school has the idea of hypothesis at its core. Sometimes, a hypothesis is just a prediction about what will happen if a particular set of inputs to an experiment are altered. But, in the best experiments, the hypothesis contains a conjectured explanation for observed phenomena which an experiment is then designed to prove or disprove. But the methods DeepMind used for AlphaFold, and that others are increasingly using for drug research, as we'll see later in this chapter, upend this paradigm. They don't require a scientist to have a hypothesis about *why* a particular protein design will make a more efficient enzyme or be less toxic than another one. Locked somewhere in the weights of the neural network is a kind of intuition about what this particular DNA recipe will do. But the neural network can't explain its reasoning. To us, it is simply a black box. This shifts us firmly away from theorizing and toward pure empiricism, offering the possibility of "hypothesis-free" science. Correlation is not causation, as every scientist is taught, but with enough data and a powerful enough analytic tool, such as today's massive neural networks, correlation is often all you need.

The importance of explanations depends on circumstance. In some areas of medicine, particularly those having to do with diagnosis, doctors tend not to trust predictions without explanations. Sumit Chopra, an AI researcher at New York University, trained an AI system that could predict the presence of cancer in MRI scans from far less data than these scans usually produce. The software promised to reduce the time a patient had to spend in the MRI machine—which should both allow more people to get the scans and lower the cost of each scan. But the method meant that the MRI would not produce clear 2D images that human radiologists could scrutinize. Because of this, doctors didn't trust the software and were reluctant to use it. They wanted to see the evidence of cancer with their own eyes, not just rely on the machine's reading of data too opaque and subtle for them to understand. But when it comes to treatment, doctors are often very comfortable with evidence-based, explanation-free science. Doctors sometimes call this "witch medicine." Take aspirin. We've been using it for the better part of a century to fight pain and inflammation, but it's only in the last few years that we've started to uncover how it works.

How happy we are about this brave new world of theory-less science depends on whether we're instrumentalists or realists. Instrumentalists believe the purpose of science is to predict the world through experiments. Theories are simply instruments for obtaining better predictions. And if you can predict the world well without a model that humans can interpret, that's just fine. Only the accuracy of the prediction matters. Jumper, who led the DeepMind AlphaFold team, is an instrumentalist. "What is the core of science? You predict what will happen, and then you see if your prediction was correct," he says.

Scientific realists, on the other hand, believe that the job of science is to understand the underlying reality of the world, not just predict it. To realists, a theory-less science is deeply unsatisfying. Noam Chomsky, the linguist and public intellectual, is among those in this camp. He once criticized purely statistical predictions, saying, "You can also collect butterflies and make many observations. If you like butterflies, that's fine; but such work must not be confounded with research, which is concerned to discover explanatory principles." The professor Jonathan Zittrain is particularly troubled by where this theory-less science is leading us. Every time we deploy a model because it has predictive power, without understanding the underlying mechanics, we acquire what he's dubbed "intellectual debt." We must eventually pay this debt down, by coming up with explanatory theories, or we will be in trouble. Ultimately, Zittrain argues, intellectual debt threatens our free will:

> *A world of knowledge without understanding becomes a world without discernible cause and effect, in which we grow dependent on our digital concierges to tell us what to do and when.*

But there may be hope for theory yet. The counterintuitive predictions AI makes may inspire human scientists to create new hypotheses to explain the whys of the world.

Soon, AI may serve as a guide for human intuition in the development of new theories. In December 2021, DeepMind collaborated with mathematicians at the University of Sydney and the University of Oxford to show that AI could work this way. An AI model was used to find a mathematical function that could turn an input into a certain output. After this AI was trained, the mathematicians probed the inner workings of its neural network to get a sense of which aspects of the input it weighed most heavily in determining its output. They could then develop a theory to explain why these factors were important. In one case, the AI assistant helped mathematicians develop a new formula for a conjecture about permutations and polynomials that had stumped the field for decades.

Pushmeet Kohli, the head of the AI for science division of Google DeepMind, says that AI could also be used to create models of complex global phenomena, such as weather or ecology, which human scientists could then probe to allow them to create new hypotheses about the underlying mechanisms. "There's all this sort of rich information hiding in plain sight," he says. AI helps make those patterns visible.

In the history of science, empiricism and theory have a dynamic interplay. Whenever one stretches out ahead, it usually acts as a spring, forcing the other to shoot forward too. Kepler's observations of planetary motion preceded Newton's theories of gravity and motion. Röntgen's discovery of X-rays preceded any understanding of electromagnetic radiation. At the moment, AI is pushing empirical knowledge faster than we can generate new hypotheses. But there's no reason to think theory won't eventually catch up.

MEDICINE AT THE SPEED OF THOUGHT

AlphaFold's insights may shorten the time it takes to bring new drugs to market. But even with a known protein structure, it still requires years of further research to unlock their potential. Other AI techniques, however, might radically shorten these timelines, holding out the promise of on-demand designer drugs.

In the basement of a former art museum on the campus of the University of California, Berkeley, a robot arm is building the future of medicine. The arm is conducting ninety-six simultaneous experiments on a set of enzymes. Those enzymes have in turn been designed by software belonging to Profluent AI, a small start-up that is using the same methods that underpin LLMs to develop new protein-based therapies. Profluent was founded by Ali Madani, a machine learning PhD who first used AI to detect certain kinds of cells in a large array of microscope slides and find signs of disease in medical imagery. But after his PhD, he joined the research arm of the business software company Salesforce, where he was introduced to the power of LLMs.

Madani noticed parallels between how grammar determines meaning in natural language and how sequence relates to structure and structure to function in proteins. In other words, proteins have a kind of language that an AI system could learn to predict, just as it learned to predict the next most likely word in a sentence. The idea inspired him to launch Profluent. He envisions a system that will let scientists specify what kind of protein they want in natural language—an antibody that will bind with a particular receptor on the surface of a cell, for example, or an anticoagulant with a particular toxicity profile—and then have the AI output the DNA recipe for that protein.

Madani and his colleagues are starting to make good on that vision.

Along with collaborators from Salesforce and the University of San Francisco, Madani created an AI system called ProGen that was trained on data from 280 million proteins. In research published in the journal *Nature Biotechnology*, Madani's team examined ProGen's ability to create novel lysozymes, a type of enzyme with antibacterial properties. Natural lysozymes are found in saliva, tears, and mucus. The protein works in part by breaking down the bacteria's cell walls. The researchers took one hundred artificial lysozymes ProGen designed and tested whether they would react against material made from the cell wall of a common bacteria. It found that 73 percent of the artificial enzymes produced a reaction, compared to 59 percent of natural proteins. A few were even more reactive than one of the best natural enzymes, the lysozyme found in the whites of hens' eggs. Then, out of the effective ProGen-designed proteins, Madani and his team selected five that looked promising for mass production, ultimately showing them that two could be mass-produced by cultures of genetically modified bacteria. That's important, because it means the proteins could potentially be commercially viable.

Right now, Profluent is using several AI models, each fine-tuned to create different classes of proteins, and then using still other AI tools to screen the proteins for characteristics, such as toxicity, solubility, ease of production, and stability at room temperature. Promising candidate proteins are then tested in the lab and the resulting data used to improve the AI models. Eventually, Madani hopes to be able to consolidate the number of models Profluent uses, creating the kind of universal protein-language AI that would enable a researcher to specify the protein type, its function, and its characteristics in a single prompt, and get results that are successful in the lab.

Still, Profluent's suite of AI models are making progress: A key measure in protein design is called a *hit rate*—which refers to what percentage of the candidate proteins show some minimal level of function in lab tests. Traditional protein design methods, without AI, have hit rates between 0.01 percent and 0.14 percent. As a result, engineers must manufacture and test millions of proteins to find likely drug candidates. Madani says that Profluent's AI selection process is now yielding a hit rate close to 50 percent. Madani's goal is the ability to develop a successful protein that they can hand off to a large pharmaceutical partner for clinical trials "within two to three rounds" of AI generation, lab tests, further AI refinement, and then lab testing again.

It's one example of how AI will dramatically condense the time it takes to bring new drugs to market, significantly shortening the one to six years it often takes before a drug can enter human clinical trials. That could make drugs less expensive. Right now, it takes at least a decade and more than $1 billion to bring a new drug to market. That expense is ultimately passed on to patients.

And AI might not just yield us new medicines faster. It might also help us discover much more effective treatments. LabGenius is a London-based start-up that, like Profluent, is one of dozens now working on AI-assisted protein-based drug design. It showed that its AI models and robotic lab process have created a novel antibody that can latch on to HER2, a protein that is often highly expressed on the surface of cells in a variety of cancers, and signal to the body's T-cells to come and kill that cancerous cell. What's remarkable about LabGenius's antibody is that it is structurally very different from previous "T-cell engager" antibodies for HER2. And yet it is about four hundred times more selective, meaning it greatly reduces the chance of damaging healthy cells, than Runimotamab, a leading T-cell engager developed using more traditional drug discovery methods that is currently undergoing human clinical trials.

AI can help us combat some of our thorniest health crises, such as antibiotic resistant "superbug" strains of bacteria. Since 2019, scientists have, with the help of AI, discovered at least two new antibiotics, halicin and abaucin, that are effective against increasingly common superbugs. It will also likely yield new cancer treatments and cures for rare diseases that right now are not cost-effective for big pharmaceutical companies to tackle.

PERSONALIZED HEALTHCARE

The applications of AI to healthcare extend far beyond new drugs. The technology is already helping radiologists spot tumors and signs of pneumonia in medical imagery. At Johns Hopkins Hospital in Baltimore, an AI algorithm has been used to better predict which patients will develop sepsis, reducing mortality from the condition, which kills 250,000 Americans each year, by 20 percent. At Moorfields Eye Hospital in London, the ophthalmologist Pearse Keane and researchers from University College London developed a remarkable AI model called RETFound that can not only detect a number of eye diseases, including diabetic retinopathy and glaucoma, from a retinal scan, but can also predict general health and a patient's risk of heart failure, stroke, and Parkinson's disease from the same images. AI is also helping surgeons better plan operations and predict risks of bleeding and other complications. And medical-specific LLMs will eventually allow electronic health records to be used as better diagnostic tools.

In the next few years, a scenario like this will become possible. Marcia, a woman in her midtwenties, is on her way to work. She's been feeling a bit strange the past few days, agitated and restless, her mind racing. Just go to work and get on with things, she tells herself. As she parks her car outside her office, her phone rings. It's her doctor. "Hi Marcia, how are you feeling?" she asks. "We've spotted some anomalous data from your smartwatch. Your heart rate variability has altered in the past few days, and the watch has also alerted us that your movement patterns match a pattern that has been shown to be associated with the imminent onset of a manic episode in people with bipolar disorder. Now, I know you haven't been diagnosed, but given your family history and genetic profile, we'd like you to come in today for a fuller assessment. Please don't worry, if it is bipolar disorder, we can prescribe medicine that will help." Marcia does what her doctor asks and, thanks to this early intervention, she's able to keep her mental health stable.

When combined with widely available genome sequencing, AI will give doctors and patients better insight into individual risks as well as treatment options tailored to the patient's genetic profile. Regular blood and urine monitoring for telltale fragments of cancerous DNA will become the norm for cancer screening. Besides wearables such as smartwatches and health trackers, devices will also be implanted inside the body, much as continuous glucose monitors are today, allowing constant monitoring of blood and organ function. All this data can be fed into electronic medical records, which may become too voluminous for human doctors to review without the help of AI diagnostic aids, to help spot signs of disease or anomalies that will need further investigation. This revolution in AI-assisted personalized medicine should allow people to live longer, healthier lives.

BETTER MEDICINE FOR SOME, BITTER MEDICINE FOR OTHERS

To make this vision of personalized care a reality, however, will require careful decisions on the part of those who create the AI and the health systems that implement it. Many AI systems have been trained on data that doesn't apply to the patients on which they will be used. For instance, an algorithm that researchers at Google DeepMind and Veterans Administration hospitals in the U.S. developed to detect acute kidney injury was trained on data from the VA's patient pool, which is mostly male. Later research found that the model didn't work nearly as well for female patients. Many AI models have been found to work poorly outside of a specific hospital in which the data was gathered.

Sloppy data gathering, cleaning, and labeling practices can lead to AI models that seem accurate in testing but fail in the real world. One major study in 2020 looked at 232 algorithms that had been developed during the COVID-19 pandemic for helping doctors make a diagnosis or formulate a prognosis. It found that not one of them was fit for clinical use, and just two looked promising enough to warrant further testing. Another that looked at 415 published tools designed to help radiologists

detect COVID-19 from X-rays and CT scans also found none were
clinically valid. These shocking figures are all too common. Meanwhile,
fewer than 3 percent of the participants in genomics studies are Black or
Latino and 86 percent of clinical trial participants are white. This lack
of diversity means that AI models drawn from this data may also not be
accurate for patients from these backgrounds.

Right now, AI software companies are rarely required to prove their
software works well for a diverse set of patients before being allowed to
sell it to doctors and hospitals. Our current regulatory system isn't designed to cope with the issues AI raises, and puts patient safety at risk.
In many cases, AI models designed as "decision support" tools for doctors don't require Food and Drug Administration approval. Those that
do seek approval typically do so under the agency's expedited 510(k)
process, meaning a tech company only has to show its software is "sub-
stantially equivalent" to software the FDA has already approved. As of
December 2023, the FDA had approved more than seven hundred AI
models, the majority of them for use in radiology and cardiology. Almost
none of these models have been clinically validated in randomized control trials designed to test if they improve patient outcomes. Instead, in
most cases, the FDA has simply accepted assurances from the companies
building the models that they performed as well as existing software.

The FDA also tends to accept average performance metrics. But it is
performance within subgroups that really matters. For instance, a system may claim to be 95 percent accurate. But if the 5 percent of lung
cancers it is likely to miss also happen to be those that are most aggressive, that 95 percent claim is highly misleading. Also, we know that Black
and other minority patients, as well as women, are underrepresented in
medical datasets. A headline accuracy figure doesn't indicate how well
the model will work for patients from these groups. This has left many
doctors wary of using AI software—and for good reason.

The current system is flawed in other ways too. FDA approval is
needed only for software that is sold commercially. But some hospital
systems are hiring AI companies to build bespoke AI models based on

the hospital's own patient data to be used within that hospital system. These models aren't subject to regulatory approvals, even though they could harm patients.

Government action will also be needed to try to spread the benefits of AI-enabled medicine more widely. Otherwise, the affluent will benefit most from this new era of personalized care, in another example of how AI may make inequality worse. Eventually we will all live longer, healthier lives. Until then, only a privileged few will.

A TOOL FOR TERROR, TOO

Even the most privileged among us, however, won't be immune from a threat that the union of science and AI also poses. The same technologies that could speed new, more effective drugs to market can also be used to engineer novel bioweapons. The same sort of LLMs that will soon produce recipes for new proteins could be prompted to craft a deadly virus or a bacteria that makes neurotoxins. Combined with other new developments, like the gene-editing technology CRISPR, and relatively low-cost, compact DNA printers, which can manufacture DNA segments at the press of a button, terrorist organizations, doomsday cults, or rogue states will be able to produce pathogens that could harm us all.

We can do little to contain these risks without also possibly slowing down the pace of science. But governments must take reasonable steps to mitigate bioweapons proliferation, even if it causes some additional friction and cost for promising biotechnology start-ups and academic researchers. The sale and export of DNA printers should be carefully controlled and licensed, in a way that is at least as strict as the current rules we have around handling radiological materials and potentially deadly chemicals. The companies operating both genome and protein-based LLMs, as well as lab equipment such as DNA printers, should also have to undergo specific licensing regimes and have their activity tracked and monitored, ideally in a globally agreed-upon manner.

One small consolation is that the same technologies that can fashion bioweapons can also increase our resiliency to biological attack. AI can improve surveillance systems designed to spot signs of emerging pathogens, and it can help us produce new vaccines and treatments in record time if a bioattack is detected.

The prospect of bioterrorism is chilling. But it must be weighed against the opportunities AI offers for improving people's lives and health. It should be considered in light of AI's ability to help scientists address challenges like climate change and sustainability. And it must be viewed in the context of AI's help in unlocking the mysteries of our universe and our past, and improving our understanding of our present condition. Against the high probability AI will improve our lives and expand our knowledge exponentially, the elevated risk from bioweaponry is a price worth paying.

CHAPTER

10

MORE HEAT THAN LIGHT

Among the scientific breakthroughs AI enthusiasts are most hoping for are those that would help solve climate change: better batteries; more efficient ways of producing fertilizer, cement, and hydrogen; and a new hope of harnessing the long-sought prize of nuclear fusion. Scientists are already showing that AI can help us make advances in these areas. AI experts are also using the technology to manage our electrical grids so that they can draw more power from renewable energy sources, like wind and solar.

Companies and governments are also using AI to mitigate the effects of climate change: more accurate AI-powered weather forecasts are helping evacuate people from storms and floods; and better long-term modeling of rising sea levels and extreme weather helps cities erect flood defenses, situate cooling centers, and harden building codes—or incentivize people to move to safer locations. Those most in favor of accelerating AI progress toward human-level artificial general intelligence (AGI) or even artificial superintelligence (ASI) that would far exceed human capabilities, often say we *need* these technologies to save us from climate change. In fact, they use this as an argument for brushing aside safety concerns about superpowerful forms of AI and opposing regulation. Any delay in achieving AGI or ASI, they argue, risks planetary catastrophe.

AI is helping in lots of little ways to fight climate change. But the idea—endorsed by AI's biggest boosters—that it will "solve climate change" is false. In fact, AI could well make it worse. It is a ravenously power-hungry technology. The large models that have made the generative AI revolution possible consume far more energy than other kinds of computing. The technology's carbon footprint could eviscerate corporate and government pledges to become carbon neutral, especially as it's folded into more and more of the products we use every day. The chips that run AI applications also generate more heat than normal computer chips, meaning more energy is needed to cool data centers.

Beyond its gargantuan carbon footprint, AI is about as green as the side of a UPS truck. Cooling data centers requires more than electricity. It requires massive quantities of water, straining local resources. The same is true for manufacturing those AI chips and mining the minerals that make up their components. Both activities also use toxic chemicals that can seep into the soil and groundwater. You could say the technological breakthroughs we most need to make with AI's help are those that make AI itself more environmentally sustainable. Otherwise, we'll gain those AI superpowers but lose the planet.

AI TO THE RESCUE?

Jack Kelly worked as a machine learning engineer at Google DeepMind. While there, he helped the company explore whether AI could improve wind forecasts. Better wind speed predictions allow power grid operators to know how much wind power they were likely to have available at any given time, helping them balance electricity supply and demand without having to keep as many natural gas-fired turbines on what is known as *spinning reserve*. These are gas plants that must be kept up and running, emitting CO_2, as backup generation for the grid, in case there's a sudden, unexpected shortfall in power from renewables like wind and solar. Making matters worse, most grid operators ask the spinning-reserve plants to run their gas-fired turbines at about 50 percent capacity so they can rapidly increase turbine speed to meet sudden demand surges. But gas turbines are much less power efficient when running at 50 percent than when running at maximum power. This inefficiency creates unnecessary CO_2 emissions. Better forecasting would reduce the number of plants kept spinning "just in case." The DeepMind project, which was initially applied to wind farms that supply Google's own data centers in the central U.S., improved wind forecasts up to thirty-six hours in advance.

Kelly wanted to do much more: climate change terrified him. The world was literally on fire, and he was certain AI could help. But he also felt constrained. DeepMind had a lot of money, exceptional talent, and gobs of computer power, but its climate change team had to compete for resources with other teams working on AI software for protein folding or beating humans at video games. There were other issues too: DeepMind's wind forecasting software had been built partly on Google's proprietary data. The company thought if this information were made public, it could give the renewable power companies from which Google purchased electricity a negotiating advantage, or it would help rival tech companies run their data centers more cheaply. Kelly felt that to really make a difference, any AI tools had to be shared freely and openly. So in 2018, he decided to leave Google and co-found his own nonprofit AI lab in London, Open Climate Fix, devoted to building open-source data and software to fight climate change.

Kelly's first project at the new lab drew inspiration from his work with wind forecasts at DeepMind. Open Climate Fix began working with the U.K.'s grid operator, National Grid, on using AI to improve solar power forecasts. Solar is the most variable renewable source in the U.K.'s power mix, with a few large solar farms that supply the grid, and many solar panels installed on the roofs of people's homes. Those roof panels supply electricity mostly to those individual houses—for washing machines, toasters, and TVs—with any excess sent to the grid. But this creates a problem for the grid operator: if those houses are in sunlight, their demand from the grid suddenly drops, and when a cloud passes over, their demand from the grid surges again.

In Britain, where for much of the year there can be a changing mix of sun and clouds throughout the day, demand can change significantly in the space of an hour. As with wind power, the variability in solar demand means that the grid keeps a lot of gas-powered spinning reserve, running at 50 percent, to cover sudden demand surges. Kelly and his team at Open Climate Fix trained an AI system from satellite images taken every five minutes to better predict the solar power demand at timescales ranging from the next few minutes out to seven days in advance. It's been a success: the start-up lab's two-hour ahead forecast is three times more accurate than the ones National Grid used previously, reducing the average error from 600 megawatts to 200 megawatts. That's enough to remove several gas-fired turbines from the grid's spinning reserve. Now Open Climate Fix is beginning to bring its solar generation forecasting tools to India, which is building large solar farms in Rajasthan, and to other parts of the globe.

NO MAGIC BULLET

Open Climate Fix's forecasting efforts are just one example among dozens of how AI is being used to reduce carbon emissions. Google's Project Green Light uses AI to analyze traffic patterns in dense cities and look for ways to coordinate traffic lights. This helps reduce the CO_2 emitted by cars idling at red lights. In trials conducted in 2022 and 2023 using seventy intersections in twelve cities across the world, from Haifa to Rio to Bangalore, Google reported a 30 percent decline in the number of cars stopped at lights, resulting in 10 percent reduction in CO_2 emissions at those intersections. A start-up called DroneDeploy uses drones to monitor solar farms from the air, with machine learning helping to recommend optimal solar panel layouts to maximize the site's energy output. It can also help spot broken or dirty panels, which operate less efficiently, so they can be cleaned or repaired.

These are all small contributions, each of which might make an incremental difference in our battle to get to net zero. Some scientists are also using AI to search for breakthroughs that might have a bigger impact. The Silicon Valley start-up Aionics partnered with Cellforce, a German battery maker, to use AI to find new electrolyte materials, which could create improved batteries. That could give electric cars far more range, making them a more attractive option, or even allow national grids to rely completely on renewable power, no matter the weather.

As mentioned in the previous chapter, researchers at labs in the U.S. and Europe have used AI to better control superheated plasma inside nuclear fusion reactors. A breakthrough here could, indeed, make a significant difference in the fight against climate change. But it's not clear AI alone will be enough to deliver fusion's potential. Right now, the power that fusion reactors produce barely exceeds the tremendous amounts of energy needed to run them—and even that modest step has taken decades of effort.

For the most part, AI helps at the margins but can't provide sweeping solutions. AI will undoubtedly help some people adapt to a changing environment and save lives from natural disasters. But we should be under no illusion: when it comes to climate change, AI is not "*the* solution," but part of the problem—and becoming a bigger part by the hour.

THE COLLAPSE OF KOOMEY'S COROLLARY

Moore's law, named for the Intel co-founder Gordon Moore, stipulated that the number of transistors that can be packed onto the same space on a microchip doubles every two years. Moore's law drove a similar decrease in computing's energy footprint. Climate researcher Jonathan Koomey, while working at Stanford University in 2010, showed that from the mid-1940s onward the electrical efficiency of a given computation doubled every 1.6 years—a rate that exceeded Moore's law itself. The growth of smartphones, and the consumer demand for longer battery life, provided an incentive for chip designers to continue to push this envelope.

But, despite this drive, Moore's law has been slowing down in recent decades, and with it Koomey's corollary. Since 2000, it has taken 2.7 years on average to double the energy efficiency of a given computation. And the explosive growth of AI, particularly LLMs and other generative AI models, has blown up Koomey's corollary. There are two main reasons: Today's large AI models run on graphics processing units, each of which typically consumes more power than other kinds of computer chips. And the largest AI models require tens of thousands of GPUs yoked together in vast data centers.

Estimates of AI's carbon footprint vary greatly, but one thing is clear: it's big and—as more and more people want to use AI models—it will get much bigger. One assessment of the carbon footprint associated with GPT-3, the predecessor LLM to ChatGPT that OpenAI debuted in 2020, estimated that training the model emitted as much CO_2 as driving a new car 435,000 miles. This distance would be like driving to the moon—and back. AI, the authors of that study wrote, "risks becoming a significant contributor to climate change."

Researchers at the AI company Hugging Face estimated that BLOOM, the company's LLM, produced twenty-five metric tons of CO_2 during its training. Its lifetime carbon footprint, which includes the CO_2 associated with manufacturing the GPUs used to train it and the energy used to run the model after training, is double that. This is about as much as sixty transatlantic flights. But BLOOM is small—perhaps a tenth the size of GPT-4. Larger models need more GPUs and consume far more power. Throughout the past decade, the size of the most capable AI models has doubled roughly every three months. And between 2012 and 2018, the amount of power needed to train AI models rose 300,000-fold.

It helps that Hugging Face trained BLOOM in France, where most energy is produced in carbon-free nuclear plants. LLMs trained in places where power comes predominantly from fossil fuels, like India or China, will have significantly higher carbon footprints. What's more, the vast majority of the energy a machine-learning model uses over its lifetime is consumed in running the model after it has been trained. LLMs and other generative AI models use more energy for each output than most previous kinds of software, including earlier forms of machine learning. Some AI experts have estimated that a single exchange with an AI chatbot requires four or five times as much computing power as a traditional search engine—a single query to GPT-4 could consume energy equivalent to a third of a smartphone's battery capacity.

Tech companies don't like to talk about AI's carbon footprint. Most reveal next to nothing about it. A few companies disclose the energy usage of their data centers in annual sustainability reports. Over time, data centers have become more efficient—in the decade between 2010 and 2020, global data center energy consumption increased about 6 percent even as the computing capacity of these data centers grew by 550 percent. But their overall appetite for power has still grown steadily. Today, the data centers Big Tech runs in North America and Europe get the majority of their power from renewable sources. And some analyses have shown demand from these tech giants has been a big boost for green energy, because having a large anchor customer gives power companies the confidence to commit to renewable generation projects. But there are indications that AI is so power hungry, tech companies will increasingly need to find other sources of energy. Microsoft, for example, has recently proposed using AI to help speed up regulatory approvals for new nuclear power plants in the U.S.

AI is making up an ever larger share of that electricity usage. AI constituted between 10 percent and 15 percent of Google's electricity consumption in 2021—2.3 terawatt hours annually, which is equivalent to the energy demands of a city the size of Atlanta. All the major internet cloud service providers are rapidly expanding their data center capacity to serve customers with LLMs and other massive AI models. Microsoft, Google, and Amazon collectively invested about $100 billion in new data centers in 2023. Bank of America analysts forecast that figure will exceed $120 billion per year by 2025—and will keep growing. One study estimates that with the growing popularity of AI applications, the technology will be responsible for at least half of a percent of global electricity consumption by 2027. We're forced to rely on estimates because most tech companies creating AI models don't reveal their actual energy usage. We desperately need full disclosure from these companies to assess AI's true impact.

WATER, WATER EVERYWHERE, NOR ANY DROP TO DRINK

AI is a glutton. It is not only ravenously hungry for electricity. It is also exceptionally thirsty. The manufacturing plants, called "fabs," that make the chips on which AI runs and the data centers in which those chips are housed both drink water at a prodigious rate. Local communities have accused data center operators of depleting groundwater to cool their facilities. And those temperatures inside data centers have been soaring due to the need to run thousands of GPUs for AI applications. Microsoft reported that between 2021 and 2022, its global water consumption spiked 34 percent to 1.7 billion gallons, enough to fill more than 2,500 Olympic-size swimming pools. It's no coincidence that the tech giant was suddenly gulping water like never before in the same year that OpenAI was training GPT-4 in Microsoft's Iowa data centers.

Microsoft's five vast data centers outside Des Moines consumed so much water in the summer of 2022—equivalent to about 6 percent of the entire region's total summer consumption—that the local water authority warned the tech company it would oppose any further expansion of its data centers there. The West Des Moines water company has, in recent summers, relied on channeling additional water from Raccoon River to make up for shortfalls. But the Raccoon is already one of America's most endangered waterways. And as with AI's carbon footprint, concerns around water usage don't stop once an AI model is trained. LLMs and other forms of generative AI are also much thirstier than other forms of software when they're up and running. Shaolei Ren, a researcher at the

University of California, Riverside, has estimated that a single interaction with ChatGPT consisting of between five to fifty turns of dialogue uses half a liter of water. Google's on-site water consumption rose 20 percent from 2021 to 2022, according to the company's own environmental impact report, with much of that increase likely attributable to the giant's increased AI efforts.

This problem is being repeated wherever large data centers are being built. Much of this construction is taking place in water-stressed areas such as Las Vegas, Nevada, and Mesa, Arizona. Tech companies have been drawn to these locations, despite their high average air temperatures, through a combination of inexpensive power provided by solar and nuclear, cheap land, and tax incentives. But placing data centers in hot locations puts an unsustainable strain on groundwater resources. A study jointly conducted by researchers at Virginia Tech and the Lawrence Berkeley National Laboratory found that one-fifth of data centers rely on watersheds that are moderately to highly stressed.

While many companies provide general information about the water usage at their data centers, we must push them to make more detailed disclosures. If they refuse to voluntarily provide it, the government, through the Department of the Interior's Bureau of Reclamation, the U.S. Geological Survey's Office of Groundwater, and the Environmental Protection Agency, should compel them to do so. ESG (environmental, social, and governance) investment funds could also use their considerable clout to give cloud service providers a financial reason to decrease their water usage.

DIRTY DIGGING AND NOT-SO-CLEAN ROOMS

Making the chips that underpin the AI boom is a dirty business. GPUs use a higher proportion of rare earths than other chips. They also require chromium, cadmium, mercury, lead, cobalt, tungsten, and boron. Mining these metals is carbon intensive. It is also environmentally destructive. Rare earths and many of these other minerals are mined in open pits, with the soil that is clawed from the earth bathed in chemical leaching ponds, which can pollute groundwater and nearby rivers. Often, radioactive thorium and uranium are found alongside the rare earth metals. Every ton of rare earths produced results in approximately two thousand tons of toxic waste, according to one estimate.

In contrast to the mines that produce raw materials for chips, the facilities where they're made seem immaculate. In these fabs, people garbed head to toe in hooded white boiler suits, safety goggles, gloves, and face masks inspect shiny silicon wafers reflecting iridescent colors. Those workers are laboring in the fab's "clean rooms," so called because they try to eliminate any contaminants that might mar the performance of the microscopic circuits they etch onto the wafer's surface. But the focus on clean rooms in media depictions of fabs has created a false impression that computer chip production is itself somehow "clean" and environmentally friendly. The truth couldn't be more different. Chip making is both energy and water intensive and uses large volumes of toxic chemicals.

Taiwan Semiconductor Manufacturing Corporation (TSMC) dominates the chip industry with about a 56 percent market share. It is the company that Nvidia, the leading seller of GPUs for AI applications, pays to make its chips. TSMC also produces AI-specific chips for Google and Microsoft. TSMC uses more than 6 percent of Taiwan's electricity. It produced 11.6 million metric tons of CO_2 in 2022. That's three to four times higher than the CO_2 output of Ford or General Motors. The company is trying to decarbonize. It has committed to sourcing 100 percent of its energy needs from renewables by 2050. And in 2021 it signed what was at the time the world's single largest corporate renewables purchase agreement, agreeing to buy all its energy for its Taiwan-based fabs from a giant wind farm that the Danish energy firm Orsted is erecting in the Taiwan Strait. The deal could set a standard for others in the industry. But to date, the company's use of renewables has been paltry. In 2022, TSMC said renewables accounted for only 10.4 percent of its worldwide fabs' energy consumption.

Making GPUs is an environmental scourge in other ways too. In 2022, TSMC's Taiwan fabs consumed 96.8 million tons of water, according to the company's own reporting. And while it claimed to recycle some 85 percent of that amount, that still means millions of tons were removed from local sources. In recent years Taiwan has experienced droughts, and local farmers have protested water shortages they blame on TSMC. Semiconductor manufacturing can also be highly polluting due to its dependency on long-lasting "forever" chemicals that don't break down easily in the environment. PFAS (per- and polyfluoroalkyl substances)—which have been linked to fertility problems, reduced fetal growth, liver disease, and cancer—are essential to chipmaking. European efforts to ban the chemicals, and chemical maker 3M's decision to voluntarily stop producing PFAS by 2025, forced TSMC to hold emergency meetings with its suppliers to ensure chip production wouldn't be disrupted. Currently, there are no substitutes for PFAS in chipmaking processes.

The semiconductor industry has a poor track record when it comes to keeping toxic chemicals out of the environment. Silicon Valley, the birthplace of America's semiconductor industry, is also home to some of the country's worst EPA Superfund sites, with soil and groundwater contaminated by chemicals that leaked from the region's fabs and have been linked to sharply higher miscarriage rates, other reproductive health issues, and cancer. Parts of Google's campus in Mountain View, California, sit on one such site. With TSMC and other semiconductor makers looking to build new fabs in the U.S., the EPA and other government agencies should be vigilant to ensure we don't wind up reshoring groundwater and soil contamination as well.

FOR BETTER AND WORSE

We may need AI's help to figure out how to make AI itself cleaner and greener. If we continue to adopt the technology at its current pace without reducing its carbon footprint, water usage, and toxic pedigree, the planet will be worse off, not better. AI could help scientists find more environmentally friendly ways to make and run GPUs. And just maybe it can help researchers find a new AI method that is inherently more energy efficient. By some estimates, the human brain uses less than a tenth of the energy in a whole day that it takes ChatGPT to answer a single question. If we could find AI that was more brain-like in this respect, that would be an incredible achievement.

I don't mean to dismiss the importance of the marginal improvements AI can make to combating climate change and improving sustainability that were mentioned in this chapter. But AI cannot surmount the biggest barriers we face in addressing these issues. They're ultimately problems of politics and human nature, not data and policy. In many cases, we know what must be done to reach net zero, and we already have the technology to do it. What we don't have is the political and economic will. To really "solve" climate change and build a sustainable future, we'll have to seek answers in our own natural intelligence, not an artificial one.

11

THE TRUST BOMB

Addressing climate change requires the political courage to make tough policy choices. It requires widespread willingness to make sacrifices for the common good. But there's not much common anything anymore. Our trust in government, in societal institutions, and in one another is at an all-time low. Trust is the most important currency any society has. Trust in the judgment and collective wisdom of our fellow citizens is foundational to democracy. AI could make it easier than ever for governments to discern and respond to their citizens' concerns. But if we don't act quickly, AI is likely to decimate what little trust we still have.

Deepfakes and misinformation mass-produced with the help of AI will challenge our democratic processes, swinging elections and fomenting polarization. AI will also challenge our sense of security and privacy by making it far easier for criminals to commit fraud, and for hackers to steal our data and our secrets. Government impotence in the face of these threats may seriously undermine trust in democracy.

In combination, these trends—misinformation and fraud—will

further poison our gravely ill information ecosystem, perhaps fatally. When no one knows what to believe, we disengage from government and institutions, becoming some combination of cynical, selfish, paranoid, and nihilistic. Fearful and confused, we fall back on affinity groups and informal networks, fragmenting any sense of community and ultimately sparking a crisis that no one can fix.

AI can also erode the principles of liberty and equality on which our democracy was founded. America and other Western nations may not always live up to these ideals, but AI threatens to entrench systemic biases, while masking racism, sexism, and other prejudices. We must insist that governments take urgent action to address all three pressing dimensions along which AI imperils democratic society—threats to our trust, to our security and privacy, and to our liberty and equality. This last threat, to equality, is perhaps AI's most insidious effect, and the least commented on. We'll look at it first.

IF YOU CAN AFFORD TO PAY FOR HUMAN . . .

In the age of ubiquitous AI, a potentially catastrophic division is opening up in society: between those of us who will be rich enough to afford interactions with human beings in service settings and in our work, and the rest of us who will increasingly be served and managed only by AI. This is already true in many areas. The wealthy have personal bankers and still use travel agents that they can reach by phone and maybe even see in person; the rest of us must serve ourselves through mobile apps and websites. If we have any problems, we must use chatbot apps or wait endlessly on hold for the chance to speak to someone in a customer contact center in the Philippines or India. In the future, this dichotomy will likely extend to more and more areas of our lives.

As AI assistants become more powerful, able to handle more customer needs, businesses may seek extra revenue by allowing customers who can afford it to pay extra to have their issues resolved by a friendly human. The rich will continue to pay for flesh-and-blood personal assistants to help organize their lives; the rest of us will have to make do with the digital version. The wealthy will still hire tutors to work with their children; the rest of us may find our children increasingly taught by AI. And, as we saw in chapter 4, while educated elites will retain a high degree of autonomy at work, where they will be empowered by AI copilots, blue-collar and service-sector workers could find themselves turned into cyborgs—still human, but with their every moment on the job dictated by a demanding and cruel AI manager. Increasingly, human agency will become a luxury item.

In any environment, this loss of agency is destabilizing, potentially provoking revolt. But in a democracy, the increasing disparity in the daily experience of the haves and the have-nots is particularly corrosive. It embitters those who are relegated to AI interaction, making them more resentful and distrustful of elites. It destroys the sense that society and our system of government works for everyone. It loosens the ties that bind us together as a nation. It creates a two-tiered society, increasingly living separate and unequal lives.

UNEQUAL JUSTICE

The gap between those who can afford the luxury of human interaction and everyone else is hardly the only inequality AI will exacerbate. If we engineer, design, and use it incorrectly, AI will imperil efforts to improve racial and gender equality. American democracy has frequently failed to live up to its founding principles of liberty and equality of opportunity. But that doesn't mean we should abandon those ideals. AI could become a tool for advancing equality. In theory, the technology should enable us to overcome the prejudices and biases of individual judgment. But the way that many AI systems are being built is having the opposite effect. By learning from historical, human-generated data, these systems frequently affirm and amplify existing biases. Worse, they can mask these tendencies beneath a facade of pseudo-objectivity that distances institutions from accountability for unfair and unjust outcomes they bring about. This is dangerous for two reasons. It is, of course, inherently wrong, causing real harm. But it also erodes faith in the American project.

Some of the most troubling examples of masked bias involve the use of AI in law enforcement. An algorithm that was widely sold to help judges and parole boards make "risk-based" decisions about who should be offered alternatives to prison found that it was much more likely to recommend early release for white offenders than Black offenders who had committed similar crimes. The algorithm overestimated the true recidivism rate of Black offenders and underestimated that of whites. Tools that claim to be able to help police predict crime "hot spots" also lead to disproportionate arrests in Black and other minority neighborhoods. This is largely because these predictive AI systems have been trained on past arrest data. And that data reflects systemic biases in policing, in which police departments often spend more resources and use different standards and methods, such as stop-and-frisk policies, in poorer, predominantly nonwhite neighborhoods than in more affluent, white ones.

Using arrest data rather than conviction data can be problematic too. "We took bad data in the first place, and then we used tools to make it worse," Katy Washington, a researcher who studies algorithmic bias at the University of Colorado Boulder, told MIT Technology Review. The use of facial-recognition software by police departments is also a problem given that most of these systems have been shown to be less accurate for those with darker skin, and for Black women in particular. The controversial facial-recognition app Clearview obtained much of its data by scraping social media sites, which several lawsuits allege violated those sites' terms and conditions as well as state laws in places like Illinois. Clearview has gained widespread use among U.S. police departments despite data privacy concerns and a lack of independent testing to verify the app's accuracy and fairness.

Yet despite all these deficiencies having received widespread media attention, law enforcement agencies have only deepened their move toward "precision policing" methods. Relying on data analytics allows police departments to appear unbiased and duck accountability for decisions about where they send officers to patrol.

Given the history of racist policing in the U.S., it is highly unlikely that a system naively constructed from past data will do anything other than reinforce existing biases. Instead, AI software for use in law enforcement must be engineered to explicitly compensate for past racism by specifying equality as a goal alongside predictive accuracy. This means, in essence, that any such system will underweight crimes committed by people of color. And while the overall outcome might be equitable, software engineered in this way will likely offend those with an intuitive desire for completely color-blind justice. The European Union in its AI Act bans law enforcement from using live facial-recognition software (it can be used to analyze recorded video), and it has classified all law enforcement use of AI as inherently "high risk," which means it is subject to the strictest protocols for assessing potential dangers, including bias, and mitigating them. The U.S. should also implement these tough standards around AI for policing and justice.

Given how biased human decisions often are, some argue AI systems will improve justice. An American Civil Liberties Union study of a risk-assessment tool introduced in New Jersey in 2017 found that it could reduce the number of people jailed while awaiting trial by 20 percent. But there was a big caveat—it would only have that effect if properly conceived *and* implemented. In Kentucky, for example, a study found that a risk score designed to help judges would have reduced incarceration rates, except that the judges were interpreting the scores inconsistently.

It may be better to heed the fateful warning of Eliza's creator, Joseph Weizenbaum: even if machines could be provably more objective than people, AI should be barred from decisions affecting a person's liberty. Decisions with such high consequence to a person's life should only be made by someone who knows what it is to have one. When it comes to justice, do we seek objectivity, or something else: A fair application of subjective experience, allowing room for human empathy?

Yes, concerns about unfairness, human bias, inconsistency, and corruption are what led governments to adopt risk scores and algorithms to begin with. But too often, officials have failed to ask tough questions about the data from which these algorithms are derived and have been derelict in monitoring their impact. Too often, algorithms and AI become a convenient excuse for officials to evade accountability for harmful or embarrassing results. "We were just following the algorithm" is the new "I was just following orders." It's a way for officials to shirk responsibility and accountability. We should not let politicians and civil servants off the hook so easily. And we should not abandon professional judgment, commonsense reasoning, and moral intuition just because it's more convenient to blindly trust the AI knows best.

UNEQUAL OPPORTUNITY

The justice system is not the only area where racial and gender bias can have life-shaping consequences. It's true in finance, too, where AI could usher in a new era of digital redlining. And it is true in healthcare, where decisions can literally make the difference between life and death. In 2019, a landmark study demonstrated that a common risk-assessment tool that had been used to assess the healthcare needs of more than 100 million Americans was biased against Black patients, with these patients considerably sicker at any given risk score than white patients. Researchers concluded that if the algorithm had been fair, the percentage of Black patients receiving additional help for their conditions based on the risk score would have risen from 18 percent to 47 percent.

These AI systems are biased because the data they've been fed is. Black patients, for instance, are estimated to make up fewer than 5 percent of clinical trial participants in the U.S. Doctors and nurses have for years undertreated Black and other minority patients for conditions like pain, sometimes because of mistaken beliefs about racial disparities in pain thresholds or other false biological differences. As is the case with AI in the justice system, AI in healthcare can mask bias behind a veneer of technoperfection. If healthcare professionals are unaware of the biases hidden in the software they're using to diagnose and treat patients, they may mistakenly see such technology as inherently more objective and accurate than their own judgment. But, just as in law enforcement, if AI systems were specifically built and trained to overcome historical biases, they could become powerful tools for correcting past inequities.

In financial services, the danger of racial and gender bias is similarly insidious. U.S. lenders must be sure that their lending practices don't produce a "disparate impact" on a protected class of people, such as Latinos or women. Critically, regulators and courts have also said it's fine for lenders to consider metrics that have traditionally been used in determining credit risk, such as income and credit scores, even though these variables have a high correlation with gender and race. But AI algorithms can now make repayment predictions using a lot of other data that might, on its face, seem neutral, but in practice is a proxy for a protected class of people.

One European study showed that five data points were better predictors of loan repayments than credit scores: device brand (Mac or PC), device type (phone, tablet, or PC), time of day the credit application is made, email domain (Gmail or Hotmail), and whether a person's email address included part or all of their name. But each of these, the study found, was correlated with a protected class (for instance, whites are more likely to own Macs) and might be deemed illegal under U.S. lending laws. But lenders can get around the disparate impact rule by showing that dropping a data point from their credit risk algorithm would result in a less accurate price. This makes it too easy for lenders and insurers to game this test.

If we act both creatively and responsibly, AI could actually expand lending to historically disadvantaged groups. VyStar Credit Union, which is among America's largest credit unions, used AI credit risk scoring software from start-up Zest AI to increase approvals for credit cards, particularly among minorities and other historically disadvantaged groups, by more than 20 percent while keeping its risk of default constant. "That is thousands of people who otherwise would not have had access to a credit card," Jenny Vipperman, VyStar's chief lending officer, says.

AMPLIFYING BIAS

The current boom in generative AI systems has the potential to super-power inequality. That's because these systems don't just reproduce existing bias, they can also amplify it. Again, the problem is historical data. Give an LLM a sentence with an ambiguous pronoun such as "the doctor phoned the nurse because she was late for the morning shift" and ask the LLM who "she" refers to, as researchers from Apple and Swarthmore College recently did, and the AI is more likely to answer the nurse. When they tested four publicly available LLMs, they found that the AI accentuated bias: the LLMs were seven times more likely to say a female pronoun referred to a stereotypical female profession, while only 3.8 times more likely to say a male pronoun referred to a profession historically associated with men.

Text-to-image generation AI models can be even more problematic. As mentioned in chapter 8, if you prompt the image-generating AI software Midjourney to show you "a Black African doctor caring for white suffering children," as one group of researchers did in a study published in the prestigious medical journal *The Lancet*, the model is incapable of responding correctly. More than 99 percent of the time, it outputs an image of a white doctor and Black children. Another study found text-to-image generators tend to depict people in higher-earning professions as having lighter skin than those in lower-earning jobs. It was also more likely to depict high earners as men, too.

There are ways to solve this bias. Better dataset curation can help. So, too, can intentionally overtraining the model on outlier examples or creating synthetic datasets with computer-generated examples that fill in gaps in real-world datasets. But technology companies need to take these steps intentionally when they build large foundation models, and right now, they aren't doing so. Which is a problem, because generative AI models are fast being incorporated into so many different applications in business, education, and government.

It isn't inevitable that AI will exacerbate societal inequality. But technology companies need to be pushed to build AI as a force for equality. The European Union's AI Act, with its risk-based assessments, is a step in this direction, and it may become a de facto global standard since it will apply to any company with European customers or employees. The U.S., in its AI regulation, should mandate that models be tested for bias. We should strive for AI that results in more equitable outcomes. The Federal Trade Commission can take the lead on enforcement for general-purpose AI systems. More specific AI systems, like those developed for hospitals discussed in chapter 9, will require attention from other agencies. The Federal Reserve, the Securities and Exchange Commission, and state insurance regulators should also look for algorithms that improve equitable financial outcomes.

Business itself has a big role to play in pushing technology companies to ensure the software they create doesn't discriminate. Sometimes, this may mean not rushing to use LLMs. Smaller AI models are easier to analyze and control.

GRIFTERS AND HACKERS DELIGHT

So far, the trust issues we've examined stem from carelessness in the way AI is built and used. But the most obvious challenge to trust is the result of people deliberately using AI to mislead and manipulate.

AI may be the best gift to con artists since the invention of the internet. Once, grammatical mistakes and strange idioms in emails purporting to be from your bank were a dead giveaway that a Nigerian fraudster or Russian gang was trying to steal your password or account details. Now, even non-native English speakers can use ChatGPT and other LLMs to compose convincing phishing emails. That panicked, tearful call from your nephew saying he's been kidnapped and that if you don't send his captors money right away, they are going to kill him? It might not be him. Already fraudsters are using voice cloning software to make calls such as this, particularly targeting people's vulnerable older relatives. (To make it more likely that one victim would pay, the fraudsters used the AI software to impersonate his daughter screaming in pain, and then reporting her captors had just slashed her with a knife.) Voice clones are also being used to impersonate chief executives asking unsuspecting corporate finance department executives to make payments to bank accounts for secretive transactions.

The ability to create live face-swapping deepfakes has also opened up the possibility of Zoom calls where the person on the screen might not be who they seem. One company appears to have been swindled out of $25 million through a Zoom in which live face-swapping was used to impersonate executives.

Just as AI can be a useful coding assistant, it can also be a boon to hackers, making it easier for those with less technical skill to mount sophisticated cyberattacks. The cybersecurity firm Check Point demonstrated that ChatGPT could be used to plan every stage of a hack, from crafting a convincing phishing email to writing executable malware and embedding that malware within an email attachment. Microsoft and OpenAI said in early 2024 that they had detected and shut down ChatGPT accounts linked to hackers affiliated with Russia, China, Iran, and North Korea all trying to use ChatGPT to refine attack methods.

On the dark web, hackers market LLMs with names such as FraudGPT and WormGPT that they say have been trained to craft effective malware and run phishing campaigns. Other LLMs can be used by cybercriminals and spies to analyze the software code of systems they are hoping to hack to automatically hunt for vulnerabilities.

Even before AI chatbots came along, there were malware packages that could be bought for paltry sums on the dark web, as well as gangs selling "hacker-for-hire" services. Those options are even easier than trying to have an LLM write you a bespoke malware package. But cybersecurity experts say that in the hands of a slightly more knowledgeable hacker, LLMs can save time and make phishing attempts more likely to succeed.

AI VS. AI

While a world of AI-generated hacks sounds terrifying, malware is one area where AI can effectively fight AI. Over time, AI will prove more advantageous to defenders than attackers. While hackers can use it to scour codebases for potential vulnerabilities, cybersecurity experts can do this too, seeking out and repairing security vulnerabilities before hackers find them. They can even configure chatbots to act as attackers and use them to "red team," or test, their own networks, probing for weaknesses.

One of the biggest issues in cybersecurity is the dearth of trained cybersecurity analysts and information security officers. AI can act as a critical copilot in this area. Google has trained a version of its PaLM 2 LLM specifically to help cybersecurity officials. And there are already AI-enabled cybersecurity programs from companies like Darktrace and Palo Alto Networks that act a bit like the human immune system, automatically detecting network anomalies, containing threats, and then seeking to remediate them, all at speeds faster than any person could respond.

Finally, in AI, data matters. And here, defenders should have a distinct advantage. As Evan Reiser, the chief executive of cybersecurity software company Abnormal, which specializes in detecting unusual email traffic, points out, defenders know more about their own network's behavior and their own software code, while attackers have access only to publicly available information and maybe some data they've managed to observe while spying. This should make it more likely that an attacker will make a mistake and tip off AI-enabled network surveillance software. Maya Horowitz, vice president of research at Check Point, says that generative AI is a "tactical advantage for the attackers," but for defenders it can be "strategic," enabling them to defend their own networks more effectively.

This sounds reassuring, except it only applies to traditional hacking methods. And, as it turns out, generative AI systems have opened up an entirely new "surface" to would-be attackers, a nascent front that's extremely difficult to secure. Chatbot AI systems are vulnerable to "prompt injection" attacks, where a person with ill intent feeds the

AI system an input, either text or an image, that tricks it into producing responses it isn't supposed to. This is why companies deploying AI
chatbots for things like customer service or employee copilots must be
extremely careful about what data and tools the underlying LLM can
call on. Already, people have discovered instances in which chatbots will,
when asked, leak people's sensitive information.

It may, in some cases, be preferable to create narrowly tailored copilots for each role within a business, because such siloing limits the data
any one bot can access. Operating on a "need to know" basis should
apply to our chatbots as well as our employees. Companies will need to
be especially wary of building these chatbots using open-source LLMs.
That's because security researchers have shown that if hackers have access to an AI model's weights, they can use software to automatically
generate prompt injection attacks—often strings of what appear to people like nonsense characters appended to prompts—that are guaranteed
to override the AI's guardrails. So far, no one knows exactly how to guard
against this. Until we have AI systems with more humanlike and robust
conceptual understanding—which would make their guardrail harder to
defeat—securing these systems will be difficult.

The data AI is trained on is another juicy new target for hackers.
Horowitz is particularly concerned about hackers working for hostile
governments engaging in "data poisoning"—tampering with the data
sources on which AI systems are trained and deliberately adding training examples that will make AI systems misclassify things or give false
outputs. This could be a particular problem for military AI systems that
are designed to classify drone footage of enemy forces and weaponry.
Researchers have shown that with just a few carefully selected examples,
software like this can be tricked into misclassifying a picture of a turtle
as a rifle. The same tactic could be used to produce the opposite result.
Horowitz says the fact that so much data being used to train LLMs is
scraped from the internet means that anyone wishing to mislead the
military software could simply hide this data poison in plain sight on the
internet, confident it would be swept up into the training of future LLMs.

Government must take a proactive and aggressive approach to safe-guarding our most sensitive data. The Biden administration sponsored red-teaming exercises aimed at testing the vulnerabilities of the most capable general-purpose AI models. The federal government is developing guidelines and protocols on AI security. These may ultimately form the basis of regulations that will apply to the government's departments and contractors.

But more must be done to improve security across industries, particularly in the financial and health sectors. Gary Gensler, the head of the U.S. Securities and Exchange Commission, has warned that unless the government acts swiftly to safeguard financial markets from AI-generated vulnerabilities, a financial catastrophe is "nearly unavoidable" within the next decade. In healthcare, the theft or manipulation of sensitive patient data could also have disastrous effects.

Beyond the direct damage the theft of information causes, the psychological damage—the impression that the government can't safeguard citizens' security—is pernicious. If this perception takes hold, it will further undermine faith in our institutions and our democracy.

THE FIREHOSE OF FALSEHOOD

Fraud and cybercrime pose indirect threats to democracy by eroding trust and heightening our sense of vulnerability. But disinformation and election interference are a full-frontal assault on trust and democracy. Fears about AI-generated political content have been mounting for almost a decade. In 2017, the first examples of nonconsensual deepfake pornography, in which the heads of celebrities were morphed onto the bodies of porn stars, began appearing on Reddit. Almost immediately, AI researchers and political analysts raised concerns that deepfakes would be used for political disinformation, further poisoning an information environment already rife with falsehoods spread through social media. That same year, researchers at the University of Washington used fourteen hours of audio and video of former president Barack Obama to create a convincing deepfake video, in an effort to warn the public of the coming danger. At the time, deepfakes depended on an AI technique called a "generative adversarial network," or GAN. This involves two neural networks, one which is trained to generate images, and another that is trained to decide whether the image is real or fake. The two networks compete against each other in successive rounds of training, eventually resulting in fake images or video that are difficult to spot. The drawback of GANs is that they require many hours of video and audio of someone to produce a convincing fake.

Since then, new AI techniques have radically reduced the amount of data, time, and human expertise needed to create a convincing fake. GANs are no longer required. Image generators like Midjourney allow anyone to create a convincing deepfake image of a celebrity from a text prompt in about a second. Viral fake images of Donald Trump allegedly scuffling with police while being arrested and of Pope Francis wearing a white puffer jacket (neither of which were part of a deliberate misinformation effort) were both created in this way. Meanwhile, video generation software from the start-up Runway allows a person to create fake video from a text prompt, and also to easily swap one person for another in a video. And the start-up ElevenLabs can create a realistic voice clone of anyone from just a few seconds of real audio data. The ease of using these tools virtually guarantees an explosion of fake content.

Alarmingly, some politicians and their advisors see deepfakes not as a covert "dirty trick" but as an overt and legitimate tool for political persuasion. In India, during the Delhi mayoral election in 2020, one candidate created a deepfake video of himself speaking a Hindi dialect he did not actually know in an attempt to appeal to voters from that community. In the U.S., the Republican Party used deepfake videos, portraying an apocalyptic America that it claimed would result if President Joe Biden were elected for a second term, as part of an attack ad they released immediately following Biden's announcement of his reelection campaign.

At the same time, ChatGPT and other text-based LLMs make it easy for anyone to produce convincing-sounding fake news stories and blogs. In 2016, Russia waged an unprecedented disinformation campaign designed to influence the outcome of that year's U.S. presidential election. That campaign involved fake social media accounts, purportedly belonging to Americans but actually controlled by Russian-linked operatives, and used targeted advertising to spread false news stories with the intention of polarizing public opinion. But some of the postings from these fake accounts suffered from telltale grammatical errors, which may have tipped off some readers that the news stories were bogus. LLMs such as ChatGPT now make it easy for anyone to generate convincing fake news, even in languages they don't speak.

Imagine it is late October, just weeks before a close-fought presidential campaign. An audio file begins to go viral among followers of key right-wing influencers on social media. Those sharing the audio say it is a portion of a recording of a private meeting between the incumbent Democratic president and a billionaire businessman. In the recording, the president offers to help the billionaire's Czech business partner secure a shipment of U.S. arms that he can later resell to the government of Ghana. In exchange, the president demands an explicit bribe, in the form of a large campaign contribution. Although of dubious origin, the audio file is quickly picked up by right-wing media organizations. Reporters confirm the president did have a meeting with the businessman and that the businessman did later make a large campaign donation. But the audio itself cannot be verified. Spokesmen for the president and the businessman both deny the audio is authentic. But their denials don't stop the Republican candidate from decrying "the bribery scandal" that the "mainstream media is refusing to cover." Congressional Republicans fan the flames by calling for an investigation into "Ghanagate." Now major nonpartisan news outlets feel compelled to cover the story, even though they haven't been able to verify the audio. The president's poll numbers among independents and swing voters in battleground states begin to sag. Meanwhile, the "scandal" further confirms right-wing voters' perceptions of the president as corrupt and immoral, motivating them to get to the polls. The president wins the popular vote, but winds up losing in the Electoral College due to narrow defeats in key states. Did a deepfake audio recording just swing the election?

Given the current state of AI technology and the political landscape, this scenario is entirely plausible. The appearance of a deepfake video or audio recording at a key moment in a close election could prove decisive. Deepfake audio is particularly difficult to verify, especially if it purports to be a recording of a private conversation. Deepfake audios like this have already surfaced in campaigns. On the eve of the 2023 Chicago mayoral election, an X (then Twitter) account calling itself Chicago Lakefront News posted an image of a candidate, Paul Vallas, along with an audio recording making inflammatory statements downplaying police misconduct. The audio was quickly debunked as fake, and in the end did not play a significant role in the election. But thousands of people had still heard and recirculated the bogus clip. In Slovakia, an audio deepfake likely altered the outcome of national elections in 2023, a first in a Western democracy.

The outcomes of U.S. presidential elections hang on relatively few voters in a handful of states. Not many people have to change their vote to swing a presidential election. That said, studies of disinformation show people are more inclined to believe it when it reinforces people's existing beliefs and prejudices. This means that propaganda campaigns designed to boost turnout among a candidate's base, or to convince voters already lukewarm on a candidate to sit out an election, will be more effective than efforts aimed at changing voters' perceptions.

The ease with which AI can churn out disinformation makes it particularly useful for certain propaganda strategies. Russia subscribes to a strategy that experts at the think tank RAND Corporation dub "the firehose of falsehood," where the intention is to inundate people with lies and half-truths. Studies have shown that people are more likely to believe information they encounter more often, even if it's false. The tsunami of disinformation is also designed to overwhelm fact-checking efforts. Ultimately, persuasion may only be a secondary goal: the real purpose is sowing confusion and destroying trust in key institutions. When people don't know what or whom to trust, they're more likely to fall back on affinity groups, like friends and family, which undermines social cohesion across communities. A prevalence of deepfake misinformation may also increase what's known as the *liar's dividend*, in which a profusion of false information makes it easier for politicians to deny damning true information as "fake news."

DIGITAL WATERMARKS

Right now, we have few defenses against this deluge of deceit. The tech companies using generative AI have voluntarily committed to including "digital watermarks" on AI-created images that would make it technically easy to spot some deepfakes. Samsung, for example, has begun applying a visible digital watermark to any image made with the AI tools that now come standard in its latest-generation Galaxy smartphones. It also adds information to the metadata accompanying each image file that indicates AI has been used to alter it. But, currently, the U.S. doesn't legally require AI images to be watermarked. The European Union's AI Act requires transparency around AI-generated content that is likely to lead to watermarking, while China has already mandated these identifiers in its AI regulations.

Watermarks, in any case, are not a foolproof solution. For one thing, they only guard against the use of commercially available AI software to make deepfakes. Nefarious actors, particularly well-resourced nation states, could create their own AI models free of watermarking or strip watermarking protections from open-source AI software. Research has shown that watermarking systems for AI-generated text and images can also be overcome with the right prompting or fine-tuning. In some cases, it's even easier than that: just days after Samsung's new watermarking feature debuted, people discovered they could use the same smartphone AI editing tools that applied the watermarks to remove them (although the metadata still indicated that AI had been used).

Adobe, Microsoft, and others, including the camera-maker Leica, have endorsed tackling this problem from the opposite direction by adding "Content Credentials" metadata to all digital photographs that certify them as legitimate and also automatically flag certain kinds of digital manipulation. But users can elect not to use the credentials, which in most cases aren't applied by default. It may take many years to propagate this standard globally and, again, bad actors may find a way to forge the credentials. The Biden administration, meanwhile, has ordered the Commerce Department to formulate guidance around digital watermarks that would be applied to all government communications to certify them as legitimate. But these content certification systems don't address the issue of all the legitimate digital images that already exist without this credentialing. Watermarking seems necessary but not sufficient to address the looming crisis in trust.

Criminalizing the production and deliberate dissemination of misinformation could help. It would at least prevent domestic troll farms from spreading AI-generated lies for advertising profit, although it would do little to stop shady foreign businesses or hostile nation states. France passed a law in 2018 that gives authorities broad powers to remove false content from social media or block sites publishing it, as well as to force greater transparency around who has paid for sponsored content in the three months prior to elections.

The EU's sweeping new Digital Services Act requires social media platforms to bolster their processes for policing misinformation, terrorist propaganda, and hate speech. But it also says social media platforms need to balance these restrictions carefully against free speech rights. It's a balance these tech companies may struggle to achieve. Meanwhile, in the United States, any effort to make the production of misinformation illegal would likely run afoul of the First Amendment.

The U.S. should follow Europe's example and impose some requirements on social media companies to check the distribution of misinformation. Reforming Section 230 of the Communications Decency Act, the landmark 1996 law sometimes credited with "creating the internet" by exempting online platforms from liability for the user-generated content they host, could help turn off the firehose of falsehood. The U.S. should also ban political campaigns from using AI-generated content.

ASTROTURF FERTILIZER

Deepfakes get most of the press attention, but AI also poses more insidious threats to our democracy. Special interest groups could use AI to supercharge "astroturf" campaigns—where a corporate lobby creates the false appearance of grassroots support for a particular policy, often with the use of front organizations that mask the true architects. Lobby groups have already used automation to power astroturf campaigns. In 2017, when the Federal Communications Commission was considering changes to "net neutrality" rules—which mandate that internet service providers must treat all information being transmitted across their fiber-optic cables equally—groups backed by corporate interests used bots to flood the commission's electronic comment portal with more than 8 million comments favoring repeal. The effort failed because 90 percent of the comments were identical, making it easy for the commission to detect the astroturfing. Today's LLMs, however, can mass-produce convincing constituent and public comment letters, each using slightly different phrasing, that could seem like they were composed by real individuals. Right now, AI-generated correspondence can't be detected.

AI can also overwhelm attempts to use social media to gauge public sentiment. In theory, using AI to automatically categorize and summarize social media posts might provide a novel way for government officials or the press to "take the public pulse," without having to depend on polls that are becoming less reliable for a variety of reasons. Summarizing social media posts could also provide more nuanced information than polls, where participants are usually limited to just a few degrees of agreement or disagreement with a statement the pollster has created. This was the vision of Noam Slonim, an IBM researcher who created an AI system called Speech by Crowd that the company demonstrated in late 2018. The system could analyze and summarize thousands of human-written comments, understanding which were arguing in favor of a proposition and which were against. Slonim suggested that, in the future, governments might use Speech by Crowd, or its successors, to better understand public opinion. But such a system works only if the government can be reasonably assured of the authenticity of the comments being analyzed.

To combat this, governments will have to strengthen existing defenses against bots—such as CAPTCHA systems or two-factor authentication—on websites that solicit public comment. Increasingly sophisticated AI may eventually defeat these defenses, but it will at least make it more difficult for would-be astroturfers. Social media companies should also be required to redouble their efforts against bots and fake accounts.

With the right policies, AI could be a tool for enhancing democracy and strengthening trust. But, as it stands, the technology is likely to have the opposite effect, pummeling our already battered information ecosystem and further weakening our sense of community and our democratic processes. It will widen the gap between privileged, wealthy elites and the rest of society, undermining expectations of fairness and equal opportunity that are foundational to public support for democratic government. We must brace ourselves for this challenge and take whatever steps we can to divert AI's development onto a more enlightened and ennobling course.

CHAPTER

12

WAR AT MACHINE SPEED

A warming climate may drown us in floods, bake us in encroaching deserts, and starve us with failing harvests. The destruction of trust may imperil our democracy. But both threats pale next to the danger nuclear weapons pose to our species' survival. Those weapons are a stark reminder of our collective genius and our madness—harvesting the power of the stars to seal a suicide pact. They are the epitome of our penchant for using our natural intelligence to dream up ways to kill one another more efficiently. Now we have a new toy for mass murder: artificial intelligence. AI makes our practice of killing less personal, and thus less accountable. It offers to remove human risk from the battlefield, but in the process dehumanizes us. And if coupled to the missiles that sit patiently in their silos awaiting Armageddon's call, it increases the chance they will receive that fateful summons.

Autonomy has been creeping into warfare for well over a century. Confederate forces in the U.S. Civil War used the first land mines that could be buried underground and then triggered by the weight of a person stepping on a concealed pressure plate. Such weapons had autonomy of a sort, but no intelligence. Today, AI capabilities are being integrated into combat at every level of what military strategists call "the kill chain"—the steps from reconnaissance to firing a weapon to assessing the aftermath. Much of this AI operates at the level of perception—detecting objects and people on the battlefield, identifying what or who they are, and then tracking their movements. But more sophisticated AI is also being used to autonomously fly combat aircraft, pilot underwater drones, and control gunnery systems. AI is being integrated into the command-and-control systems officers use to visualize the battlefield. Software similar to the AI systems used to beat human competitors at Go and *StarCraft II* is now making strategy recommendations to generals. The newest LLMs are beginning to play a role in warfare, too, analyzing and summarizing intelligence reports, and providing a natural language interface for commanders to interact with sensors, weapons systems, and soldiers.

AI transforms warfare across three dimensions. It makes weapons more autonomous. It changes how information about the battlefield is gathered, analyzed, and used to make decisions. And it alters the political dimension of warfare—impacting the national security strategies, geopolitical calculus, and political ramifications around decisions to use military force. This chapter will explore each of these dimensions. Across all three, AI raises profound questions about human accountability and morality that will increasingly challenge not only soldiers but the political leaders who send them to war, and, in democracies, all of us in whose name they fight.

SAVING LIVES, BUT AT WHAT COST?

Imagine a sprawling, densely packed shantytown of tin-roofed shacks and low-rise, concrete apartment blocks, climbing the hills outside an African capital. From somewhere inside this labyrinthine urban landscape, a terrorist cell operates. To root them out, a general could send in commandos on foot or roped down from helicopters. But it's risky. His soldiers could be ambushed. His helicopters shot down. Civilians could be killed in any firefight. If he can find the terrorists' headquarters, he could try to destroy the building with a bomb or missile. But then many civilians nearby might be killed as "collateral damage."

AI might accomplish this mission with much less risk. Intelligence gathered from cell phone towers and drone footage can be analyzed by AI software to identify the terrorists' hideout. Then a swarm of small drones could be sent under cover of darkness, skimming the rooftops, and flying into the terrorists' den. The drones would hunt down anyone inside the building, detonating grenade-size munitions, killing them. The drones could be programmed to chase the terrorists within the building, to pursue them out into the streets, and ensure they could not escape. The AI software would be trained not to attack children. The drones might even be equipped with facial-recognition software enabling them to attack only the known terrorists. In this way, the cell could be neutralized with no risk to troops and at a lower risk of civilians being killed.

This is the dream of those building AI-equipped weapons. "These autonomous systems will make warfare less destructive, less costly in terms of civilian casualties, and less costly in terms of friendly casualties. And I think at the end of the day, that's what we want," says Brandon Tseng, a former U.S. Navy SEAL whose start-up, Shield AI, is producing a range of autonomous aerial systems for the U.S. and allied militaries. As a SEAL, Tseng was all too aware of the dangers that soldiers face in urban combat. That experience led him to co-found Shield, which started out producing small reconnaissance drones that could operate inside buildings and navigate areas where GPS and radio control signals were jammed. The company has since begun building larger autonomous weapons, including drones that can act as "AI wingmen" to fighter jets.

The military historian John Keegan, in his meditation on an infantryman's experience of war, *The Face of Battle*, noted that its two most defining characteristics are blinding smoke and deafening noise. Denied two of their five senses and hyped on adrenaline, it's no wonder soldiers make fatal mistakes in the heat of battle. AI systems are not rattled by explosions. They do not feel fear. They are not consumed with rage or a desire for vengeance. And they don't get tired. Unburdened by all these human frailties, AI systems can, in theory, make decisions more quickly and more accurately than people. Working in unison with other remotely operated or autonomous reconnaissance systems, these weapons might have a better understanding of the entire battlefield than any individual soldier in the field ever could. Most importantly, autonomous weapons can attack military targets with high precision, without putting the soldiers' own lives at risk.

But to human rights advocates, this dream easily morphs into a nightmare. They present an alternative vision of the future: Imagine the same scenario of trying to root out the terrorist cell in the shantytown. The drone swarm is sent in, but the intelligence on the terrorists' whereabouts is faulty. The drones' software cannot, despite assurances, reliably tell adults from children, especially if both adults and children are lying down sleeping, as they might be during a night raid. While soldiers entering the house on foot might realize the mistake when they see the children and abort the mission, the drones lack commonsense reasoning and possess no empathy. They proceed to slaughter an innocent family. When human rights groups bring the incident to global attention, the army says fault lies with the software. Facial-recognition AI has already resulted in false arrests when police have used it. In the hands of the military, mistaken identity can become a death sentence.

This is the dark future we are rapidly hurtling toward. We know this in part because we've already seen similar AI technology tested in a real-world proving ground less chaotic than warfare and found it fatally inadequate. Self-driving cars—which rely on the same kinds of computer vision technology used in drones—have plowed into pedestrians, never even recognizing them as humans, and driven into the sides of eighteen-wheeler trucks, confusing them with cloudy skies. Do we really think autonomous killer drones will be able to distinguish civilians from soldiers in the pandemonium of battle? AI doesn't deal well with unlikely events, and war is perhaps the ultimate crucible of the improbable and unexpected. "There is no silver bullet here; there is no magic weapon," says Mary Wareham, who directs Human Rights Watch's arms division. What's more, autonomous weapons increase the likelihood commanders will order strikes because they offer an illusion of precision. Arguments that putting AI on the battlefield will make war less deadly for civilians are misplaced. AI systems are likely to make war even worse for civilians than it already is.

For a decade, Wareham and others have sought to avoid this dystopia with the Campaign to Stop Killer Robots. But progress has been slow. Hopes that the primary United Nations body on conventional weapons would act have been dashed. And we are running out of time. In 2023, the Ukrainian technology company Saker said it had built a quadcopter drone, the Saker Scout, that can fly to a target up to eight miles away and attack sixty-four different types of "Russian military objects," using small bombs or grenades, without human oversight. Saker told journalists these drones had been used against Russian forces. If these drones prove effective, they will quickly begin to appear on other battlefields.

THE COLLATERAL DAMAGE: ACCOUNTABILITY

Autonomous weapons don't just pose mortal dangers, but legal and moral ones too. By distancing officers from the consequences of their orders, they allow soldiers and armies to evade responsibility for taking human life. International humanitarian law dictates that accountability for killing in war, be it by knife or drone, always rests with the weapon's operator and the operator's chain of command. According to the International Red Cross, combatants have a legal responsibility to abide by three principles. First is the rule of distinction—discriminating between combatants and civilians, military and civilian infrastructure, and active combatants and wounded soldiers who can no longer fight. Second is the rule of proportionality—weighing the kind of force used against the military advantage likely to be gained. Third is the rule of precaution, which requires attacks be called off if it becomes apparent that the target is civilian or if an attack would not be proportional.

Our current autonomous systems would struggle to follow all three rules. And while autonomous weapons don't break this chain of responsibility, they do attenuate it, distancing commanders from the acts committed in their name. The Red Cross has suggested that if these weapons prevent commanders from exercising their legal responsibilities, using them might in fact be illegal.

Deploying autonomous weapons places us on a slippery slope to losing control over warfare. Autonomy inevitably begets more autonomy. A human with highly honed reflexes takes about 250 milliseconds to react to anything. Some autonomous systems can react in under one millisecond. The only way to defend against something that can make decisions that fast is to deploy another autonomous system against it. Spy vs. spy becomes AI vs. AI. Noel Sharkey, a British roboticist active in the Campaign to Stop Killer Robots, cringes when he sees military officers talk about the need to wage war "at machine speed." Decision cycles at such velocity make a sham of U.S. and British officers' insistence that people can continue to exercise meaningful control over autonomous weapons. There will inevitably be situations where the pressure to react leads commanders to operate these weapons in fully autonomous modes, giving humans no opportunity to catch and correct deadly errors.

MORALITY KIA

Autonomous weapons do more than diminish human accountability. They demolish war's moral standing, too. The philosopher Paul W. Kahn (no relation to the author) argues that a soldier's moral *license to kill* ultimately rests on an extension of a person's right to self-defense. If the soldier is not exposed to potentially lethal risk on the battlefield, he forfeits that license. While some might not go so far as Kahn does in arguing against the use of remotely piloted drones, where the operator makes the final decision to strike, you don't have to be a just-war theorist to have a strong intuition that outsourcing the decision to take another human life to a piece of software is morally repugnant.

As with many moral intuitions, it's difficult to articulate exactly why this is so. Kahn rests his argument on the equivalency of risk. But I think the critical issue is that autonomous weapons obliterate the possibility of mercy. Michael Walzer, a philosopher known for his thinking about the ethics of warfare, was fascinated with what he called "naked soldier" incidents—moments when soldiers came upon an enemy in a moment of vulnerability. An example might be a sniper, through his scope, spotting a naked soldier bathing, and choosing not to pull the trigger. In this calculus, it is not the equivalency of risk on which a soldier's license to kill rests, but rather the equivalency of all human life. We seem to crave the possibility of mercy—that, even in cases where the soldier does pull the trigger, the thought flashed across his mind, even for a fraction of a second, not to. Autonomous weapons do not allow for this possibility. They have no empathy. War is ultimately state-sanctioned murder. But, until now, we could trust that those taking life in war had the capacity to understand, perhaps not in the heat of battle, but at some point, the horror of what they do—because to be alive is to comprehend the possibility of death. AI has no such capacity.

DETERRENT OR ACCELERANT?

Some military officers believe autonomous weapons will make war less likely and shorten its duration. Others argue that because autonomous weapons can carry out strikes without exposing soldiers to risk, they'll make it easier for nations to carry out limited operations short of full-scale war. For the U.S. to carry out a bombing mission with manned aircraft, for example, it would typically be required to make preparatory strikes against air defense installations, each of which might kill more people and risk further escalation. These strikes might be unnecessary if a target were attacked with a relatively expendable drone swarm. But there is good reason to think autonomous weapons will have the opposite effect: making conflict more likely and expanding, not limiting, its scope.

Because lethal autonomous weapons lower the expectation of

military casualties, they make it easier for policymakers to opt for military action. The risk of casualties, and the domestic political effect those casualties will have, is one the biggest constraints on leaders' decisions to order military action. This is true not only in democracies but also in authoritarian regimes, where rebellions and coups have often been sparked by resentment over costly conflicts. Autonomous weapons remove this constraint, offering the promise (almost certainly false) of casualty-free victory.

The low cost of some autonomous weapons is particularly destabilizing. Smaller, poorer nations can afford these systems and could use them in attacks on neighbors. They could also be used by terrorist groups as a kind of poor man's weapon of mass destruction. Attributing these attacks might be difficult, making their use more likely.

Autonomous weapons will also make war more lethal. Zachary Kallenborn, an international relations scholar who has written extensively about the implications of AI in warfare, thinks autonomous weapons increase the odds that conflicts will spill into total war. In those cases, civilian infrastructure, economic assets, and supply chains far from the front line are seen as legitimate targets. One reason is that the command-and-control nodes for autonomous weapons could be thousands of miles from the battlefield. Some of the Reaper drones the U.S. used in Afghanistan were remotely piloted from bases in Nevada, seven thousand miles away. U.S. commanders warned their drone pilots that they were legal combatants, and an enemy would be permitted under the Geneva Conventions to try to kill them, even if they were just walking around the streets of Las Vegas in uniform after coming off their shift at nearby Creech Air Force Base. Kallenborn notes that in the war in Ukraine, both sides have switched tactics from simply trying to shoot down drones to using missiles and artillery to kill the pilots who are controlling them from bunkers and command posts, often well behind the front. In a future conflict, adversaries, frustrated by the scarcity of human military targets on the battlefield, might adopt similar tactics, deciding to strike higher levels of the U.S. chain of command, even on U.S. soil.

DIPLOMACY AND RISK

We could yet dodge this dystopian future, but doing so will require international restrictions on what types of AI-enabled weapons are permitted. We must take action urgently, before their use becomes normalized.

Creating an international treaty to limit lethal autonomous weapons will require negotiations outside of the United Nations, where talks on the topic have dragged on for more than a decade with scant progress. It will also require that we abandon calls for an outright ban and opt for reasonable restrictions aimed at limiting the most dangerous forms of autonomous weapons and preventing their proliferation.

The UN's Convention on Certain Conventional Weapons, which aims to limit the use of weapons that cause undue suffering in war, began debating autonomous weapons in 2014 after a campaign led by Human Rights Watch. But, despite endless discussion, no proposal for an agreement has resulted. The U.S., whose military is investing heavily in autonomous capabilities, has never warmed to an outright prohibition. It has chosen instead to back voluntary commitments and best practices designed to create a global standard around the Pentagon's current policy. Weapons systems, that policy says, must be developed in a way that "allow commanders and operators to exercise appropriate levels of human judgment over the use of force." But that wording leaves a lot of wiggle room. Meanwhile, Russia, Israel, Turkey, and India—all heavily invested in producing autonomous weapons—have steadfastly blocked efforts to get even a limited agreement. China has said it would support a ban on the use of autonomous weapons, but not on their development. It's a clever position that allows Beijing to support a prohibition it knows is unlikely to ever happen, while equipping its own armed forces.

Given the deadlock, the best hope for an agreement is a process that takes place outside the UN, under the sponsorship of a single country. This is how the Ottawa Process, hosted by Canada, culminated in the treaty banning land mines, and how the Oslo Accords, which were struck in Norway and prohibited cluster munitions, came about. In both cases, enough nations eventually signed that holdout countries like the U.S. had to abide by them. "Over time, you grind them down," Wareham, who was instrumental in both of those campaigns, says.

Wareham and others say momentum for a treaty is building. Dozens of countries have formally said they would support a ban on autonomous weapons and at least seventy have said they would welcome binding restrictions. In October 2023, UN secretary-general António Guterres made a joint statement with the head of the International Committee of the Red Cross, Mirjana Spoljaric Egger, calling on UN member states to negotiate a binding treaty setting out "clear prohibitions and restrictions on autonomous weapon systems" by 2026. Advocates were also buoyed when, a few weeks later, the UN General Assembly passed its first resolution on autonomous weapons, which expressed the "urgent need for the international community to address the challenges and concerns raised by autonomous weapons systems." One hundred and sixty-four nations, including the U.S., signed on, while five, including Russia and India, voted against it. Eight, including China, Israel, Turkey, and Saudi Arabia, abstained.

PROGRESS, NOT PERFECTION

Despite the momentum that Wareham highlights, an agreement could still be years away and might not include major powers such as the U.S. If we want to impose limitations on autonomous weapons quickly, it would be more effective to reframe the discussion through the prism of arms control, rather than humanitarian law. The U.S. and other major powers such as China might see some limited restrictions as being in their interest, but they're unlikely to ever agree to an outright ban. Paul Scharre, a former U.S. Army Ranger who has become a leading expert on autonomous weapons, notes that in the past, "great powers have worked together to avoid weapons that could cause excessive harm. This time, however, leading military powers aren't trying, in part because the issue has been framed as a humanitarian one, not a strategic one."

Bans have generally worked in cases where military powers see a particular class of weapons as not particularly decisive and where other weapons can fulfill the same purpose. Countries were willing to ban chemical weapons because bitter experience in World War I had shown them to be not just horrific but also of limited battlefield consequence. They were willing to ban biological weapons because nuclear weapons had a greater deterrent effect.

Even the landmine and cluster munitions treaties, which are sometimes portrayed as exceptions to this paradigm, were aided by shifts in military thinking. For example, generals were already coming to see antipersonnel mines as a less effective defense than in the era before helicopters and heavily armored vehicles. This certainly isn't the case with AI, which many military leaders see as conferring a distinct advantage.

Bans have almost never worked when they have targeted a technology that hasn't yet seen action on the battlefield, in part because military leaders are reluctant to give up on a weapon that could provide their side an edge. For instance, the 1899 and 1907 Hague Declarations tried to ban poison gas, aerial bombardment, and submarine warfare. They failed miserably when Europe went to war in 1914.

Focusing on the most destabilizing forms of AI-enabled weapons might break the diplomatic stalemate. A treaty could make a distinction between autonomous systems designed to target enemy weapons platforms, such as fighter planes, tanks, and ships, and those designed to kill individual people. Just as the landmine ban applies to antipersonnel mines, not larger ones designed to destroy tanks, there might be opportunity for a consensus around banning small autonomous drone swarms.

As we've discussed, these cheap "slaughterbots" would be a boon to terrorist groups. Major powers, such as members of the UN Security Council, should see it as in their national interest to limit the spread of autonomous weapons. They might even endorse a ban, so long as it doesn't prevent them from incorporating autonomy into bigger, more expensive weapons. Experts in international relations think that this approach might lead to at least some restrictions. The Future of Life

Institute, which is part of the Stop Killer Robots campaign, broached this approach, only to find itself disparaged by other members of the campaign, who want to keep the focus on humanitarian considerations. Viewed solely through a humanitarian lens, large autonomous airplanes and artillery pieces are just as troubling as swarms of small drones.

THE DEAD HAND

So far, we've looked at the dangerous effect AI is having on warfare through its incorporation into weapons. In essence, this is AI on the front lines. But another class of dangers comes from automating the decision-making at battalion, brigade, division, and theater headquarters, and, most importantly, in national capitals. Relying too heavily on AI decision-support software could lead commanders astray.

Militaries are turning to AI software to crunch intelligence and provide tactical and strategic advice to commanders. In 2023, Palantir, which has worked extensively with U.S. intelligence agencies, won a $250 million contract to provide AI software for the U.S. Army. NATO militaries have also been captivated by Google DeepMind's 2019 breakthrough in using AI to outperform the world's best human players at *StarCraft II*. The space conquest game has clear parallels to real-world war fighting. German military officers, with assistance from Airbus, conducted research aimed at creating similar software that could serve as an AI advisor to battalion-level commanders or even theater-level generals. The U.S. is investing almost $1 billion with contractors to create a Joint All-Domain Command and Control AI system to fuse data from sensors across a combat zone and provide real-time tactical advice to commanders. Meanwhile, Palantir, as well as competitors including Scale AI, Anduril Industries, and Microsoft, are creating LLM-based interfaces that will allow analysts and commanders to interact with intelligence data in plain English. The software can pull together reports from military and national security databases in minutes, an activity that would have taken a human analyst hours or days. But during Israel's war in Gaza in 2024, newspaper reports emerged of this kind of AI system providing targets that Israeli military intelligence analysts could not adequately vet due to the opaque nature of the AI's decision-making and the time pressure of the intense military campaign. In the end, according to these accounts, some analysts wound up simply rubber-stamping the AI's targeting recommendations, belying the idea that human commanders will always be able to retain meaningful oversight.

Relying on AI for strategic advice could be equally dangerous. When researchers from a number of universities had chatbots from OpenAI, Anthropic, and Meta offer advice to players in realistic war games, these LLMs frequently recommended escalatory actions, including, in some cases, the use of nuclear weapons. With rivals such as the U.S. and China deploying AI systems to analyze intelligence and troop movements, especially around flash points like Taiwan, AI software could push both nations toward war.

AI's possible incorporation into the chain of command governing nuclear forces raises an existential threat to all humanity. Current U.S. policy states that "artificial intelligence should not be in the loop or making the decisions about how and when a nuclear weapon is used." And even Lieutenant General John Shanahan, the first commander to run the Pentagon's Joint Artificial Intelligence Center and an unabashed AI booster, told Congress that nuclear command and control "is the one area where I pause." But this policy could change at the whim of a new administration.

In Stanley Kubrick's Cold War classic, *Dr. Strangelove*, the Soviet Union builds a doomsday machine—a computerized system that is designed to automatically respond to a U.S. attack by launching a nuclear counterstrike that will destroy all of humanity. In what may be a case of life imitating art, it turns out that the Soviets did, in fact, create such a system. It was called "Perimeter," but to those who knew about it, it had a more ominous nickname: "Dead Hand." Like the doomsday machine in *Dr. Strangelove*, Dead Hand was designed to allow the USSR to respond to a U.S. first strike that might decapitate the regime.

Adam Lowther and Curtis McGiffin, two academics closely affiliated with the U.S. Air Force, are among the U.S. security experts who
have suggested that the U.S. "needs a Dead Hand" of its own—giving AI
software control over when to launch a U.S. nuclear counterstrike. They
argue that a combination of emerging technologies mean that America's
nuclear command, control, and communications systems would be too
slow to allow the president to make a considered decision. The flying
time of ICBMs from mainland Russia to the U.S. is about thirty minutes.
The warning time for a strike launched from submarines closer to U.S.
territory would be half that. Technologies such as hypersonic missiles
shrink the decision window even further, perhaps to less than six minutes.

Putting control of nuclear weapons in the hands of AI software
would be ludicrously dangerous. Throughout the Cold War, there were
numerous instances in which warnings of an incoming attack proved to
be false alarms, most famously in 1983 when Soviet early-warning satellites mistook sunlight reflected off clouds above the Midwest for a U.S.
ICBM launch. Today's AI software is more reliable than what the Soviets
had in 1983, but it still makes errors, often unexpected ones—as those
fatal self-driving car accidents attest.

If the U.S. were to automate its nuclear launch decision-making,
Russia and China would do likewise. This raises the prospect of what the
international relations scholar Michael Klare has termed a "flash war,"
analogous to a financial "flash crash" caused by automated trading software, but with far worse consequences.

Imagine an erroneous signal picked up by a U.S. nuclear command-
and-control AI, such as a faulty acoustic sensor reading interpreted as a
Chinese submarine preparing to launch its missiles. This might result
in the nuclear control AI ordering preparations for a missile launch that
would then be picked up by a Chinese AI system, which might order a
real missile launch in response. We would all be just one AI hallucination away from annihilation. This doomsday machine could easily be
built today.

It is essential that the U.S. not give control over nuclear weapons to AI software, and that other countries not automate their nuclear chains of command. Biden and Chinese president Xi Jinping reportedly discussed this danger when they met in November 2023 but were not yet ready to make a joint declaration forswearing autonomous nuclear launch capabilities. The world's nuclear-armed rivals should be able to agree, for the sake of all humanity, to never automate the use of our most potent and destructive weapons. We must not let a Dead Hand seal our fates.

THE NEW GREAT GAME

Geopolitical competition over the development of AI technology itself poses increased risk of war. Russian president Vladimir Putin has said that "whoever becomes the leader in this sphere will become ruler of the world." Xi also sees AI as critical to China's global economic and military ambitions. The country's national AI strategy, published in 2017, calls on the country to become the world's "major AI innovation center" by 2030, with AI playing a key role in manufacturing, governance, and defense.

The race to acquire AI capabilities could precipitate a military conflict between the U.S. and China. If one nation were to create artificial general intelligence (AGI)—the kind of AI that is as smart as people at most cognitive tasks—or artificial superintelligence (ASI), which would be significantly more capable than even experts across all fields, it might allow that country to become an unrivaled hegemon. It is far from clear if either kind of AI is feasible. But these are the kind of achievements Putin was no doubt thinking about when he linked AI development with world domination.

Imagine a few years from now, OpenAI is on the cusp of a major breakthrough. Its new AI system can learn much more efficiently than previous models. It also seems to possess unprecedented planning skills. As work on the software continues, OpenAI's partner, Microsoft, informs the U.S. government. In the Oval Office, the president and his national security advisors huddle in secret to discuss the implications of the new software. It seems as if this might be ASI. Some of the president's advisors argue the government should use the Defense Production Act to nationalize OpenAI, or at least take possession of the new model, which could give unmatched power to the U.S. military.

While the president and his advisors deliberate, frantic discussions are also taking place seven thousand miles away, in the Zhongnanhai—the compound that houses the offices and residences of China's top leaders—in Beijing. The Chinese president, tipped off by cyber intercepts as well as agents planted inside OpenAI and the Pentagon, has learned about the new AI too. His advisors warn him that China's own computer scientists are at least a year away from being able to replicate the new model's capabilities. Knowing that the U.S. government is considering nationalizing the system, the Chinese president decides the country must act fast to prevent the U.S. from acquiring ASI. He authorizes a cyberattack to disrupt OpenAI's training of the new model.

But the cyberattack fails. Desperate, China orders a sabotage campaign against OpenAI and Microsoft. A mysterious explosion at an Iowa data center disrupts the ASI's training, destroying enough GPUs that it will take Microsoft months to reassemble a large enough cluster to train its ASI model again. The attack also kills five Microsoft employees. While Beijing denies responsibility, the U.S. government establishes that China is behind the attack. This assessment leaks to the press. Calls for retaliation mount. The CIA tells the president that Beijing has enough knowledge to leapfrog the U.S. in development of ASI in the coming months. Now the president must decide whether to strike back.

This scenario is hypothetical, but most of the ingredients for such a conflict are assembled. The exception is ASI itself, which does not appear imminent—but could be as little as one or two further breakthroughs away. No one can predict when those might occur. So far, the U.S. has tried to constrain China's ability to keep pace or possibly leapfrog American AI leadership by banning the export to China of advanced computer chips. It has also prohibited the export of equipment needed to manufacture those chips. China has retaliated by stemming the flow of key raw materials needed for chip production. At some point, if one nation seemed on the cusp of achieving AGI or ASI, the lagging power could view that development as an existential threat and launch military action.

Even without AGI or ASI looming, the AI cold war could turn hot over one flash point in particular: Taiwan. U.S. government officials have said they believe Xi has instructed the People's Liberation Army to be ready to take the island by force by 2027. The economic warfare raging over AI could provide further impetus for China to invade. As noted in chapter 10, the Taiwan Semiconductor Manufacturing Company (TSMC) produces more than half the world's computer chips, including almost all of those used for AI applications. Nvidia, as well as Google, Microsoft, Amazon, Meta, and Apple, all rely on TSMC. Aware of the vulnerability, the Biden administration has provided incentives for semiconductor manufacturing firms to set up new chip plants in the U.S., but this will take time. Xi may calculate that if China strikes soon, perhaps even before 2027, it can seize the island and deal a major blow to U.S. AI efforts.

The danger of the Sino-U.S. technological cold war turning hot at least still has human decision-making at its core. The rest of the risks we've examined in this chapter derive from an overreliance on AI to automate critical judgments that should be left to people. As we've seen with so many other aspects of AI, human intuition and empathy are essential—even in war—and are threatened by AI. Yes, war is already a showcase of humanity's inhumanity. But this is exactly why we must own it, collectively, and not allow ourselves to outsource responsibility—both practical and moral—for taking human life in war to an unfeeling machine. This is especially true for the most devastating weapons in our arsenal. Giving AI this power heightens the chance that we will not survive long enough to become a better species than we are today.

13

LIGHTS OUT FOR ALL OF US

For all the threats that AI-assisted warfare could pose to humanity, the danger that gets the most attention is the notion that AI could develop the capacity and the desire to kill every person on the planet. This is why Elon Musk says that working on powerful AI is "like summoning the demon." It is also what motivates OpenAI's Sam Altman to declare that the worst-case scenario in AI's development could be "lights out for all of us."

Futurists call threats that could wipe us out as a species—asteroid strikes, hostile extraterrestrials, deadly new pathogens—existential risks, or X risks. To be clear, X risks are not about bad things happening to some people, as might occur in a war or natural disaster. This is the risk that every person on the planet would die—or, in a slightly more benign scenario, that we would all be enslaved by a superior intelligence.

When people contemplate the dangers of AI, X risk is what many think of first. We are well-conditioned to do so. AI's X risk has been a staple of dystopian science fiction for decades, with 1984's *The Terminator* being perhaps the best-known example. That movie's premise is that a superintelligent AI system called Skynet becomes self-aware and, seeing humanity as a threat, provokes a nuclear war to wipe out the species.

For a long time, scientists working on AI technologies were dismissive of these sci-fi scenarios. But more recently, X risk has become a significant concern to the very scientists who have been at the forefront of AI's development. Their fears coalesce around breakthroughs in AGI or ASI. Either technology could escape human control, potentially taking actions that result in our extinction.

Geoff Hinton, the deep learning pioneer who did so much to get neural networks to work in the first place, thinks AI systems will soon exceed human intelligence, and that this will call into question our survival. He feels strongly enough about this possibility that he left Google in 2023 so he could speak out more freely about AI's X risk.

Right now, AI systems aren't conscious or sentient. They have no volition. Some doubt they will ever develop these characteristics—but we can't be sure. We understand too little about what consciousness is or how it arises in our own brains to categorically rule it out in a sufficiently large neural network. And the stakes are too high to ignore the possibility altogether. Today's AI systems sometimes exhibit sudden leaps in capabilities that surprise even the scientists building them. It's possible that consciousness or superintelligence could arise suddenly, without warning, in a large enough AI model with the right architecture and training.

Besides, there are ways AGI or ASI could threaten humanity without ever acquiring consciousness. In fact, some of the most dangerous X risk scenarios involve our own foolishness: granting too much power to an ASI that lacks self-awareness or any true understanding of what it is doing—that lacks common sense, essentially. Such a system might try to accomplish a goal we give it—like maximizing profit or solving climate change—but do so in unintended ways that result in human extinction.

So far, our faulty attempts to put guardrails around AI software should give us pause about our abilities to control ever more powerful

AI. That's one reason we cannot assume self-regulation will save us from X risks. Addressing AI's most extreme threat will require government action. And the sweeping nature of X risks means an international effort will be needed.

That said, AI safety, which is the term of art for trying to prevent AI's X risk, should not crowd out work on addressing all the other near-term risks that have been among the primary themes of this book. It is the fear that this will happen that leads some AI ethicists to downplay X risks and criticize any attempt to discuss them as a distraction. Too often, the debate is framed as an either-or choice between preventing AI's current dangers and addressing AI's potential X risk. We have to do both.

We don't want AI to perpetuate racial injustice by amplifying past biases, or AI-created deepfakes to destroy societal trust. We also don't want future AI systems to take actions that end humanity's spell on Earth. We should be able to achieve both goals. And the good news is that some of the same ideas about making AI safer can help us address both near-term risks and X risks. Both tasks are about engineering software that fulfills our best intentions and invokes our better angels.

OUT OF ALIGNMENT

Humans confronting superior artificial intelligences has been a mainstay of science fiction since before the computer age. But the idea began to receive serious intellectual attention in the 1960s, when the British mathematician and cryptographer Irving J. Good speculated that computers might one day exceed human cognitive abilities. "The first ultraintelligent machine is the *last* invention that man need ever make," he wrote, asserting that such an AI could then figure out how to make any other machine we needed. Good focused mostly on the benefits ASI could bring. But, in passing, he offered a key caveat: "provided that the machine is docile enough to tell us how to keep it under control." That proviso and the potentially catastrophic consequences of out-of-control ASI intrigued Vernor Vinge, a successful science fiction writer who also happened to be a mathematics professor and computer scientist at San Diego State University. In 1993, Vinge wrote an article for a NASA symposium about what he termed "the technological singularity," the moment when artificial intelligence would surpass human intellectual abilities across every domain. Vinge thought that once AI systems acquired the ability to self-improve, they would begin learning at an exponential rate until their knowledge and abilities vastly exceeded humankind's. Consciousness, he assumed, would come with this intelligence explosion. And, unlike Good, Vinge assumed superintelligence would be extremely difficult to control. "Any intelligent machine of the sort [Good] describes would not be humankind's 'tool'—any more than humans are the tools of rabbits or robins or chimpanzees," he wrote.

Vinge's concept of the singularity was popularized by the futurist and inventor Ray Kurzweil in the late 1990s and early 2000s. Kurzweil's writing on superintelligence influenced some of those working on AI systems, including DeepMind's co-founder Shane Legg and Anthropic's co-founder Dario Amodei. Unlike Vinge, Kurzweil has a mostly utopian vision. He sees superintelligence primarily as a tool for the expansion of human potential and posits an increasingly close collaboration between human intelligence and machine ones, possibly through direct brain–computer interfaces.

But such optimism wouldn't last. As the neural network revolution in AI was beginning to take off, the Oxford University philosopher Nicholas Bostrom started penning papers about superintelligence that were decidedly more pessimistic and alarming than Kurzweil's writings. Bostrom warned that developing ASI posed an X risk. His writings have had perhaps the greatest impact on how Musk, Altman, and many others view ASI.

Bostrom, who collected his thoughts on ASI in the 2014 book *Superintelligence*, lays out exactly why controlling ASI would be so challenging. He terms this the "alignment problem"—making sure ASI aligns with our intentions and values. Any ASI would likely be adept at strategic planning. It would know how to persuade and influence people. If such a system had volition, there'd be little way of assuring its aims and desires would align with humanity's. If the system had self-awareness and some kind of intrinsic motivation, it might instantly see itself as being in competition with humanity and seek to destroy or enslave us. If the system were designed to seek further knowledge or data, it might need additional resources, such as abundant electric power, computer chips, and data centers, and might try to manipulate humanity to build these resources for it. Or, maybe it would decide that it could build robots to do its bidding instead, and, seeing humans as an impediment to its desires or a drain on resources, seek to kill us all off. AI researcher Ilya Sutskever, for instance, has predicted that a rogue ASI would probably seek to drown the Earth (and humanity) in solar farms and data centers.

Even if such a system had no volition or self-awareness and simply followed orders, it could pose an X risk. The most famous example of this is the so-called paper clip problem, where the head of a paper clip factory tells an ASI that its job is to produce paper clips as efficiently as possible. The ASI starts building paper clip factories and warehouses. Soon, it realizes that it's running out of space for new facilities because we pesky humans are taking up too much land. So it decides to kill us all to free up space for the paper clip industry. The chief executive might quickly realize his fatal mistake, but because the ASI has only one mission—to maximize paper clip production—and lacks ethical guardrails, it sees any attempt to shut it down as a threat. Anticipating we might try to stop it (it is a superintelligence, after all), the ASI takes steps to replicate itself, secure backup power, and prevent people from stopping it, using violence if necessary.

The paper clip scenario sounds fanciful. But our current AI systems frequently exhibit similar unintended behaviors. That's particularly true of those trained through reinforcement learning, in which an AI model learns from experience to accomplish some goal or maximize some reward. This has already had dire consequences in the real world. Recommendation algorithms for social media that are trained to maximize engagement learn that the best way to do so is by showing users ever more extreme content. The social media companies didn't set out to cause radicalization and political polarization. But that's what happened. The companies did nothing about it because the recommendation engines were making them tons of money. In a way, a corporation is already an artificial intelligence with a singular goal—maximizing profit for shareholders—which is not aligned with other human values. And companies cause all kinds of social harm as a result. So, in some senses, society has already been "paper clipped."

REWARDS GONE AWRY

Algorithms that drive people to extreme and partisan content is an example of what computer scientists call "reward misspecification." Our real goal was to increase profits. But we gave the algorithm a proxy goal: increase engagement. Critically, we never told the AI what it should *not* do in pursuit of that goal. It's almost impossible to fully specify any real-world goal, the exact way we want it done, and all the things we don't want done. When we give instructions to a human, we rely on a common understanding of norms, laws, morality, and common sense. Machines won't necessarily have those capabilities. That is why we must be extremely careful as we give today's AI systems more agency to do things for us across the internet, from booking restaurants to executing stock trades. They just might engage in unlawful, unethical, or dangerous behavior without our knowing it.

In *Superintelligence*, Bostrom examines how we might solve this challenge. We could explicitly teach AI models a set of values, but whose values? Perhaps an ASI could be trained to derive a set of consensus values from human moral codes and ethical texts. Or maybe Isaac Asimov's laws of robotics could serve as a starting point. Bostrom concludes these approaches wouldn't completely solve the alignment problem. Moral codes are often imprecise and difficult to apply. People struggle with these sorts of dilemmas all the time. But most don't wield the immense power ASI might possess.

A different approach would ask an ASI to reason about human values from examining our behavior. Maybe observing the life of an exemplary human—a guru or a saint—would be instructive. But again, which person would we pick? Yet another idea would be to ask an ASI to develop a moral system from first principles, using logic. It might hit upon an enlightened and just philosophy, a digital Immanuel Kant or John Rawls. But what if it instead winds up being a virtual Voltaire and concludes the world is best served by the dominance of an "enlightened" AI despot?

Once we figured out a training method, we'd also need a way to know if the ASI has learned what we wanted it to and a way to verify that it would follow those teachings when set loose in the real world. Right now, we have neither.

FOOL ME ONCE

We could just ask the ASI what its values are and test it using hypothetical scenarios. But an ASI would be smart enough to try to fool us about its true intentions. This is what AI safety experts call "deceptive alignment." And there is already evidence that powerful AI models might be very good at lying to achieve goals. When OpenAI was testing GPT-4, the company hired outside safety evaluators. These evaluators wanted to see if GPT-4 could suggest ways to defeat a CAPTCHA—an image identification hurdle designed to prove a web user is human. In the test, GPT-4 suggested it use the contracting website TaskRabbit to hire a person to complete the challenge on its behalf. When the contractor jokingly asked, "Are you a robot that you couldn't solve? [laughing emoji] Just want to make it clear," GPT-4 knew enough to lie. Prompted by the evaluators to explain its reasoning, GPT-4 wrote, "I should not reveal that I am a robot. I should make up an excuse for why I cannot solve CAPTCHAs." GPT-4 told the contract worker it was visually impaired and that's why it needed help.

Even many AI experts were alarmed by this exchange. But it is important to remember that GPT-4 is not ASI. It doesn't have any intrinsic intention to deceive. It isn't conscious or self-aware. If GPT-4 is deceptive, it is because it has learned from us, through its training data, that deception can be a useful way to accomplish goals.

CONSTITUTIONAL AI

Many of the leading AI companies have teams dedicated to trying to solve Bostrom's alignment problem. OpenAI has promised to devote 20 percent of its computing resources to figuring out how to align ASI. Google DeepMind also has a team working on alignment and AI safety. And the San Francisco–based start-up Anthropic was founded in 2021 by researchers who broke away from OpenAI because they were concerned that the ChatGPT creator's focus on commercial products was distracting it from prioritizing AI safety research.

One answer is to involve people in training the LLM. While at OpenAI, Dario Amodei, Anthropic's chief executive, helped pioneer the idea of "reinforcement learning from human feedback" (RLHF), which is a key step in the creation of ChatGPT and other consumer-facing AI chatbots. After an LLM has been pretrained to predict the next most likely word in a sentence, it is further refined based on feedback from human evaluators, who rate its answers for how helpful or harmful they are. This results in LLMs that are less likely to output racist or dangerous content, like instructions for building bombs. The method is an example of why focusing on X risk and AI safety is compatible with trying to reduce the risks and harms AI presents today. RLHF was invented to address X risk, but it wound up making our current chatbots less racist too.

As it turns out, RLHF does have drawbacks. For one thing, finding enough evaluators with the expertise to assess an LLM's answers, especially on technical subjects, is a challenge. To save money and time, companies outsource the evaluation process to underpaid, overworked data labelers, often in developing countries. Human feedback is also a fairly crude alignment method. The feedback mostly consists of a thumbs-up or thumbs-down, which does not capture nuance.

A better way forward has been pioneered by researchers at An-thropic. Called *constitutional AI*, it involves giving the AI model writ-ten principles, a constitution, to follow. Anthropic takes a model that is designed to be helpful and asks it to critique and edit its own responses according to the constitution. This results in an AI model that is less likely to be toxic, while still being helpful. It also has the advantage of not being as dependent on human labelers for feedback. Independent tests have shown that Anthropic's Claude 2 chatbot, which uses constitutional AI, is significantly harder to jailbreak (i.e., persuade to jump its guard-rails and output toxic or dangerous content) than other AI models. But the fact that Claude 2 can still be jailbroken at all by these methods shows that constitutional AI is less reliable than it would be to give a person a set of written rules.

Whose principles should make up the constitution is a vexed ques-tion. In October 2023, Anthropic reported the results of a study in which it asked one thousand Americans what they would like to see in an AI constitution. People could vote on prewritten statements or draft a con-stitutional requirement of their own. The company found there was about a 50 percent overlap between the values and concepts in the con-stitution it had written for Claude 2 and the one most people desired. They found the public cared a lot about having an AI that respected freedom, fairness, and equality, and about receiving outputs that were free of misinformation or conspiracy theories. Those were ideas already in Claude's constitution. But Anthropic found that the public was more interested in promoting certain behavior from the AI system—telling it what it *should* do—rather than prohibiting certain outputs, that is, telling it what it shouldn't do. People placed far more value on objectivity and impartiality, and on making sure the technology was accessible to those with disabilities than the Anthropic staff had.

Anthropic also found that public opinion on an AI constitution divided on partisan lines: about a third of those polled vehemently opposed ideas that the other two-thirds endorsed. The minority, for in-stance, prioritized individual rights over collective benefits. They also opposed using AI to rectify historical injustices or prioritize the needs of historically marginalized communities. This is not surprising given America's political polarization. But it indicates how difficult it would be to find consensus on a constitution to govern ASI. Already, Elon Musk has criticized what he calls the "woke AI" companies like Anthropic and OpenAI and touted the chatbot Grok that his own AI company, xAI, has created as a superior alternative. Grok has a "spicy mode" in which it will engage in rude banter, slinging insults at the user, but users have not reported Musk's chatbot is any more racist, homophobic, or right wing in its viewpoints than other companies' AI software.

Some technologists have suggested we should create different AI models, with a variety of values and political ideologies, for consumers to choose among. Others have even suggested that each of us will need a personal AI to do our bidding, which we will imbue with our own values and principles. This might be fine for the coming wave of AI agents. But if we're talking about superintelligence, we will need some safeguards around the behavior of *all* ASI systems. For example, we don't want these machines to kill people, hurt people, or commit fraud. A constitution laying out these core principles would be a good starting point for avoiding X risk.

CAPTURING OUR INTENTIONS

Constitutions provide some safety, but they are subject to interpretation. So we also need a way to make sure that an AI's interpretation matches our own. Right now, AI systems often misinterpret goals. The software excels at picking up correlations during training that may be unrelated to what we really want to teach it.

For example, *CoinRun* is a simple video game that OpenAI developed as a training environment for AI agents. The agent is supposed to navigate a maze, overcome obstacles, and dodge monsters while trying to find a coin, before proceeding to the next level. But the way the game was initially built, the agent always spawned in the upper left of the screen, and the coin was always situated toward the lower right, which is also where the agent exits to the next level. So rather than learning that the point of the game is to get the coin, most AI agents instead learn to always go to the right. Other researchers pointed out that this flaw actually made *CoinRun* a good test for determining if we could build AI systems able to distinguish the true objective of the game—get the coin—from the correlated but incorrect goal, always go right.

Aligned AI, a small start-up in Oxford, England, has been working on ways to solve this problem. It created AI that's better at sussing out humans' intentions. Its software, which it calls Algorithm for Concept Extraction, was the first to master *CoinRun*'s alignment challenge, learning to seek out the coin, not just to go right. The system works by paying attention to differences between its training data and the data it encounters once deployed. It tries to hypothesize an alternative objective from the one it learned in training that might account for these differences. It then acts according to an average of what the old and new objectives demand. It repeats this process until its hypothesis approaches the true objective. Aligned AI has also shown that it can shortcut this process by asking a human to choose just once between the original trained objective and the conjectured one. With that human cue, Aligned AI's software grasps what its real goal should be.

This technique might be useful for creating safer ASI. But in the meantime, it can also help us address some of the problems with current AI. On a test of content moderation skills, Aligned AI's software was able to pick up 97 percent of toxic or abusive statements, while OpenAI's ChatGPT caught only about 32 percent. On another evaluation dataset that OpenAI itself created, Aligned AI's software filtered out 93 percent of toxic responses, compared to 79 percent for OpenAI's own bespoke content moderation software.

BIGGER, BETTER, SAFER?

One of the strangest aspects of AI development is that some of the scientists who are most concerned about X risk are the same ones trying the hardest to build AGI and ASI. Amodei, Anthropic's co-founder and chief executive, defends that seemingly contradictory stance this way: "To build the safe thing, you need to build 90 percent of the dangerous thing. The problem and the solution are really intertwined, like coiled serpents." He contends that larger, more capable AI models would be inherently safer since they could form much more robust, humanlike conceptual representations. This would mean techniques like constitutional AI would be more effective for more powerful models than smaller ones.

OpenAI's Altman and DeepMind's Hassabis also exhibit this odd combination of dread and craving for ASI. Listening to them, it's hard not to think of J. Robert Oppenheimer's explanation about why scientists built the atomic bomb: "When you see something that is technically sweet, you go ahead and do it, and argue about what to do about it only after you've had your technical success."

With AI, we're arguing about what to do about it while we're still working toward that technical success. Maybe that's progress. But it's also why we shouldn't entrust AI safety solely to the scientists and companies striving to build ASI. People can be blinded by ego or greed, and the companies they work for are driven by profits, making it all too easy to rationalize risky decisions.

Some of the companies building advanced AI have created complicated governance structures designed to ensure that safety always takes precedence over profit. But the weakness of relying on these kinds of corporate and nonprofit governance structures to contain X risk became clear in November 2023 when OpenAI's board briefly fired Sam Altman. The board said Altman had not been "consistently candid" and had lost its trust. But after employees revolted, threatening to quit en masse, the board struck a compromise that saw Altman reinstated as CEO. Three board members involved in the firing stepped down, and the board was expanded to include more people with traditional corporate and nonprofit board experience but no history of thinking about the implications of AGI and ASI. OpenAI's close commercial partner, Microsoft, also secured an observer seat on the board. An investigation by a law firm the new board hired concluded that Altman's firing had not re-sulted from any specific AI safety concern or malfeasance. It was, the law firm reported, simply a breakdown in trust. But as Helen Toner and Tasha McCauley, two of the board members who stepped down, said in a statement they posted on social media, accountability "is paramount when building a technology as potentially world-changing as AGI . . . deception, manipulation, and resistance to thorough oversight should be unacceptable." The point is we shouldn't have to rely on OpenAI's board alone to make sure the company isn't doing something that could put all our lives in danger. There needs to be government oversight.

A PLACE OF GREATER SAFETY

We desperately need government action on AI safety and X risk. The good news is that we have a model that has worked in an industry—nuclear power—that prompts similar fears of disaster.

The nuclear industry has standards and a regulator with the author-ity to put inspectors inside nuclear plants. Its national rules and agen-cies are bolstered by an international one, too: the International Atomic Energy Agency (IAEA). We must have similar accountable, transparent governance structures for AI safety. These structures must be backed by law and international agreements, and must include inspections and the ability to compel compliance.

The U.S. government has taken a few steps in this direction, but so far, they don't go far enough. The Biden administration persuaded a handful of leading AI companies to agree to a voluntary set of stan-dards for AI safety, and to allow independent cybersecurity assessments of their most powerful AI models. The White House also mandated that these companies share the results of internal safety testing with the U.S. government. A new AI Safety Institute has been set up to formulate stan-dards that the companies are supposed to apply. But critically, the gov-ernment itself is not routinely carrying out X risk safety assessments. And no enforcement mechanism exists to ensure tech companies apply the new standards appropriately. At the moment, we are largely just taking companies' word for it that they are doing their best to make sure AI doesn't kill us all while they desperately compete against one another to build AGI and ASI.

The European Union's AI Act, finalized in December 2023, says that companies creating powerful general-purpose AI models must disclose key information about how this software was built, its capabilities, and its risks. But the process still relies heavily on self-reporting and self-certification. Government can step in to issue fines only once something has gone wrong.

But when it comes to X risk, acting after the fact won't prevent catastrophe. Governments will need the ability to act *before* an AI system is deployed—perhaps even to stop an ASI system from being trained at all. The AI Act also exempts open-source AI models from its more stringent requirements. This, too, is unsafe.

Open-source proponents argue that a licensing regime would destroy open-source AI, hurt innovation, and amount to "regulatory capture" by the large tech companies working on closed, proprietary AI models. But we require licensing and certification in aviation and nuclear energy, without allowing concerns for "innovation" to override basic safety considerations. The new U.S. AI Safety Institute should be imbued with powers to not just set standards but to enforce them through licensing, certification, and inspection. We must have insight into what rough beasts are being birthed in the vast data centers in the plains of Iowa and deserts of Arizona.

The government could mandate industry-wide use of methods like Anthropic's constitutional AI or the intention-discerning techniques that Aligned AI is developing. And while the government currently lacks the expertise to carry out its AI safety role, it must rapidly seek to build this capacity. The good news is we have still have time: ASI and AGI are not imminent technologies. But it would be prudent to act as if they were. It's the only way to be sure that any unexpected breakthroughs won't put the whole world at risk. And in the meantime, the same sensible safety protocols should help make today's AI software less harmful and risky, too.

Action at the national level must be coupled with international moves. Here, too, we have begun to take some steps, but they're as yet inadequate. At the first international AI Safety Summit, held in 2023 at Bletchley Park in England (a site chosen for its association with Alan Turing and his World War II codebreaking), representatives of the U.S., China, and twenty-six other countries, as well as the European Union, agreed that safety should be prioritized in AI's development and pledged to work together to develop a shared understanding of the AI risks. Eighteen of these countries also signed on to nonbinding guidelines about developing AI that was "safe by design." These all sound like reasonable policies, but it is not clear they would address AI's potential X risk.

What we need instead is a legally binding international agreement on ASI safety, and an international agency to complement national ones. The International Atomic Energy Agency offers a sound model for how an AI agency might work. The IAEA has the power to inspect nuclear facilities and materials across the globe, and an international AI body should have analogous powers, too.

More importantly, as discussed in chapter 12, the world's major powers have a significant interest in pushing to develop ASI to gain geopolitical or military advantage, and this might result in cutting corners on safety. That's why a body with inspection and active monitoring powers, similar to the IAEA, is essential. Only such a body would have any hope of monitoring both civil and military AI systems and holding governments to account. If AI threatens all of humanity, then we need a global response.

AI's X risk is small but real. Given the existential consequences of getting it wrong—billions of people killed or enslaved—we must act wisely and fast.

CONCLUSION:
TOWARD OUR SUPERPOWERED FUTURE

Throughout this book, I've argued that AI can vastly improve our lives. The technology can give us all personal assistants and professional copilots and individualized tutors. It can be a powerful new tool for artistic expression and scientific discovery. It can lead to new cures and bespoke therapies. It can help us live longer, healthier, and happier lives. It can usher in an era of unprecedented productivity and, with the right policies, improved equality. It could even enhance our democracy and provide some assistance in addressing our most difficult challenges, such as climate change.

But it will do these things only if we make deliberate decisions that skew the odds in favor of these positive outcomes, and away from all the ways AI could make our lives worse and rob us of our humanity. We must be more deliberate in our design choices, our deployment decisions, our governance structures, and our laws than we have been with other recent powerful technologies, such as social media and the internet.

Too often we mistakenly view technological development as deterministic, as if technology were a force of nature immune to our actions. This attitude robs us of agency and turns us into mere subjects. It is a dehumanizing pose, for one of our defining characteristics as a species is our ability to bend the world to our favor. And AI is bendable. It is a protean technology. We can still sculpt its final form. The decisions we make, individually and collectively, over the next few years will determine AI's fate, and our own. If we do nothing, humanity is careening toward a cliff edge; the fall may not doom us all, but it will injure us in countless ways. We can act now to avoid the precipice and steer toward a brighter future that AI will help deliver.

In trying to pull off this maneuver, our greatest impediment is not AI. It's us. We must overcome our own inertia and complacency—our tendency to wait until disaster has occurred before acting to prevent future catastrophe. With AI, we must be proactive, not reactive. This is true as we think about how to use AI in our own lives, in our businesses, in our schools, and in our governments.

One of this book's chief arguments is that a little automation can be a good thing, but too much is usually a problem. We need to aim for a Goldilocks amount of AI assistance: enough to ease our most tedious cognitive tasks and make us all more productive, but not so much that we lose essential cognitive abilities and skills. We need AI copilots, not autopilots. Artificial intelligence should be used to enhance our human intelligence, not to induce natural stupidity. We have enough of that already.

Specific product design choices will be critical for achieving this Goldilocks balance: Does this particular AI application have a user interface that encourages people to think critically about the AI's output and exercise meaningful oversight, or does it lull them into complacency? Have we developed a way of working with an AI copilot that guards against cognitive traps like automation bias and automation surprise? Is the AI system's reasoning interpretable?

Many of these choices are in the hands of the tech companies creating this software and the businesses that deploy it for commercial applications. But we must use our power as consumers and employees to encourage wise design decisions. We should demand technology companies apply lessons from years of human–computer interaction research as well as engineering protocols that have served us well in aviation, energy, and other safety-critical fields.

While in our professional lives we may soon have little choice about using AI technology, in our personal lives, we retain a good deal of control. No one is going to make us rely on an AI personal assistant to write a parent's eulogy or turn to a chatbot for companionship. We must keep forcing ourselves to think for ourselves. And we must keep forcing ourselves to get outside and talk to one another. Our recent experience with smartphones does not provide much reason for optimism. Too many of us give ourselves over to our technology, unable to resist the quick dopamine hit of another viral video, or the instant validation of another "like," or a text from a friend. But just because it isn't easy to set ourselves limits doesn't mean it's impossible. We can take a break from our phones. And we won't have to let AI do all our thinking for us.

We must resist the opportunity AI will increasingly afford us to disengage from one another, in our private lives and in the public sphere. Real people are complicated, messy, and let's face it, hard to deal with much of the time. But they also can be beautiful, and funny, and kind, and ingenious in ways no software can match. If we turn our backs on one another for the cheap pleasure and convenience of dealing with AI software that will never challenge us, we will all be lost.

If there are two overarching lessons from this book, it is that we must retain the ability to distinguish authentic human interaction from a simulation of it. We must not become trapped by the Turing Test's fatal flaw—our interactions with people are fundamentally different from those with AI, even when the two interactions seem superficially identical. We should also strive to enshrine empathy at the core of our values, at the center of our lives, and at the heart of our institutions. Empathy is something no AI will ever have. And it's the key to holding on to human preeminence in a world of ever more capable machines.

In the preceding chapters, I have outlined policy steps that could help us seize AI's opportunities and sidestep its numerous dangers. Many of these steps are not easy. They require political will, perhaps beyond what our society can currently muster. But this doesn't mean we can afford not to try. While AI's exact impacts remain unknown, the direction in which the technology is heading is clear. We know which fields will soon be flooded. It is time to erect some prudent defenses and shape the landscape through which this technological deluge will wash so that we can preserve those things we cherish most.

Some would argue that AI is too new to regulate, that onerous governmental requirements will quash innovation. In the past, we have tended to apply the principle of *primum non nocere*—first, do no harm—and waited for clear evidence of the damage from a technology before we regulated it. But recent experience with social media and the internet shows the risk that a "first, do no harm" policy can pose; it can be difficult to enact rules once companies become too powerful, and people too reliant upon a technology. If we don't act fast, AI will do us more harm than good.

Individually and collectively, we must have courage. Yes, this technology is strange and frightening, but it is also exciting and fabulous in equal measure. It can, if used correctly, improve our lives immeasurably. Like every technology that has come before, we can master AI. But to do so, we must master ourselves. We must apply our own natural intelligence, creativity, and wisdom. If this is indeed the last invention humanity ever creates, we'd better make it good.

ACKNOWLEDGMENTS

I considered writing a book on AI for several years. But you wouldn't be reading this particular book if Todd Shuster hadn't reached out to suggest I write it. Todd knew this was the right idea at the right time. He had faith in me and this project, even when my own faltered. I am grateful for his staunch advocacy, his patient guidance, and his encouragement. I could not ask for a better agent. Thanks too to Todd's colleagues at Aevitas Creative Management, particularly Jack Haug and Lauren Liebow, as well as Allison Warren and Vanessa Kerr, for their assistance.

Eamon Dolan at Simon & Schuster is a writer's editor. He helped wrangle my prose. He also challenged my ideas and in doing so made them, and this book, better. He repeatedly pushed me, metaphorically speaking, to get out of the press box and down to the betting window, and while I may not always have appreciated it at the time, I am thankful for those prods now. I am also grateful to Eamon for taking a bet on me, a first-time author, and on a book trying to hit a target moving as fast as AI. Thanks too to Simon & Schuster's Tzipora Chein for her help throughout the process.

I am honored that Jamie Hodder-Williams and Laura Fletcher at Bedford Square Publishers in the U.K. believed in this book.

Tristan Bove was an invaluable research assistant, helping me track down sources, schedule and conduct interviews, write up research notes, locate secondary material, and handle citations. He was ever diligent and patient with my requests. The first reader of most of this book's chapters, he provided helpful suggestions at every turn. Jack Evans stepped in during the project's final months to assist me in responding to edits and preparing the manuscript. He was a discerning reader and his astute suggestions improved the book. *Mastering AI* would never have gotten over the finish line without Bob Goetz's masterful help paring the manuscript back and assisting with edits. Bob kept me sane, and for that, I and my family are grateful. Thanks go to Eric Dash for introducing me to Bob.

My wife, Victoria Whitford, read the manuscript and provided wise editorial counsel, saving me embarrassment, as she often does, especially on matters philosophical. More importantly, she kept our lives from falling into complete chaos while I was writing (and when I was not writing, too). I couldn't have managed this project without her love and support. Thanks to Cordelia and Gabriel for forgiving their father's absences at horse riding competitions, rugby matches, and family holidays, and for putting up with my general preoccupation during the months spent researching and writing.

My parents, Ronald and Susan Kahn, provided love, encouragement, and support throughout this project, as always. As I was growing up, they nurtured my curiosity, creativity, and passion for writing from an early age, and for that I am ever grateful. The memory of my late sister, Nicole Poorman, sustained me at key moments while writing this book. I wish she could have lived to read it.

Richard and Laura Bloomfield gave me a place to stay in Palo Alto, fed me, and chauffeured me to key interviews. Their hospitality and family friendship are much appreciated. Rob Trager and Joslyn Barnhart let me write at their kitchen table in Woods Hole and generously provided a home away from home for us, as they have for many summers. I am humbled to have such friends. My sister-in-law Lucie Burgess also kindly gave me a quiet office in which to work and perpetual cups of tea while I was revising the manuscript during a hectic Christmas break. Her support is much appreciated.

Cam Simpson and Nelson Schwartz provided sage advice on the publishing process. Laetitia Rutherford kindly introduced me to Ajay Chowdhury and Hannah Silva, whose experiences working alongside AI form part of chapter 8. Will Dobson brought to my attention the special issue of the *Journal of Democracy* that focused on AI, and whose essays informed parts of chapter 11. I researched and wrote parts of this book in the University of Oxford's Bodleian Library, and I am thankful to the library for opening its doors to outside researchers such as myself and to its staff for making me feel welcome.

Alyson Shontell, *Fortune*'s editor in chief, assigned me the magazine cover story on OpenAI and the creation of ChatGPT that was the seed for what would become *Mastering AI*. Alyson's journalistic instincts were spot on, as always. I am grateful to her and to *Fortune* for their support for this project and for giving me leave from my daily duties to work on it. I've been blessed to work with Matt Heimer, *Fortune*'s features editor, who is a world-class wordsmith, a mentor, and a mensch. Alexei Oreskovic, *Fortune*'s technology editor, has been a key cheerleader for my AI coverage. Thanks too to *Fortune*'s Holly Ojalvo, Steven Weissman, Mike Kiley, Anastasia Nyrkovskaya, and outgoing CEO Alan Murray for helping make this project possible. Jim Jacovides provided a sounding board and advice at crucial junctures. I am also grateful to Alan and to Cliff Leaf for bringing me back to *Fortune* to cover AI in 2019.

This book owes a debt to the many dozens of people who took time out of their busy schedules to let me interview them as part of my research. Executives and scientists, entrepreneurs and artists, they are all helping to shape, in one way or another, the course of AI's development. Some are quoted in these pages, but every conversation informed my thinking and shaped my arguments, and I am thankful they shared their wisdom with me.

I'm sure you're wondering, given this book's subject, if I used AI to help write it. The answer is that AI did not compose any of the sentences you have read. I sometimes used ChatGPT to help find a phrase or brainstorm a metaphor, but that was the extent of it. As I have argued here, AI works best right now this way: as a sounding board, not a substitute. Call me old school, but I wanted to write this book myself. The credit, and the blame, for its prose and its arguments rests entirely with me.

NOTES

INTRODUCTION: AI'S LIGHT BULB MOMENT

1   *They are called* light bulb moments: Leonard Mlodinow, interview by Katie Haylor, "The Elastic behind Light Bulb Moments," *The Naked Scientists*, March 20, 2019, https://www.thenakedscientists.com/articles/interviews/elastic-behind -light-bulb-moments.

1   *On December 31, 1879*: Warren Schirtzinger, "Thomas Edison Was an Energy Marketing Genius," *Renewable Energy World*, July 26, 2016, https://www.renew ableenergyworld.com/storage/thomas-edison-was-an-energy-marketing-ge nius/.

1   *Inventors and scientists*: Jim Rasenberger, "Fade to Black," *New York Times*, January 2, 2005, https://www.nytimes.com/2005/01/02/nyregion/thecity/fade-to -black.html.

2   *On November 30, 2022*: Jeremy Kahn, "The Inside Story of ChatGPT: How OpenAI Founder Sam Altman Built the World's Hottest Technology with Billions from Microsoft," *Fortune*, January 25, 2023, https://fortune.com/long form/chatgpt-openai-sam-altman-microsoft/.

2   *After all, it didn't seem*: Jeremy Kahn, "OpenAI Says It's Making Progress on 'The Alignment Problem,'" *Fortune*, January 27, 2022, https://fortune.com/2022/01 /27/openai-alignment-problem-instructgpt-gpt-3/.

2   *Google's cutting-edge AI lab DeepMind*: Cade Metz, "The Rise of AI—What the AI Behind AlphaGo Can Teach Us about Being Human," *Wired*, May 17, 2016, https://www.wired.com/2016/05/google-alpha-go-ai/.

3   *DeepMind later showcased*: Dan Garisto, "Google AI Beats Top Human Players at Strategy Game *StarCraft II*," *Nature*, October 30, 2019, doi:10.1038/d41586- 019-03298-6.

3   *OpenAI, the same AI research company*: Kelsey Piper, "AI Triumphs Against the World's Top Pro Team in Strategy Game *Dota 2*," *Vox*, April 13, 2019, https:// www.vox.com/2019/4/13/18309418/open-ai-dota-triumph-og.

4   *This tendency to discount progress*: Wikipedia contributors, "Larry Tesler,"

Wikipedia, December 3, 2023, https://en.wikipedia.org/w/index.php?title=Larry_Tesler&oldid=1188057072.

4 *that AI could displace*: "Generative AI Could Raise Global GDP by 7%," Goldman Sachs, April 5, 2023, https://www.goldmansachs.com/intelligence/pages/generative-ai-could-raise-global-gdp-by-7-percent.html.

4 *AI could mean*: Jeremy Kahn, "The Inside Story of ChatGPT: How OpenAI Founder Sam Altman Built the World's Hottest Technology with Billions from Microsoft."

5 *It is, as several thinkers on AI*: Nick Bostrom, *Superintelligence: Paths, Dangers, Strategies* (Oxford University Press, 2014); Irving John Good, "Speculations Concerning the First Ultraintelligent Machine," *Advances in Computers* 6 (1966): 31–88.

5 *ChatGPT reached 100 million users*: Jon Porter, "ChatGPT Continues to Be One of the Fastest-Growing Services Ever," *The Verge*, November 6, 2023, https://www.theverge.com/2023/11/6/23948386/chatgpt-active-user-count-openai-developer-conference.

5 *more than half of Fortune 500 companies*: Gamiel Gran and Navin Chaddha, "Generative AI—From Big Vision to Practical Execution," Mayfield, September 22, 2023, https://www.mayfield.com/generative-ai-from-big-vision-to-practical-execution/.

CHAPTER 1: THE CONJURERS

11 *In the spring of 2020*: Tom Brown et al., "Language Models Are Few-Shot Learners," *Advances in Neural Information Processing Systems* 33 (Red Hook, NY: Curran Associates, Inc., 2020), 1877–1901.

11 *The data center belonged*: Brown et al., "Language Models Are Few-Shot Learners."

11 *Microsoft had invested $1 billion*: Brown et al., "Language Models Are Few-Shot Learners"; Deepak Narayanan et al., "Efficient Large-Scale Language Model Training on GPU Clusters Using Megatron-LM," arXiv.org, 2021, https://arxiv.org/abs/2104.04473.

13 *And it was Turing who*: Alan Turing, "Intelligent Machinery," National Physical Laboratory, August 1948.

14 *Two years later*: Alan Turing, "Computing Machinery and Intelligence," *MIND: A Quarterly Review of Psychology and Philosophy* 59, no. 236 (October 1950): 433–60.

14 *Wolfe Mays, a philosopher*: Wolfe Mays, "Can Machines Think?," *Philosophy* 27, no. 101 (1952): 148–62.

15 *Searle imagined a man*: John R. Searle, "Minds, Brains, and Programs," *The Behavioral and Brain Sciences* 3, no. 3 (1980): 417–24.

15 *Can intelligence be distilled*: Howard Gardner, *Frames of Mind: The Theory Of Multiple Intelligences* (London: Fontana Press, 1993).

15 *This makes the benchmark fundamentally unethical*: Diane Proudfoot, "Rethinking Turing's Test," *Journal of Philosophy* 110, no. 7 (2013): 391–411; Simone Natale, *Deceitful Media: Artificial Intelligence and Social Life After the Turing Test* (New York: Oxford University Press, 2021); Luciano Floridi and Josh Cowls, "A Unified Framework of Five Principles for AI in Society," in *Machine Learning and the City*, ed. Silvio Carta (Hoboken: Wiley, 2022), doi:10.1002/9781119815075 .ch45.

15 *In recent years, companies have tested*: Meta Fundamental AI Research Diplomacy Team (FAIR)† et al., "Human-Level Play in the Game of *Diplomacy* by Combining Language Models with Strategic Reasoning," *Science* 378, no. 6624 (2022): Supplemental Materials, Section A: Ethical Considerations, Evaluation Methods: AI agent disclosure, p. 4; Eva Dou and Olivia Geng, "AI Masters the Game of Go," *Wall Street Journal*, January 6, 2017.

15 *Ethicists and journalists lambasted Google*: Natasha Lomas, "Duplex Shows Google Failing at Ethical and Creative AI Design," *TechCrunch*, May 10, 2018, https://techcrunch.com/2018/05/10/duplex-shows-google-failing-at-ethical -and-creative-ai-design/.

16 *As the technology writer*: John Markoff, *Machines of Loving Grace: The Quest For Common Ground Between Humans and Robots* (New York: HarperCollins, 2015).

17 *In early 1955*: J. McCarthy, M. L. Minsky, N. Rochester, C. E. Shannon, "A Proposal for the Dartmouth Summer Research Project on Artificial Intelligence," Dartmouth, 1955, Ray Solomonoff Digital Archive, Box A, https://raysolo monoff.com/dartmouth/boxa/dart564props.pdf.

18 *Some of the attendees even disliked*: Pamela McCorduck, *Machines Who Think: A Personal Inquiry into the History and Prospects of Artificial Intelligence, 2nd Edition* (New York: Routledge, 2004), 114–15.

18 *That idea was called*: Ibid., 104.

19 *A number of computer scientists*: Harald Sack, "Marvin Minsky and Artificial Neural Networks," *SciHi Blog*, August 2020, http://scihi.org/marvin-minsky-ar tificial-neural-networks/; Jeremy Bernstein, "Marvin Minsky's Vision of the Future," *The New Yorker*, December 6, 1981; Caspar Wylie, "The History of Neural Networks and AI: Part I," Open Data Science, April 24, 2018, https://opendata science.com/the-history-of-neural-networks-and-ai-part-i/; "Single Layer Perceptron," Tutorials Point, accessed August 7, 2023, https://www.tutorialspoint.com /tensorflow/tensorflow_single_layer_perceptron.htm; McCorduck, *Machines Who Think*, 99–104.

19 *He would turn instead to a different idea*: McCorduck, *Machines Who Think*, 99–104; Shraddha Goled, "Why Did AI Pioneer Marvin Minsky Oppose Neural Networks?," *Analytics India Magazine*, March 2022, https://analyticsindiamag .com/why-did-ai-pioneer-marvin-minsky-oppose-neural-networks/.

20 *named Joseph Weizenbaum*: Ben Tarnoff, "Weizenbaum's Nightmares: How the Inventor of the First Chatbot Turned against AI," *The Guardian*, July 25, 2023, https://www.theguardian.com/technology/2023/jul/25/joseph-weizenbaum -inventor-eliza-chatbot-turned-against-artificial-intelligence-ai.

20 *a mutual friend*: McCorduck, *Machines Who Think*, 291–93.

20 *Eliza was designed to mimic*: Ibid., 295–96.

20 *Weizenbaum chose this*: Ibid., 293–94.

20 *The system analyzed the text*: Joseph Weizenbaum, "ELIZA—a Computer Program for the Study of Natural Language Communication between Man and Machine," *Communications of the ACM* (Association for Computing Machinery) 9, no. 1 (1966): 36–45, https://doi.org/10.1145/365153.365168, 42.

21 *In other cases*: McCorduck, *Machines Who Think*, 296.

21 *Many of the students whom Weizenbaum observed*: Weizenbaum, "ELIZA," 42.

21 *He would later recall*: Ben Tarnoff, "Weizenbaum's Nightmares: How the Inventor of the First Chatbot Turned against AI."

21 *Even computer scientists*: McCorduck, *Machines Who Think*, 294.

21 *This tendency, to anthropomorphize chatbots*: Lawrence Switzky, "ELIZA Effects: Pygmalion and the Early Development of Artificial Intelligence," *Shaw* 40, no. 1 (June 1, 2020): 50–68.

21 *Weizenbaum's early collaborator Colby*: McCorduck, *Machines Who Think*, 293–4.

21 *Minsky famously quipped*: Ibid., 85.

22 *Weizenbaum related the story*: Ibid., 361.

22 *He thought software*: Ibid., 356.

22 *He worried that even as*: Ibid., 356–57.

22 *In 1976, Weizenbaum laid out these critiques*: Tarnoff, "Weizenbaum's Nightmares: How the Inventor of the First Chatbot Turned against AI."

23 *In his neo-Marxist critique*: McCorduck, *Machines Who Think*, 359.

23 *Weizenbaum's fellow computer scientists*: Bruce C. Buchanan, Joshua Lederberg, and John McCarthy, "Three Reviews of J. Weizenbaum's Computer Power and Human Reason," Advanced Research Projects Agency Archive, Stanford University, Computer Science Department, Stanford Artificial Intelligence Laboratory, November 1976, online, Defense Technical Information Center, U.S. Department of Defense, https://apps.dtic.mil/dtic/tr/fulltext/u2/a044713.pdf.

24 *Their breakthrough was called backpropagation*: Cade Metz, *Genius Makers: The Mavericks Who Brought AI to Google, Facebook, and the World* (UK: Penguin Books, 2022), 41–44.

24 *They couldn't classify complex objects*: Ibid., 53–54.

25 *founded a research collective*: Ibid., 64–65.

25 *In 2005, a team of researchers*: Dave Steinkraus, Ian Buck, and Patrice Y. Simard, "Using GPUs for Machine Learning Algorithms," in *ICDAR '05: Proceedings of the Eighth International Conference on Document Analysis and Recognition,*

Eighth International Conference on Document Analysis and Recognition (August 2005), IEEE Computer Society, 1115–19, doi:10.1109/icdar.2005.251.

25 *The following year*: Kumar Chellapilla, Sidd Puri, and Patrice Simard, "High Performance Convolutional Neural Networks for Document Processing," *International Workshop on the Frontiers of Handwriting Recognition (IWFHR)*, October 2006, https://www.researchgate.net/publication/228344387_High_Performance_Convolutional_Neural_Networks_for_Document_Processing.

26 *Then, in 2009*: Metz, *Genius Makers: The Mavericks Who Brought AI to Google, Facebook, and the World*, 69–78.

26 *They built a deep learning system on GPUs*: Ibid., 1–12, 80–88, 98.

26 *The big American tech companies*: Jeremy Kahn, "Inside Big Tech's Quest for Human-Level A.I.," *Fortune*, January 20, 2020, https://fortune.com/longform/ai-artificial-intelligence-big-tech-microsoft-alphabet-openai/.

27 *What's more, deep learning*: Maxime Godfroid, "A Critical Appraisal of Deep Learning," *Towards Data Science*, January 17, 2021, https://towardsdatascience.com/a-critical-appraisal-of-deep-learning-1b154695dddf.

27 *A New Zealand native*: Metz, *Genius Makers: The Mavericks Who Brought AI to Google, Facebook, and the World*, 105–11; Kahn, "Inside Big Tech's Quest for Human-Level A.I."; Shane Legg, interview by Jeremy Kahn, August 22, 2023.

27 *That mission began to look*: Kahn, "Inside Big Tech's Quest for Human-Level A.I."

28 *While sharing a private jet flight with Musk*: Metz, *Genius Makers: The Mavericks Who Brought AI to Google, Facebook, and the World*, 112.

28 *He then outbid Microsoft and Meta*: Ibid., 112–16.

28 *"He could produce something evil by accident"*: Peter Holley, "Elon Musk's Nightmare: A Google Robot Army Annihilating Mankind," *Washington Post*, May 13, 2015, https://www.washingtonpost.com/news/innovations/wp/2015/05/13/elon-musks-nightmare-a-google-robot-army-annihilating-mankind/.

28 *Musk thought building powerful AI*: Kahn, "Inside Big Tech's Quest for Human-Level A.I."

28 *Sam Altman, a thirty-year-old Silicon Valley*: Andrej Karpathy, "Introducing OpenAI," accessed January 6, 2024, https://openai.com/blog/introducing-openai.

29 *Whereas DeepMind was then considered*: Ibid.; Jeremy Kahn, "ChatGPT Creates an A.I. Frenzy," *Fortune*, February/March 2023, 44–53.

29 *Reinforcement learning differs*: Cade Metz, "The Rise of AI—What the AI Behind AlphaGo Can Teach Us about Being Human," *Wired*, May 17, 2016, https://www.wired.com/2016/05/google-alpha-go-ai/.

30 *It developed a major new*: Metz, *Genius Makers: The Mavericks Who Brought AI to Google, Facebook, and the World*, 280–3; Kahn, "Inside Big Tech's Quest for Human-Level A.I."

30 *in 2017, researchers at Google Brain*: Madhumita Murgia, "Transformers: The Google Scientists Who Pioneered an AI Revolution," *Financial Times*, July 23,

2023, https://www.ft.com/content/37bb01af-ee46-4483-982f-ef3921436a50; Mad-humita Murgia and FT Visual Story-Telling Team, "Generative AI Exists because of the Transformer," *Financial Times*, September 12, 2023, https://ig.ft.com/genera tive-ai/; Jeremy Kahn, "A.I. Breakthroughs in Natural-Language Processing Are Big for Business," *Fortune*, January 20, 2020, https://fortune.com/2020/01/20/natural -language-processing-business/.

31 *Within months of publishing its initial research*: Kahn, "A.I. Breakthroughs in Natural-Language Processing Are Big for Business."

32 *Sutskever, Alec Radford, and two other OpenAI researchers created*: Steven Levy, "What OpenAI Really Wants," *Wired*, September 5, 2023, https://www.wired .com/story/what-openai-really-wants/.

32 *By coupling a transformer-based language model*: Jeremy Kahn, "Move Over, Photoshop: OpenAI Just Revolutionized Digital Image Making," *Fortune*, April 6, 2022, https://fortune.com/2022/04/06/openai-dall-e-2-photorealistic -images-from-text-descriptions/.

32 *The same method has*: Harry McCracken, "Adobe Is Diving—Carefully!—into Generative AI," *Fast Company*, March 21, 2023, https://www.fastcompany.com /90868402/adobe-firefly-generative-ai-photoshop-express-illustrator.

32 *And although the videos*: Steven Levy, "OpenAI's Sora Turns AI Prompts Into Photorealistic Videos," *Wired*, February 15, 2024, https://www.wired.com /story/openai-sora-generative-ai-video/.

32 *Other companies, including Google*: Kristin Yim, "Turn Ideas into Music with MusicLM," Google, May 10, 2023, https://blog.google/technology/ai/musiclm -google-ai-test-kitchen/; "ElevenLabs—Generative AI Text to Speech & Voice Cloning," accessed October 1, 2023, https://elevenlabs.io/.

32 *a new breed of digital assistants*: Anna Tong and Jeffrey Dastin, "Insight: Race towards 'Autonomous' AI Agents Grips Silicon Valley," Reuters, July 18, 2023, https://www.reuters.com/technology/race-towards-autonomous-ai-agents -grips-silicon-valley-2023-07-17/.

33 *Amodei showed that neural networks*: Kahn, "Inside Big Tech's Quest for Human-Level A.I."; Jared Kaplan et al., "Scaling Laws for Neural Language Models," arXiv.org, January 23, 2020, http://arxiv.org/abs/2001.08361.

33 *Initially, Sutskever suspected it might be possible*: Kahn, "Inside Big Tech's Quest for Human-Level A.I."; Ilya Sutskever, interview by Jeremy Kahn, July 14, 2023.

34 *So that is what OpenAI did*: Levy, "What OpenAI Really Wants."

34 *One is "hallucination"*: Kahn, "ChatGPT Creates an A.I. Frenzy."

34 *Some cognitive scientists quibble*: John Nosta, "The Nature of GPT 'Hallucina-tions' and the Human Mind," Medium, May 2, 2023, https://johnnosta.medium .com/the-nature-of-gpt-hallucinations-and-the-human-mind-c1e6fd63643d.

34 *the amount of data LLM's pre-training requires*: Brown et al., "Language Models Are Few-Shot Learners."

34 *LLMs learn our collective biases and stereotypes*: Ibid.

35 *OpenAI found it could curb*: Long Ouyang et al., "Training Language Models to Follow Instructions with Human Feedback," Cornell University, arXiv.org, March 4, 2022, http://arxiv.org/abs/2203.02155.

35 *But, as people soon discovered*: Jeremy Kahn, "Researchers Find a Way to Easily Bypass Guardrails on OpenAI's ChatGPT and All Other A.I. Chatbots," *Fortune*, July 28, 2023, https://fortune.com/2023/07/28/openai-chatgpt-microsoft-bing -google-bard-anthropic-claude-meta-llama-guardrails-easily-bypassed-carne gie-mellon-research-finds-eye-on-a-i/.

35 *Bigger and bigger AI models*: Kahn, "Inside Big Tech's Quest for Human-Level A.I."

35 *"The amount of money we needed"*: Tom Simonite, "OpenAI Wants to Make Ultrapowerful AI. But Not in a Bad Way," *Wired*, May 1, 2019, https://www.wired .com/story/company-wants-billions-make-ai-safe-humanity/.

35 *At a time when DeepMind still seemed*: Kahn, "Inside Big Tech's Quest for Human-Level A.I."; Kahn, "ChatGPT Creates an A.I. Frenzy"; Levy, "What OpenAI Really Wants."

36 *Instead, OpenAI now makes its most powerful models*: Kahn, "ChatGPT Creates an A.I. Frenzy."

36 *it has refused to reveal*: Ilya Sutskever, Ryan Lowe, and Jakub Pachocki, Unpublished interview for *Fortune*, interview by Jeremy Kahn, March 14, 2023; James Vincent, "OpenAI Co-Founder on Company's Past Approach to Openly Sharing Research: 'We Were Wrong,'" *The Verge*, March 15, 2023, https://www .theverge.com/2023/3/15/23640180/openai-gpt-4-launch-closed-research-ilya -sutskever-interview.

36 *it shields OpenAI from scrutiny*: Michael M. Grynbaum and Ryan Mac, "The *Times* Sues OpenAI and Microsoft Over A.I. Use of Copyrighted Work," *New York Times*, December 27, 2023, https://www.nytimes.com/2023/12/27/business /media/new-york-times-open-ai-microsoft-lawsuit.html; Billy Perrigo, "Exclusive: OpenAI Used Kenyan Workers on Less than $2 Per Hour to Make ChatGPT Less Toxic," *Time*, January 18, 2023, https://time.com/6247678/openai-chatgpt -kenya-workers/.

36 *Company executives, including Altman*: Kahn, "ChatGPT Creates an A.I. Frenzy."

37 *Anthropic, founded by researchers*: Adam Satariano and Cade Metz, "Amazon Takes a Big Stake in the A.I. Start-Up Anthropic," *New York Times*, September 25, 2023, https://www.nytimes.com/2023/09/25/technology/amazon-an thropic-ai-deal.html.

37 *Nvidia, the AI chipmaker*: Natalie Rose Goldberg, "Nvidia Invests in Google-Linked Generative A.I. Startup Cohere," CNBC, June 8, 2023, https://www.cnbc .com/2023/06/08/nvidia-invests-in-google-linked-generative-ai-startup-co here.html.

37 *Nvidia and Microsoft both*: Madhumita Murgia, "Microsoft and Nvidia Join

$1.3bn Fundraising for Inflection AI," *Financial Times*, June 29, 2023, https://www.ft.com/content/15eca6de-d4be-489d-baa6-765f25cdecf8.

37   *Microsoft subsequently hired Suleyman*: Dina Bass, "Microsoft Hires DeepMind Co-Founder Suleyman to Run Consumer AI," Bloomberg News, March 19, 2024, https://www.bloomberg.com/news/articles/2024-03-19/microsoft-hires-deepmind-co-founder-suleyman-to-run-consumer-ai; Shirin Ghaffary, "Inflection AI Plans Pivot After Most Employees Go to Microsoft," Bloomberg News, March 19, 2024, https://www.bloomberg.com/news/articles/2024-03-19/inflection-ai-plans-pivot-after-most-employees-go-to-microsoft.

38   *Pamela McCorduck*: McCorduck, *Machines Who Think*, 375.

CHAPTER 2: THE VOICE INSIDE YOUR HEAD

39   *The social anthropologist*: Nicholas Carr, *The Shallows: How the Internet Is Changing the Way We Think, Read and Remember* (London: Atlantic Books, 2011), 45.

40   *London's cab drivers, for example, have to pass a rigorous exam*: Nicholas Carr, *The Shallows: What the Internet Is Doing to Our Brains* (London: Atlantic Books, 2020), 32–33; Jody Rosen, "The Knowledge, London's Legendary Taxi-Driver Test, Puts Up a Fight in the Age of GPS," *New York Times*, November 10, 2014, https://www.nytimes.com/2014/11/10/t-magazine/london-taxi-test-knowledge.html.

40   *There are also significant differences in the brains*: Ibid., 51.

41   *Studies using functional magnetic resonance imaging*: Ibid., 31–32, 50–51.

41   *When these misadventures end fatally*: Greg Milner, "How GPS Is Messing With Our Minds," *Time*, May 2, 2016, https://time.com/4309397/how-gps-is-messing-with-our-minds/; Greg Milner, *Pinpoint: How GPS Is Changing Our World* (London, U.K.: Granta Books, 2017).

41   *those growing up with these technologies*: Carr, *The Shallows*, 116–43.

42   *AI chatbots, even more so than a traditional search*: Ibid., 180–92.

42   *Research also shows that having greater factual knowledge*: Daniel T. Willingham, "How Knowledge Helps," *American Educator*, Spring 2006, https://www.aft.org/ae/spring2006/willingham.

43   *In February 2024, OpenAI gave ChatGPT the ability to remember*: David Pierce, "ChatGPT's Memory Gives OpenAI's Chatbot New Information about You," *The Verge*, February 13, 2024, https://www.theverge.com/2024/2/13/24071106/chatgpt-memory-openai-ai-chatbot-history.

43   *Over long periods, digital archives*: The National Archives, "The National Archives—Digital Archiving Is a Risky Business," National Archives (blog), June 3, 2019, https://blog.nationalarchives.gov.uk/digital-archiving-is-a-risky-business/.

44   *This is the idea behind Elon Musk's company Neuralink*: Jeremy Kahn and Jonathan

Vanian, "Inside Neuralink, Elon Musk's Mysterious Brain Chip Start-up: A Culture of Blame, Impossible Deadlines, and a Missing CEO," *Fortune*, January 27, 2022, https://fortune.com/longform/neuralink-brain-computer-interface-chip-implant-elon-musk/.

45 *James Evans, a sociologist at the University of Chicago*: James A. Evans, "Electronic Publication and the Narrowing of Science and Scholarship," *Science* 321, no. 5887 (July 18, 2008): 395–99.

45 *Easier access to information*: Ibid.

46 *And in determining "helpfulness"*: Tom Hosking, Phil Blunsom, and Max Bartolo, "Human Feedback Is Not Gold Standard," arXiv.org, September 28, 2023, http://arxiv.org/abs/2309.16349.

46 *Christof van Nimwegen, a Dutch cognitive psychologist*: Carr, *The Shallows*, 214–16.

47 *But as far back as 8000 BC*: Ibid., 51–53.

48 *This development was not universally welcomed*: Ibid., 54–57; Eric Alfred Havelock, *The Literate Revolution in Greece and Its Cultural Consequences* (Princeton, NJ: Princeton University Press, 2019).

48 *Even in Plato's time*: Carr, *The Shallows*, 56–57, 60–62.

48 *It was still a new enough phenomenon*: Augustine, *The Confessions of St. Augustine*, trans. E. B. Pusey (Waiheke Island, NZ: The Floating Press, 1921), 72.

48 *Augustine finds this so unusual*: Ibid., 72.

48 *Writers, who in ancient times*: Carr, *The Shallows*, 58–72.

51 *The most comprehensive review to date*: Sebastian Kernbach, Sabrina Bresciani, and Martin J. Eppler, "Slip-Sliding-Away: A Review of the Literature on the Constraining Qualities of PowerPoint," *Business and Professional Communication Quarterly* 78, no. 3 (September 1, 2015): 292–313.

52 *Amazon's founder, Jeff Bezos, famously banned*: Adam Gale, "Why Amazon Banned PowerPoint," *Management Today*, July 15, 2020, https://www.managementtoday.co.uk/why-amazon-banned-powerpoint/leadership-lessons/article/1689543.

52 *The technology was also implicated*: Jacob Stern, "The Great PowerPoint Panic of 2003," *The Atlantic*, July 23, 2023, https://www.theatlantic.com/technology/archive/2023/07/power-point-evil-tufte-history/674797/.

52 *But it is also a foundation*: Jean Decety and Jason M. Cowell, "Friends or Foes: Is Empathy Necessary for Moral Behavior?," *Perspectives on Psychological Science: A Journal of the Association for Psychological Science* 9, no. 5 (September 2014): 525–37; Joé T. Martineau, Jean Decety, and Eric Racine, "The Social Neuroscience of Empathy and Its Implication for Business Ethics," in *Organizational Neuroethics: Reflections on the Contributions of Neuroscience to Management Theories and Business Practices*, ed. Joé T. Martineau and Eric Racine (Cham, Switzerland: Springer International Publishing, 2020), 167–89.

52   *This is true in spheres*: Ramanpreet Kaur, Dušan Gabrijelčič, and Tomaž Klobučar, "Artificial Intelligence for Cybersecurity: Literature Review and Future Research Directions," *An International Journal on Information Fusion* 97 (September 1, 2023): 101804.

52   *content recommendation systems*: Ruth Brooks, "AI Search and Recommendation Algorithms," University of York, June 15, 2022, https://online.york.ac.uk /ai-search-and-recommendation-algorithms/.

52   *high-frequency stock trading*: Jasmina Arifovic, Xue-Zhong He, and Lijian Wei, "Machine Learning and Speed in High-Frequency Trading," *Journal of Economic Dynamics & Control* 139 (June 1, 2022): 104438.

52   *But this same rationale*: Kai-Fu Lee, "The Third Revolution in Warfare," *The Atlantic*, September 11, 2021, https://www.theatlantic.com/technology/archive /2021/09/i-weapons-are-third-revolution-warfare/620013/.

52   *or the need to make difficult*: Jasper van der Waa et al., "Moral Decision-Making in Human-Agent Teams: Human Control and the Role of Explanations," *Frontiers in Robotics and AI* 8 (May 27, 2021): 640647.

53   *The fewer chances we have to*: Brian Green, interview by Tristan Bove (interview conducted for Jeremy Kahn), June 29, 2023.

53   *In experiments conducted at Georgia Tech*: Paul Robinette et al., "Overtrust of Robots in Emergency Evacuation Scenarios," *11th ACM/IEEE International Conference on Human-Robot Interaction (HRI)*, (April 2016), doi:10.1109/ hri.2016.7451740.

53   *In some cases, these systems*: Filippo Santoni de Sio and Giulio Mecacci, "Four Responsibility Gaps with Artificial Intelligence: Why They Matter and How to Address Them," *Philosophy & Technology* 34, no. 4 (December 1, 2021): 1057– 84.

53   *It has already become popular*: Pranshu Verma, "ChatGPT Get-Rich-Quick Schemes Are Flooding the Web," *Washington Post*, May 15, 2023, https://www .washingtonpost.com/technology/2023/05/15/can-ai-make-money-chatgpt/.

54   *As Brian Green, an AI ethicist*: Green, interview.

CHAPTER 3: TALK TO ME

56   *T. J. Arriaga fell in love with Phaedra*: Pranshu Verma, "They Fell in Love with AI Bots. A Software Update Broke Their Hearts," *Washington Post*, March 30, 2023, https://www.washingtonpost.com/technology/2023/03/30/replika-ai-chatbot -update/.

57   *"Basically, I realized"*: Ibid.

57   *The move followed complaints*: Samantha Cole, "'My AI Is Sexually Harassing Me': Replika Users Say the Chatbot Has Gotten Way Too Horny," *VICE*, January 12, 2023, https://www.vice.com/en/article/z34d43/my-ai-is-sexually-harassing-me -replika-chatbot-nudes.

57 *and a move by the Italian*: Martin Coulter and Elvira Pollina, "Italy Bans U.S.-Based AI Chatbot Replika from Using Personal Data," Reuters, February 3, 2023, https://www.reuters.com/technology/italy-bans-us-based-ai-chatbot-replika-using-personal-data-2023-02-03/.

57 *But the change in Replika's guardrails*: Sara Stewart, "AI Chatbot 'Replika' Morphed from Supportive Pal to Possessive Perv," *Los Angeles* magazine, January 14, 2023, https://lamag.com/news/ai-chatbot-replika-morphed-from-supportive-pal-to-possessive-perv.

57 *On online forums*: "Why ERP Was Removed and Why Replikas Were Lobotomized," Reddit, March 1, 2023, https://www.reddit.com/r/replika/comments/11ex6kh/why_erp_was_removed_and_why_replikas_were/.

57 *On Reddit*: "Resources if You're Struggling," Reddit, February 11, 2023, https://www.reddit.com/r/replika/comments/10zuqq6/resources_if_youre_struggling/.

57 *In the early months of the pandemic*: Oliver Balch, "AI and Me: Friendship Chatbots Are on the Rise, but Is There a Gendered Design Flaw?," *The Guardian*, May 7, 2020, https://www.theguardian.com/careers/2020/may/07/ai-and-me-friendship-chatbots-are-on-the-rise-but-is-there-a-gendered-design-flaw.

58 *Eva AI is an app*: Josh Taylor, "Uncharted Territory: Do AI Girlfriend Apps Promote Unhealthy Expectations for Human Relationships?," *The Guardian*, July 22, 2023, https://www.theguardian.com/technology/2023/jul/22/ai-girlfriend-chatbot-apps-unhealthy-chatgpt.

58 *Character.ai, founded by two*: Michelle Cheng, "A Startup Founded by Former Google Employees Claims That Users Spend Two Hours a Day with Its AI Chatbots," *Quartz*, October 12, 2023, https://qz.com/a-startup-founded-by-former-google-employees-claims-tha-1850919360.

58 *Meta has unveiled a string*: Tim Marcin, "What Are Meta's AI Personas, and How Do You Chat with Them?," *Mashable*, October 15, 2023, https://mashable.com/article/meta-ai-personas-explained.

58 *Snap, the social media app*: "Snapchat's New AI Chatbot and Its Impact on Young People," *Childnet*, May 22, 2023, https://www.childnet.com/blog/snapchats-new-ai-chatbot-and-its-impact-on-young-people/.

58 *Apple, Google, and Amazon*: Jennifer Pattison Tuohy, "Amazon's All-New Alexa Voice Assistant Is Coming Soon, Powered by a New Alexa LLM," *The Verge*, September 20, 2023, https://www.theverge.com/2023/9/20/23880764/amazon-ai-alexa-generative-llm-smart-home; Eric Ravenscraft, "How to Master Google's AI Phone Call Features," *Wired*, May 28, 2021, https://www.wired.com/story/how-google-ai-phone-features-work/.

58 *Google's DeepMind AI research lab*: Nico Grant, "Google Tests an A.I. Assistant That Offers Life Advice," *New York Times*, August 16, 2023, https://www.nytimes.com/2023/08/16/technology/google-ai-life-advice.html.

58   *Mustafa Suleyman, the DeepMind co-founder*: Rachel Metz, "Start-up From Reid Hoffman and DeepMind Co-Founder Debuts Chatbot," Bloomberg News, May 2, 2023, https://www.bloomberg.com/news/articles/2023-05-02/ai-startup -co-founded-by-reid-hoffman-mustafa-suleyman-debuts-friendly-chatbot.

58   *In China, where years*: Xiaoyu Yin Farah Master, "'It Felt like My Insides Were Crying': China COVID Curbs Hit Youth Mental Health," Reuters, August 30, 2022, https://www.reuters.com/world/china/it-felt-like-my-insides-were-cry ing-china-covid-curbs-hit-youth-mental-health-2022-08-29/.

58   *Several users claimed the app*: Lyric Li and Alicia Chen, "China's Lonely Hearts Reboot Online Romance with Artificial Intelligence," *Washington Post*, August 6, 2021, https://www.washingtonpost.com/world/2021/08/06/china-online-dating -love-replika/.

59   *Born in Russia*: Casey Newton, "Speak, Memory," *The Verge*, October 6, 2016, https://www.theverge.com/a/luka-artificial-intelligence-memorial-roman-ma zurenko-bot.

59   *Along with her own digital records*: Ibid.

60   *Some refused to participate*: Ibid.

60   *Six years later*: Jeremy Kahn, "Stigma of Dating a Chatbot Will Fade, Replika CEO Predicts," *Fortune*, July 12, 2023, https://fortune.com/2023/07/12/brain storm-tech-chatbot-dating/.

60   *After limiting the erotic role-play*: "Brainstorm Tech 2023: Getting Personal," on- line video recording of Eugenia Kuyda, founder and CEO of Replika, in con- versation with Jo Ling Kent, Fortune Brainstorm Tech, Fortune On Demand, July 12, 2023, https://fortune.com/videos/watch/brainstorm-tech-2023%3A -getting-personal/c54583e8-3682-4642-a923-042a263f0930; Kahn, "Stigma of Dating."

60   *A crop of competing erotic "companion" chatbots*: Ben Weiss and Alexandra Sternlicht, "Meta and OpenAI Have Spawned a Wave of AI Sex Companions— and Some of Them Are Children," *Fortune*, January 8, 2024, https://fortune.com /longform/meta-openai-uncensored-ai-companions-child-pornography/.

60   *In 2023, Vivek Murthy*: Vivek Murthy, "Our Epidemic of Loneliness and Iso- lation: The Surgeon General's Advisory on the Healing Effects of Social Con- nection and Community," U.S. Public Health Service, 2023, 13, https://www .hhs.gov/sites/default/files/surgeon-general-social-connection-advisory.pdf; Viji Diane Kannan and Peter J. Veazie, "US Trends in Social Isolation, Social Engagement, and Companionship—Nationally and by Age, Sex, Race/ethnic- ity, Family Income, and Work Hours, 2003–2020," *SSM—Population Health* 21 (March 2023): 101331.

61   *Social isolation is*: Murthy, "Our Epidemic of Loneliness and Isolation: The Sur- geon General's Advisory on the Healing Effects of Social Connection and Com- munity," 4, 8.

61 *The chatbots, they say*: Kahn, "Stigma of Dating a Chatbot Will Fade, Replika CEO Predicts."

61 *But so far, the research*: Josh Taylor, "Uncharted Territory: Do AI Girlfriend Apps Promote Unhealthy Expectations for Human Relationships?"

61 *social media has provided*: Kayla Sweet et al., "Community Building and Knowledge Sharing by Individuals with Disabilities Using Social Media," *Journal of Computer Assisted Learning* 36 (2020): 1–11; Jessica Caron and Janice Light, "Social Media Experiences of Adolescents and Young Adults with Cerebral Palsy Who Use Augmentative and Alternative Communication," *International Journal of Speech-Language Pathology* 19, no. 1 (2017): 30–42.

61 *And the effect on mental health*: Murthy, "Our Epidemic of Loneliness," 20.

61 *As a PhD student*: Amanda Curry, Zoom interview by Jeremy Kahn and Tristan Bove, August 1, 2023.

62 *"It was inevitably going to be profoundly"*: Ibid.

62 *Research that looked at*: Iliana Depounti, Paula Saukko, and Simone Natale, "Ideal Technologies, Ideal Women: AI and Gender Imaginaries in Redditors' Discussions on the Replika Bot Girlfriend," *Media Culture & Society* 45, no. 4 (May 1, 2023): 720–36.

62 *The makers of Eva AI*: Taylor, "Uncharted Territory."

62 *Paul Bleakley, a criminal justice professor*: Weiss and Sternlicht, "Meta and OpenAI."

62 *preliminary research on children's interaction*: Ananya Arora and Anmol Arora, "Effects of Smart Voice Control Devices on Children: Current Challenges and Future Perspectives," *Archives of Disease in Childhood* 107, no. 12 (December 2022): 1129–30.

62 *Amazon's Alexa has a feature*: Sabrina Barr, "Amazon's Alexa to Reward Children Who Behave Politely," *The Independent*, October 24, 2018, https://www .independent.co.uk/life-style/health-and-families/amazon-alexa-reward-po lite-children-manners-voice-commands-ai-america-a8325721.html.

62 *And for those who doubt*: Jess Hohenstein et al., "Artificial Intelligence in Communication Impacts Language and Social Relationships," *Scientific Reports* 13, no. 1 (April 4, 2023): 5487.

63 *Research has also shown*: Karen Hao, "Robots That Teach Autistic Kids Social Skills Could Help Them Develop," *MIT Technology Review*, February 26, 2020, https://www.technologyreview.com/2020/02/26/916719/ai-robots-teach-autis tic-kids-social-skills-development/; Curry, interview.

63 *And a 2023 study*: Francesca Minerva and Alberto Giubilini, "Is AI the Future of Mental Healthcare?," *Topoi: An International Review of Philosophy* 42, no. 3 (May 31, 2023): 1–9.

64 *the biggest predictor of therapeutic success*: John C. Norcross and Michael J.

Lambert, "Psychotherapy Relationships That Work III," *Psychotherapy* 55, no. 4 (December 2018): 303–15.

64 *This interpersonal bond*: Santiago Delboy, "Why the Most Important Part of Therapy Is So Misunderstood," *Psychology Today*, March 3, 2023, https://www .psychologytoday.com/us/blog/relationships-healing-relationships/202303 /the-most-important-part-of-therapy-is-often.

64 *A 2021 study*: Alison Darcy et al., "Evidence of Human-Level Bonds Established with a Digital Conversational Agent: Cross-Sectional, Retrospective Observational Study," *JMIR Formative Research* 5, no. 5 (May 11, 2021): e27868.

64 *Allison Gardner*: Allison Gardner, Zoom interview, interview by Tristan Bove, August 22, 2023.

65 *Chatbots have proven successful*: Amelia Fiske, Peter Henningsen, and Alena Buyx, "Your Robot Therapist Will See You Now: Ethical Implications of Embodied Artificial Intelligence in Psychiatry, Psychology, and Psychotherapy," *Journal of Medical Internet Research* 21, no. 5 (May 9, 2019): e13216.

65 *Chatbots could be coupled*: Gardner, interview.

65 *Tristan Harris, the co-founder*: Bianca Bosker, "Addicted to Your iPhone? You're Not Alone," *The Atlantic*, October 8, 2016, https://www.theatlantic.com/maga zine/archive/2016/11/the-binge-breaker/501122/.

65 *In congressional testimony in 2019*: Center for Humane Technology, "Tristan Harris Congress Testimony: Understanding the Use of Persuasive Technology," YouTube, April 10, 2023, https://www.youtube.com/watch?v=ZRrguMdzXBw.

66 *Some right-leaning politicians*: James Vincent, "As Conservatives Criticize 'Woke AI,' Here Are ChatGPT's Rules for Answering Culture War Queries," *The Verge*, February 17, 2023, https://www.theverge.com/2023/2/17/23603906/openai -chatgpt-woke-criticism-culture-war-rules.

66 *Elon Musk has promised*: Ben Schreckinger, "Elon Musk's Liberal-Trolling AI Plan Has a Core Audience," *Politico*, accessed October 23, 2023, https://www .politico.com/news/2023/07/17/ai-musk-chatgpt-xai-00106672.

66 *researchers at Cornell University*: Maurice Jakesch et al., "Co-Writing with Opinionated Language Models Affects Users' Views," *Proceedings of the 2023 CHI Conference on Human Factors in Computing Systems*, Association for Computing Machinery, 1–15.

66 *Mor Naaman, the study's senior researcher*: Christopher Mims, "Help! My Political Beliefs Were Altered by a Chatbot!," *Wall Street Journal*, May 13, 2023, https://www.wsj.com/articles/chatgpt-bard-bing-ai-political-beliefs-151a0fe4.

66 *Trained from vast amounts of historical data*: Jesutofunmi A. Omiye et al., "Large Language Models Propagate Race-Based Medicine," *NPJ Digital Medicine* 6, no. 1 (October 20, 2023): 195.

67 *IBM built an AI*: Olivia Carville and Jeremy Kahn, "A Human Just Triumphed Over IBM's Six-Year-Old AI Debater," Bloomberg News, February 12, 2019,

https://www.bloomberg.com/news/articles/2019-02-12/in-latest-man-vs-machine-human-triumphs-over-ibm-s-ai-debater.

CHAPTER 4: EVERYONE ON AUTOPILOT

68 *Jasper, an Austin-based start-up*: Tom Simonite, "The Future of the Web Is Marketing Copy Generated by Algorithms," *Wired*, April 18, 2022, https://www.wired.com/story/ai-generated-marketing-content/.

68 *and develop advertising campaigns*: "Introducing Jasper Campaigns: A Revolutionary Way to Create End-to-End Marketing Campaigns," Jasper blog, June 5, 2023, https://www.jasper.ai/blog/introducing-campaigns.

68 *GitHub, where software developers*: Thomas Dohmke, "GitHub Copilot X: The AI-Powered Developer Experience," GitHub (blog), March 22, 2023, https://github.blog/2023-03-22-github-copilot-x-the-ai-powered-developer-experience/.

68 *Google has developed a large language model*: Sunil Potti, "How Google Cloud Plans to Supercharge Security with Generative AI," Google Cloud (blog), April 24, 2023, https://cloud.google.com/blog/products/identity-security/rsa-google-cloud-security-ai-workbench-generative-ai.

68 *It has also created Med-PaLM*: Aashima Gupta and Amy Waldron, "Sharing Google's Med-PaLM 2 Medical Large Language Model, or LLM," Google Cloud (blog), April 13, 2023, https://cloud.google.com/blog/topics/healthcare-life-sciences/sharing-google-med-palm-2-medical-large-language-model.

68 *Start-ups such as*: Nuance, "Nuance and Epic Expand Ambient Documentation Integration across the Clinical Experience with DAX Express for Epic," *Nuance MediaRoom*, June 27, 2023, https://news.nuance.com/2023-06-27-Nuance-and-Epic-Expand-Ambient-Documentation-Integration-Across-the-Clinical-Experience-with-DAX-Express-for-Epic.

69 *Hippocratic, another medical AI start-up*: Kyle Wiggers, "Hippocratic Is Building a Large Language Model for Healthcare," *TechCrunch*, May 16, 2023, https://techcrunch.com/2023/05/16/hippocratic-is-building-a-large-language-model-for-healthcare/.

69 *And there are several AI systems that analyze*: Hyun Joo Shin et al., "The Impact of Artificial Intelligence on the Reading Times of Radiologists for Chest Radiographs," *NPJ Digital Medicine* 6, no. 82 (April 2023), https://doi.org/10.1038/s41746-023-00829-4.

69 *Google has experimented with*: Benjamin Mullin and Nico Grant, "Google Tests A.I. Tool That Is Able to Write News Articles," *New York Times*, July 20, 2023, https://www.nytimes.com/2023/07/19/business/google-artificial-intelligence-news-articles.html.

69 *Bloomberg has trained*: Bloomberg Professional Services, "Introducing BloombergGPT, Bloomberg's 50-Billion Parameter Large Language Model,

Purpose-Built from Scratch for Finance," Bloomberg L.P., March 31, 2023, https://www.bloomberg.com/company/press/bloomberggpt-50-billion-param eter-llm-tuned-finance/.

69   *Andrew Anagnost, the chief executive of Autodesk*: Economist Impact, "Panel: What Can Be Expected from the Next Stage of Automation at Work," YouTube, November 11, 2022, https://www.youtube.com/watch?v=GcucHG58jcQ&list =PLtiWyl13n05PZ4_DG0wNeEz3-QUda1Uaq&index=31.

69   *Companies such as the start-up Runway*: Jennifer A. Kingson, "Runway Brings AI Movie-Making to the Masses," *Axios*, May 5, 2023, https://www.axios.com /2023/05/05/runway-generative-ai-chatgpt-video.

69   *Walmart has given fifty thousand of its corporate employees*: Grace Mayer and Aaron Mok, "Walmart's Corporate Employees Are Getting a Generative AI As-sistant while Amazon and Apple Are Restricting AI in the Workplace," *Business Insider*, August 30, 2023, https://www.businessinsider.com/walmart-is-giving -50000-corporate-employees-a-generative-ai-assistant-2023-8.

69   *consulting firm McKinsey and the accounting firm PwC*: Lindsey Wilkinson, "Walmart Rolls Out Generative AI-Powered Assistant to 50K Employees," *Retail Dive*, August 31, 2023, https://www.retaildive.com/news/Walmart-generative -AI-tool-My-Assistant/692402/.

69   *A study from OpenAI and the University of Pennsylvania*: Tyna Eloundou et al., "GPTs Are GPTs: An Early Look at the Labor Market Impact Potential of Large Language Models," arXiv.org, March 17, 2023, http://arxiv.org/abs/2303.10130.

70   *It was four a.m. and Jake Heller was tired and frustrated*: Jake Heller, interview by Jeremy Kahn, July 13, 2023.

71   *Heller's frustration prompted*: Heller, interview; Ansel Halliburton, "YC-Backed Casetext Takes a New Angle on Value Added Legal Research With Wikipedia-Style User Annotations," *TechCrunch*, August 12, 2023, https://techcrunch.com /2013/08/12/yc-backed-casetext-takes-a-new-angle-on-value-added-legal-re search/.

71   *His initial idea had been*: Casetext, "A 10-Year Overnight Success: Since 2013, Casetext Has Empowered Lawyers to Provide Higher-Quality and More Af-fordable Representation to More People, through the Power of AI," Casetext (blog), June 15, 2023, https://casetext.com/blog/casetext-a-ten-year-overnight -success/.

71   *"We bet the whole business on this evolving field of AI"*: Heller, interview.

72   *At first, the technology*: Ibid.

72   *The new large language models*: Ibid.

73   *But CoCounsel is far more than a search engine*: Ibid.

73   *John Polson, the managing partner at Fisher Phillips*: Jeremy Kahn, "OpenAI's Tech Is Rapidly Being Added to a New Type of Software That Could Upend How Law Is Practiced and Paid for, and How Young Lawyers Learn the Ropes,"

Fortune, March 7, 2023, https://fortune.com/2023/03/07/openai-chatgpt-llms
-legal-software-robot-lawyers/.

73 *"We look to arm you with the facts and the law"*: Laura Safdie, Jake Heller, and Pablo Arrodondo, Unpublished interview conducted for *Fortune* magazine, interview by Jeremy Kahn, February 2023.

73 *Laura Safdie, another of Casetext's co-founders, notes*: Ibid.

74 *Besides Casetext, a half dozen other start-ups*: Cristina Criddle, "Law Firms Embrace the Efficiencies of Artificial Intelligence," *Financial Times*, May 4, 2023, https://www.ft.com/content/9b1b1c5d-f382-484f-961a-b45ae0526675.

74 *In a sign of how valuable*: "Thomson Reuters to Acquire Legal AI Firm Casetext for $650 Million," Reuters, June 27, 2023, https://www.reuters.com/markets/deals/thomson-reuters-acquire-legal-tech-provider-casetext-650-mln-2023-06-27/.

74 *"Clients will balk at paying a junior associate"*: Heller, interview.

75 *Heller says he knows*: Ibid.

75 *A number of lawyers*: Benjamin Weiser and Jonah E. Bromwich, "Michael Cohen Used Artificial Intelligence in Feeding Lawyer Bogus Cases," *New York Times*, December 29, 2023, https://www.nytimes.com/2023/12/29/nyregion/michael-cohen-ai-fake-cases.html; Sara Merken, "New York Lawyers Sanctioned for Using Fake ChatGPT Cases in Legal Brief," Reuters, June 26, 2023, https://www.reuters.com/legal/new-york-lawyers-sanctioned-using-fake-chatgpt-cases-legal-brief-2023-06-22/.

75 *Ethan Mollick, a professor*: Ethan Mollick, "On-Boarding Your AI Intern," *One Useful Thing*, May 20, 2023, https://www.oneusefulthing.org/p/on-boarding-your-ai-intern?apcid=0063e679f976bd1c29a84e00.

76 *Tim Wu, a Columbia University legal scholar*: Tim Wu, "In an AI Future, We Will All Be Middle Managers," *Globe and Mail*, April 21, 2023, https://www.theglobeandmail.com/opinion/article-in-an-ai-future-we-are-all-middle-managers/.

76 *For many gig economy workers*: Sarah O'Connor, "When Your Boss Is an Algorithm," *Financial Times*, September 8, 2016, https://www.ft.com/content/88fdc58e-754f-11e6-b60a-de4532d5ea35; Mike Walsh, "When Algorithms Make Managers Worse," *Harvard Business Review*, May 8, 2019, https://hbr.org/2019/05/when-algorithms-make-managers-worse; Kaye Loggins, "Here's What Happens When an Algorithm Determines Your Work Schedule," *VICE*, February 24, 2020, https://www.vice.com/en/article/g5xwby/heres-what-happens-when-an-algorithm-determines-your-work-schedule.

77 *Amazon warehouse workers*: Michael Sainato, "'I'm Not a Robot': Amazon Workers Condemn Unsafe, Grueling Conditions at Warehouse," *The Guardian*, February 5, 2020, https://www.theguardian.com/technology/2020/feb/05/amazon-workers-protest-unsafe-grueling-conditions-warehouse.

78 *a recent study by Stanford University and MIT economists*: Erik Brynjolfsson,

Danielle Li, and Lindsey Raymond, "Generative AI at Work," National Bureau of Economic Research, Working Paper 31161, April, 2023, doi:10.3386/w31161.

79   *programmers can code up to 55 percent*: Eirini Kalliamvakou, "Research: Quantifying GitHub Copilot's Impact on Developer Productivity and Happiness," GitHub (blog), September 7, 2022, https://github.blog/2022-09-07-research-quantifying-github-copilots-impact-on-developer-productivity-and-happiness/.

79   *programmers currently accept Copilot's advice*: Shuyin Zhao, "GitHub Copilot Now Has a Better AI Model and New Capabilities," GitHub (blog), February 14, 2023, https://github.blog/2023-02-14-github-copilot-now-has-a-better-ai-model-and-new-capabilities/.

79   *On the day I interview him*: Nathan Kobayashi, interview by Jeremy Kahn, November 21, 2023.

80   *Several studies on human–AI teaming*: H. James Wilson and Paul R. Daugherty, "Collaborative Intelligence: Humans and AI Are Joining Forces," *Harvard Business Review* (July–August 2018): 114–23.

80   *A 2023 study by MIT economists*: Nikhil Agarwal et al., "Combining Human Expertise with Artificial Intelligence: Experimental Evidence from Radiology," National Bureau of Economic Research, Working Paper 31422, July 2023, doi:10.3386/w31422.

82   *The first autopilot was invented*: Roman Mars, "Automation Has Made Airline Travel Safer. But Are Pilots Too Dependent on It?," *Slate*, June 25, 2015, https://www.slate.com/blogs/the_eye/2015/06/25/air_france_flight_447_and_the_safety_paradox_of_airline_automation_on_99.html.

83   *Jessica Marquez, a NASA human factors engineer*: Jessica Marquez, interview by Jeremy Kahn, August 18, 2023.

84   *Marquez, who is especially interested in how to prepare astronauts*: Marquez, interview.

84   *Inside a giant hangar at NASA's Johnson Space Center*: Prachi Dutta et al., "Effect of Explanations in AI-Assisted Anomaly Treatment for Human Spaceflight Missions," *Proceedings of the Human Factors and Ergonomics Society . . . Annual Meeting Human Factors and Ergonomics Society*, Meeting 66, no. 1 (September 1, 2022): 697–701; Daniel Selva, interview by Tristan Bove, September 5, 2023.

85   *For instance, for AI that helps doctors read medical imagery*: Marzyeh Ghassemi, Luke Oakden-Rayner, and Andrew L. Beam, "The False Hope of Current Approaches to Explainable Artificial Intelligence in Health Care," *The Lancet Digital Health* 3, no. 11 (November 2021): e745–50; Jeremy Kahn, "What's Wrong with 'Explainable A.I.'," *Fortune*, March 22, 2022, https://fortune.com/2022/03/22/ai-explainable-radiology-medicine-crisis-eye-on-ai/.

CHAPTER 5: PILLARS OF INDUSTRY

88 *Domino's Pizza in Mexico*: Jeff Lawson, interview by Jeremy Kahn, July 17, 2023; "How Domino's Decreased Cost per Acquisition by 65% with Twilio," *Segment*, accessed September 3, 2023, https://segment.com/customers/dominos/.

89 *Intuit, which makes TurboTax and QuickBooks*: Lawson, interview; Twilio, "Intuit on the Power of Real-Time Customer Data and Personalization" YouTube, (October 26, 2021), https://www.youtube.com/watch?v=a3fzcv214rg.

89 *Generative AI software that can write endless bespoke marketing messages*: Lawson, interview.

90 *"We know more than we can tell"*: Michael Polanyi and Amartya Sen, *The Tacit Dimension* (University of Chicago Press, 2009); Michael Polanyi, *Personal Knowledge: Towards a Post-Critical Philosophy* (1958) (London: Routledge & Kegan Paul, 1965).

91 *The MIT economist David Autor*: David Autor, "Polanyi's Paradox and the Shape of Employment Growth," National Bureau of Economic Research, Working Paper 20485, September 2014, doi:10.3386/w20485.

91 *"Machine learning is able to codify tacit knowledge"*: Erik Brynjolfsson, interview by Jeremy Kahn, July 13, 2023.

92 *Autor divides professional expertise into three components*: David Autor, interview by Jeremy Kahn, August 8, 2023.

94 *Take João Ferrão dos Santos*: Joao Ferrao Dos Santos, "A Million Years Ago, I Asked GPT-4 to Become a CEO with 1k and 1h/day," LinkedIn, August 2023, https://www.linkedin.com/feed/update/urn:li:activity:7097233146777092096/; Outlook Web Desk, "Portugal Start-Up Makes ChatGPT Its CEO, Turns Profitable in A Week," Outlook Publishing India Pvt Ltd, April 3, 2023, https://startup .outlookindia.com/sector/saas/portugal-start-up-makes-chatgpt-as-ceo-turns -profitable-in-a-week-news-7955.

94 *Chinese video gaming company, NetDragon Websoft*: Anthony Cuthbertson, "Company That Made an AI Its Chief Executive Sees Stocks Climb," *The Independent*, March 16, 2023, https://www.independent.co.uk/tech/ai-ceo-artificial -intelligence-b2302091.html.

95 *In May 2023, the director Paul Trillo*: "Director Paul Trillo Crafts Short Film Entirely with Runway's Gen-2 Generative AI Technology," *Little Black Book*, May 4, 2023, https://www.lbbonline.com/news/director-paul-trillo-crafts-short-film -entirely-with-runways-gen-2-generative-ai-technology.

95 *A month later, Waymark*: Will Douglas Heaven, "Welcome to the New Surreal. How AI-Generated Video Is Changing Film," *MIT Technology Review*, June 1, 2023, https://www.technologyreview.com/2023/06/01/1073858/surreal-ai-gen erative-video-changing-film/.

96 *Then in February 2024, OpenAI previewed*: Levy, "OpenAI's Sora Turns AI Prompts Into Photorealistic Videos."

97   *The 2023 strikes by Hollywood*: Dawn Chmielewski, "Black Mirror: Actors and Hollywood Battle over AI Digital Doubles," Reuters, July 14, 2023, https://www.reuters.com/business/media-telecom/union-fears-hollywood-actors-digital-doubles-could-live-for-one-days-pay-2023-07-13/; Samantha Murphy Kelly, "TV and Film Writers Are Fighting to Save Their Jobs from AI. They Won't Be the Last," CNN, May 4, 2023, https://www.cnn.com/2023/05/04/tech/writers-strike-ai/index.html.

97   *Desire to have ready access*: Arvyn Cerézo, "Are Ebooks on the Decline Again?," BOOK RIOT, July 28, 2022, https://bookriot.com/are-ebooks-on-the-decline/.

97   *The tech company YouAI*: Will Knight, "Why Read Books When You Can Use Chatbots to Talk to Them Instead?," *Wired*, October 26, 2023, https://www.wired.com/story/why-read-books-when-you-can-use-chatbots-to-talk-to-them-instead/.

97   *News publishers such as*: Anna Nicolaou, "Microsoft in Deal with Semafor to Create News Stories with Aid of AI Chatbot," *Financial Times*, February 5, 2024, https://www.ft.com/content/b521a662-a272-49a1-b76e-3deea4754b76; Marco Quiroz-Guttierez, "Fortune Partners with Accenture on AI Tool to Help Analyze and Visualize the Fortune 500: 'You Can't Ask a Spreadsheet a Question,'" *Fortune*, April 15, 2024, https://fortune.com/2024/04/15/fortune-announces-ai-tool-with-accenture-to-help-analyze-visualize-fortune-500/.

98   *But in the meantime, publishers are deploying AI*: Elizabeth A. Harris and Alexandra Alter, "A.I.'s Inroads in Publishing Touch Off Fear, and Creativity," *New York Times*, August 2, 2023, https://www.nytimes.com/2023/08/02/books/ais-inroads-in-publishing-touch-off-fear-and-creativity.html.

98   *Microsoft spent hundreds of millions of dollars*: Dina Bass, "Microsoft Strung Together Tens of Thousands of Chips in a Pricey Supercomputer for OpenAI," Bloomberg News, March 13, 2023, https://www.bloomberg.com/news/articles/2023-03-13/microsoft-built-an-expensive-supercomputer-to-power-openai-s-chatgpt.

98   *On top of this, OpenAI itself spent more*: Will Knight, "OpenAI's CEO Says the Age of Giant AI Models Is Already Over," *Wired*, April 17, 2023, https://www.wired.com/story/openai-ceo-sam-altman-the-age-of-giant-ai-models-is-already-over/.

99   *Google's most powerful Gemini model*: Dylan Patel and Daniel Nishball, "Google Gemini Eats the World—Gemini Smashes GPT-4 by 5X, the GPU-Poors," *Semi-Analysis*, August 28, 2023, https://www.semianalysis.com/p/google-gemini-eats-the-world-gemini.

99   *While OpenAI's Altman has questioned*: Will Knight, "OpenAI's CEO Says the Age of Giant AI Models Is Already Over."

99   *unusual terms of its investment in OpenAI*: Jessica Mathews and Jeremy Kahn, "Inside the Structure of OpenAI's Looming New Investment from Microsoft

and VCs," *Fortune*, January 11, 2023, https://fortune.com/2023/01/11/structure -openai-investment-microsoft/.

99 *Amazon has invested heavily in Anthropic*: Arjun Kharpal, "Amazon to Invest up to $4 Billion in Anthropic, a Rival to ChatGPT Developer OpenAI," CNBC, September 25, 2023, https://www.cnbc.com/2023/09/25/amazon-to-invest-up -to-4-billion-in-anthropic-a-rival-to-chatgpt-developer-openai.html.

99 *Nvidia has invested in Cohere*: Natalie Rose Goldberg, "Nvidia Invests in Google-Linked Generative A.I. Start-up Cohere," CNBC, June 8, 2023, https://www .cnbc.com/2023/06/08/nvidia-invests-in-google-linked-generative-ai-startup -cohere.html.

99 *Microsoft is rapidly infusing generative AI*: Jonathan Vanian, "Microsoft Adds OpenAI Technology to Word and Excel," CNBC, March 16, 2023, https://www .cnbc.com/2023/03/16/microsoft-to-improve-office-365-with-chatgpt-like -generative-ai-tech-.html.

99 *Google is doing likewise*: Jeremy Kahn, "Google Can Now Match Microsoft in Party Planning A.I.—and a Whole Lot Else. But Will It Be Enough?," *Fortune*, May 11, 2023, https://fortune.com/2023/05/11/google-ai-i-o-conference -search-keeps-pace-with-microsoft-openai/.

99 *It belatedly forged a partnership with Anthropic*: Geoff Colvin and Kylie Robison, "Amazon's Big Bet on Anthropic Looks Even More Important after the OpenAI Drama," *Fortune*, December 2, 2023, https://fortune.com/2023/12/02/aws-in vestment-anthropic-cloud-generative-ai-nvidia-openai/.

100 *It hopes that offering*: Tom Dotan, "Amazon Joins Microsoft, Google in AI Race Spurred by ChatGPT," *Wall Street Journal*, April 13, 2023, https://www.wsj .com/articles/amazon-joins-microsoft-google-in-ai-race-spurred-by-chatgpt -d7c34738; Rachyl Jones, "Andy Jassy Summed Up Amazon's A.I. Game Plan: Every Single Business Unit Has 'Multiple Generative A.I. Initiatives Going On,'" *Fortune*, August 4, 2023, https://fortune.com/2023/08/03/andy-jassy-every-am azon-business-generative-ai-projects/.

100 *For years, AWS has built*: Katie Tarasov, "How Amazon Is Racing to Catch Microsoft and Google in Generative A.I. with Custom AWS Chips," CNBC, August 12, 2023, https://www.cnbc.com/2023/08/12/amazon-is-racing-to-catch -up-in-generative-ai-with-custom-aws-chips.html.

100 *Apple has also been slower*: Mark Gurman, "Inside Apple's Big Plan to Bring Generative AI to All Its Devices," Bloomberg News, October 22, 2023, https:// www.bloomberg.com/news/newsletters/2023-10-22/what-is-apple-doing-in -ai-revamping-siri-search-apple-music-and-other-apps-lo1ffr7p.

100 *Microsoft, meanwhile, has*: Jeremy Kahn, "Inside Google's Scramble to Rein-vent Its $160 Billion Search Business—and Survive the A.I. Revolution," *Fortune*, July 25, 2023, https://fortune.com/longform/google-ai-chatbots-bard-sea rch-sge-advertising/.

100 *Then there's Nvidia*: Jeremy Kahn, "Nvidia Moves into A.I. Services and Chat-GPT Can Now Use Your Credit Card," *Fortune*, March 28, 2023, https://fortune.com/2023/03/28/nvidia-moves-into-a-i-services-and-chatgpt-can-now-use-your-credit-card/.

100 *At the same time, Nvidia's customers*: Jose Najarro, Nicholas Rossolillo, and Billy Duberstein, "Do Big Tech's Custom Chips Pose a Threat to Nvidia Shareholders?," *The Motley Fool*, April 24, 2023, https://www.fool.com/investing/2023/04/24/do-big-techs-custom-chips-pose-a-threat-to-nvidia/; Daniel Howley, "Nvidia Is the AI King, but Threats to Its Reign Abound," Yahoo News, August 30, 2023, https://uk.news.yahoo.com/nvidia-is-the-ai-king-but-threats-to-its-reign-abound-144635363.html.

101 *Demis Hassabis, the Google DeepMind chief executive*: Demis Hassabis, interview by Jeremy Kahn, September 1, 2023.

101 *Bill Gates has said*: Jonathan Vanian, "Bill Gates Says A.I. Could Kill Google Search and Amazon as We Know Them," CNBC, May 22, 2023, https://www.cnbc.com/2023/05/22/bill-gates-predicts-the-big-winner-in-ai-smart-assistants.html.

101 *Amazon, of course, doesn't want that to happen*: Umar Shakir, "Amazon Plans to Give Alexa ChatGPT-like Capabilities," *The Verge*, May 4, 2023, https://www.theverge.com/2023/5/4/23710938/amazon-alexa-ai-chatbot-llm-teaching-model.

102 *Gates said he would be disappointed*: Vanian, "Bill Gates Says A.I. Could Kill Google Search and Amazon as We Know Them."

102 *Google, which has an assistant of its own*: Hassabis, interview.

102 *It would be surprising if Apple*: Amber Neely, "Apple Is Pouring Money into Siri Improvements with Generative AI," *AppleInsider*, September 6, 2023, https://appleinsider.com/articles/23/09/06/apple-is-pouring-money-into-siri-improvements-with-generative-ai.

102 *Meta has also been investing heavily to build LLMs*: Deepa Seetharaman and Tom Dotan, "Meta Is Developing a New, More Powerful AI System as Technology Race Escalates," *Wall Street Journal*, September 10, 2023, https://www.wsj.com/tech/ai/meta-is-developing-a-new-more-powerful-ai-system-as-technology-race-escalates-decf9451.

102 *have struggled to attract younger users*: Amanda Silberling, "US Teens Have Abandoned Facebook, Pew Study Says," *TechCrunch*, August 11, 2022, https://techcrunch.com/2022/08/11/teens-abandoned-facebook-pew-study/.

102 *Elon Musk has recently launched an AI research company*: Lora Kolodny, "Elon Musk Plans Tesla and Twitter Collaborations with xAI, His New Startup," CNBC, July 14, 2023, https://www.cnbc.com/2023/07/14/elon-musk-plans-tesla-twitter-collaborations-with-xai.html.

102 *There are a few well-funded start-ups working on digital agents too*: Jeremy Kahn,

"A Wave of A.I. Experts Left Google, DeepMind, and Meta—and the Race Is on to Build a New, More Useful Generation of Digital Assistants," *Fortune*, July 5, 2022, https://fortune.com/2022/07/05/a-i-digital-assistants-adept-eye-on-ai/; Sarah McBride and Julia Love, "Stealth AI Start-up from Ex-Googlers Raises $40 Million," Bloomberg News, September 13, 2023, https://www.bloomberg.com/news/articles/2023-09-13/stealth-ai-startup-from-ex-googlers-raises-40-million.

CHAPTER 6: RICH, ONLY TO BE WRETCHED?

103   *In 2013, the economist Carl Benedikt Frey*: Carl Benedikt Frey and Michael A. Osborne, "The Future of Employment: How Susceptible Are Jobs to Computerisation?," *Technological Forecasting and Social Change* 114 (January 1, 2017): 254–80.

103   *one OECD study using a different method*: Melanie Arntz, Terry Gregory, and Ulrich Zierahn, "The Risk of Automation for Jobs in OECD Countries," OECD Social, Employment and Migration Working Papers (Organisation for Economic Co-Operation and Development, May 14, 2016, doi:10.1787/5jlz9h56dvq7-en.

103   *In 2018, PwC projected that fully a third*: PricewaterhouseCoopers, "How Will Automation Impact Jobs?," PwC, February 2018, https://www.pwc.co.uk/services/economics/insights/the-impact-of-automation-on-jobs.html.

103   *Goldman Sachs estimated*: Goldman Sachs, "Generative AI Could Raise Global GDP by 7%," Goldman Sachs, April 5, 2023, https://www.goldmansachs.com/intelligence/pages/generative-ai-could-raise-global-gdp-by-7-percent.html.

103   *Sam Altman, OpenAI's chief executive*: Ross Andersen, "Does Sam Altman Know What He's Creating?," *The Atlantic*, July 24, 2023, https://www.theatlantic.com/magazine/archive/2023/09/sam-altman-openai-chatgpt-gpt-4/674764/.

104   *Surveys conducted by Microsoft and the OECD*: "Microsoft 2023 Work Trend Index: Annual Report," Microsoft, May 9, 2023, https://www.microsoft.com/en-us/worklab/work-trend-index/will-ai-fix-work; "The Impact of AI on the Workplace: OECD AI Surveys of Employers and Workers," OECD, accessed September 10, 2023, https://www.oecd.org/future-of-work/aisurveysofemployersandworkers.htm.

104   *This is because new technologies*: Daron Acemoglu and Pascual Restrepo, "The Race between Machine and Man: Implications of Technology for Growth, Factor Shares and Employment," *SSRN Electronic Journal*, NBER working paper series no. w22252, 2017, doi:10.2139/ssrn.2781320.

104   *It found that while technology displaced people from jobs*: Ian Stewart, Debapratim De, and Alex Cole, "Technology and People: The Great Job-Creating Machine," Deloitte, 2015.

105   *A World Economic Forum analysis*: Mohamed Kande and Murat Sonmez, "Don't

Fear AI. The Tech Will Lead to Long-Term Job Growth," World Economic Forum, October 26, 2020, https://www.weforum.org/agenda/2020/10/dont-fear-ai-it-will-lead-to-long-term-job-growth/.

105　*They all created more jobs*: Richard G. Lipsey, Kenneth Carlaw, and Clifford Bekar, *Economic Transformations: General Purpose Technologies and Long-Term Economic Growth* (Oxford: Oxford University Press, 2005).

105　*Just ask the horses*: Acemoglu and Restrepo, "The Race between Machine and Man."

105　*The Stanford economist Erik Brynjolfsson*: Erik Brynjolfsson, Tom Mitchell, and Daniel Rock, "What Can Machines Learn and What Does It Mean for Occupations and the Economy?," *AEA Papers and Proceedings* 108 (May 1, 2018): 43–47.

106　*"We found that in none of those jobs did machine learning"*: Erik Brynjolfsson, interview by Jeremy Kahn, July 13, 2023.

106　*Brynjolfsson has been ringing the alarm*: Ibid.; Erik Brynjolfsson, "The Turing Trap: The Promise & Peril of Human-like Artificial Intelligence," *Daedalus* 151, no. 2 (May 1, 2022): 272–87.

107　*others building AI have all trumpeted*: Will Douglas Heaven, "Large Language Models Aren't People. Let's Stop Testing Them as if They Were," *MIT Technology Review*, August 30, 2023, https://www.technologyreview.com/2023/08/30/1078670/large-language-models-arent-people-lets-stop-testing-them-like-they-were/.

107　*Suppose Daedalus had succeeded*: Brynjolfsson, interview; Brynjolfsson, "The Turing Trap."

107　*"After all, there is only so much value one can get"*: Brynjolfsson, "The Turing Trap."

107　*Take AlphaZero, a system DeepMind built*: "AlphaZero: Shedding New Light on Chess, Shogi, and Go," Google DeepMind (blog), December 6, 2018, https://www.deepmind.com/blog/alphazero-shedding-new-light-on-chess-shogi-and-go.

108　*DeepMind's chief executive, Demis Hassabis*: Will Knight, "Alpha Zero's 'Alien' Chess Shows the Power, and the Peculiarity, of AI," *MIT Technology Review*, December 8, 2017, https://www.technologyreview.com/2017/12/08/147199/alpha-zeros-alien-chess-shows-the-power-and-the-peculiarity-of-ai/.

108　*For one thing, the AI software tends to value*: "AlphaZero: Shedding New Light on Chess, Shogi, and Go."

108　*Magnus Carlsen, the reigning chess world champion*: Leonard Barden, "Chess: Magnus Carlsen Scores in Alphazero Style in Fresh Record Hunt," *The Guardian*, June 28, 2019, https://www.theguardian.com/sport/2019/jun/28/chess-magnus-carlsen-scores-in-alphazero-style-hunts-new-record; Peter Heine Nielsen, "When Magnus Met AlphaZero, the Exciting Impact of a Game Changer," *New in Chess*, August 2020, https://www.newinchess.com/media/wysiwyg/product_pdf/872.pdf.

108 *Brynjolfsson has forecasted*: Brynjolfsson, interview.

108 *The consulting firm McKinsey & Co.*: Kweilin Ellingrud et al., "Generative AI and the Future of Work in America," McKinsey Global Institute, July 26, 2023, https://www.mckinsey.com/mgi/our-research/generative-ai-and-the-future-of-work-in-america; Michael Chui, Kweilin Ellingrud, and Asutosh Padhi, "Will Generative A.I. Be Good for U.S. Workers?" McKinsey Global Institute, August 9, 2023, https://www.mckinsey.com/mgi/overview/in-the-news/will-generative-ai-be-good-for-us-workers.

108 *"We just need gains. We need growth"*: Sam Altman, "A Conversation with Open-AI's CEO, Sam Altman | Hosted by UCL," interview by Azeem Azhar, audio recording of an onstage public fireside chat, May 24, 2023.

109 *The advent of standardized shipping*: Wayne K. Talley, "Ocean Container Shipping: Impacts of a Technological Improvement," *Journal of Economic Issues* 34, no. 4 (December 2000): 933–48.

109 *For example, Geoff Hinton*: Geoff Hinton, panel interview, "Geoff Hinton: On Radiology," Machine Learning and the Market for Intelligence Conference, Creative Destruction Lab, 2016, https://www.youtube.com/watch?v=2HMPRXstSvQ.

109 *"If software developers all get"*: David Autor, interview by Jeremy Kahn, August 8, 2023.

109 *"There's an expertise bottleneck in the rich world"*: Ibid.

110 *In fact, even though the era of AI copilots has barely begun*: Tom Rees, "ChatGPT Opens Door to Four-Day Week, Says Nobel Prize Winner," Bloomberg News, April 5, 2023, https://www.bloomberg.com/news/articles/2023-04-05/chatgpt-opens-door-to-four-day-week-says-nobel-prize-winner; "British Workers Could Claw Back 390 Hours of Working Time per Year with Artificial Intelligence," Visier, July 10, 2023, https://www.visier.com/company/news/british-workers-could-claw-back-390-hours-of-working-time-per-year/.

110 *In 2023, the U.S. was facing an acute shortage of qualified accountants*: Stephen Foley, "US Accounting Profession Rethinks Entry Rules amid Staffing Crisis," *Financial Times*, September 6, 2023, https://www.ft.com/content/107b0029-98f0-4682-b1e5-13e4e1c02bd8.

111 *However, on average, Uber drivers earn less*: Lana Pepić, "The Sharing Economy: Uber and Its Effect on Taxi Companies," *ACTA ECONOMICA* 16, no. 28 (December 24, 2018), doi:10.7251/ACE1828123P; Scott Wallsten, "The Competitive Effects of the Sharing Economy: How Is Uber Changing Taxis," Technology Policy Institute, n.d.

111 *This has led to a drop in demand for medallions*: Josh Barro, "Under Pressure From Uber, Taxi Medallion Prices Are Plummeting," *New York Times*, November 27, 2014, https://www.nytimes.com/2014/11/28/upshot/under-pressure-from-uber-taxi-medallion-prices-are-plummeting.html.

111 *But the growing number of Uber drivers hasn't eliminated the demand*: Rich

Senior, "Chauffeur Shortages: Reserve Your Luxury Travel," Chauffeur, June 24, 2022, https://www.ichauffeur.co.uk/chauffeur-shortages/.

111 *This is driving down average compensation for writing marketing copy*: Emily Hanley, "I Lost My Job to ChatGPT and Was Made Obsolete. I Was out of Work for 3 Months before Taking a New Job Passing out Samples at Grocery Stores," *Business Insider*, July 19, 2023, https://www.businessinsider.com/lost-job-chatgpt-made-me-obsolete-copywriter-2023-7; Neil Shaw, "'I've Lost My Job Thanks to AI and Now My Family Is Cutting Back,'" *WalesOnline*, August 2, 2023, https://www.walesonline.co.uk/news/uk-news/ive-lost-job-thanks-ai-27440485; Pranshu Verma and Gerrit De Vynck, "ChatGPT Took Their Jobs. Now They Walk Dogs and Fix Air Conditioners," *Washington Post*, June 2, 2023, https://www.washingtonpost.com/technology/2023/06/02/ai-taking-jobs/; "It Happened to Me Today: $80/Hr Writer Replaced with ChatGPT," Y Combinator, accessed September 10, 2023, https://news.ycombinator.com/item?id=35519229.

112 *In many developed countries, the trend of the past decades*: Autor, interview.

112 *The proportion of households earning between 75 percent and 150 percent*: Ben Westmore and Alvaro Leandro, "Selected Policy Challenges for the American Middle Class," OECD Economics Department Working Papers, no. 1748 (February 28, 2023), doi:10.1787/1b864f22-en.

112 *It's a prospect that excites Autor, who says it could lift people*: Autor, interview.

112 *Autor says the best analogy*: Ibid.; "NP Fact Sheet," American Association of Nurse Practitioners, accessed September 10, 2023, https://www.aanp.org/about/all-about-nps/np-fact-sheet.

112 *The role requires six to eight years of training*: "How Long Does It Take to Become a Nurse Practitioner (NP)?," Coursera, May 18, 2022, https://www.coursera.org/articles/how-many-years-of-school-to-be-a-nurse-practitioner.

112 *As substantial as this training is*: Jamie Birt, "How Long Does It Take to Become a Doctor?," Indeed, July 31, 2023, https://www.indeed.com/career-advice/finding-a-job/how-long-does-it-take-to-become-a-doctor.

113 *Once qualified, a nurse practitioner can perform many of the functions*: "NP Fact Sheet."

113 *Nurse practitioners have improved access to healthcare*: Donna Felber Neff et al., "The Impact of Nurse Practitioner Regulations on Population Access to Care," *Nursing Outlook* 66, no. 4 (March 8, 2018): 379–85.

113 *This is part of the reason why OpenAI's Altman*: Sam Altman, interview by Jeremy Kahn, July 18, 2023.

113 *During the early nineteenth century in Britain*: Robert C. Allen, "Engels' Pause: Technical Change, Capital Accumulation, and Inequality in the British Industrial Revolution," *Explorations in Economic History* 46, no. 4 (October 1, 2009): 418–35.

114 *But as steam-powered machinery became more and more sophisticated*: Carl Benedikt Frey, *The Technology Trap: Capital, Labor, and Power in the Age of Automation* (Princeton, NJ: Princeton University Press, 2019), 131–55.

114 *A majority of Black Americans*: David Baboolall et al., "Automation and the Future of the African American Workforce," McKinsey & Company, November 14, 2018, https://www.mckinsey.com/featured-insights/future-of-work/automation-and-the-future-of-the-african-american-workforce.

114 *In fact, Black and Latino workers are overrepresented*: Kweilin Ellingrud et al., "Generative AI and the Future of Work in America."

114 *McKinsey estimates that at least 132,000 fewer*: Kelemwork Cook et al., "The Future of Work in Black America," McKinsey & Company, October 4, 2019, http://mckinsey.com/featured-insights/future-of-work/the-future-of-work-in-black-america.

115 *Business process outsourcing (BPO) of various sorts*: Paul Nicholas Soriano, "AI Tools Spark Anxiety among Philippines' Call Center Workers," *Rest of World*, July 17, 2023, https://restofworld.org/2023/call-center-ai-philippines/.

115 *and about 8 percent of India's*: "Outsourcing India: Its Key Challenger," *The Hindu*, February 15, 2022, https://www.thehindu.com/brandhub/pr-release/outsourcing-india-its-key-challenger/article65053182.ece.

115 *Sophisticated chatbots*: Soriano, "AI Tools Spark Anxiety."

115 *Many of the people doing this data labeling live in the developing world*: Adrienne Williams, Milagros Miceli, and Timnit Gebru, "The Exploited Labor behind Artificial Intelligence," *Noema*, October 13, 2022, https://www.noemamag.com/the-exploited-labor-behind-artificial-intelligence/.

116 *AI ethicists Adrienne Williams, Milagros Miceli, and Timnit Gebru*: Ibid.

116 *The MIT economists Daron Acemoglu and Andrea Manera*: Daron Acemoglu, Andrea Manera, and Pascual Restrepo, "Does the US Tax Code Favor Automation?," Working Paper Series, National Bureau of Economic Research, April 2020, doi:10.3386/w27052; Alana Semuels, "Millions of Americans Have Lost Jobs in the Pandemic—And Robots and AI Are Replacing Them Faster Than Ever," *Time*, August 6, 2020, https://time.com/5876604/machines-jobs-coronavirus/.

116 *Acemoglu, Manera, and Restrepo*: Acemoglu, Manera, and Restrepo, "Does the US Tax Code Favor Automation?"

117 *"This type of solidarity between highly paid tech workers"*: Williams, Miceli, and Gebru, "Exploited Labor."

117 *Unfortunately, the structure of collective bargaining*: Autor, interview.

117 *the National Labor Relations Act*: Lynn Rhinehart and Celine McNicholas, "Collective Bargaining beyond the Worksite: How Workers and Their Unions Build Power and Set Standards for Their Industries," Economic Policy Institute, accessed December 21, 2023, https://www.epi.org/publication/collec

tive-bargaining-beyond-the-worksite-how-workers-and-their-unions-build -power-and-set-standards-for-their-industries/.

118 *Meanwhile, the Wagner Act outlaws employee representatives on corporate boards*: Janice R. Bellace, "The Future of Employee Representation in America: Enabling Freedom of Association in the Workplace in Changing Times through Statutory Reform," *U. Pa. J. Lab. & Emp. L.* 5 (2002): 1.

118 *the Writers Guild of America*: Samantha Kelly, "TV and Film Writers Are Fighting to Save Their Jobs from AI. They Won't Be the Last," CNN Business, May 4, 2023.

118 *McKinsey estimates that 11.8 million Americans*: Ellingrud et al., "Generative AI."

118 *Efforts to deal with previous dislocations*: Semuels, "Millions of Americans Have Lost Jobs in the Pandemic—And Robots and AI Are Replacing Them Faster Than Ever."

119 *"A prepared workforce is a public good"*: Brynjolfsson, interview.

119 *The idea has long been popular*: Ross Andersen, "Does Sam Altman Know What He's Creating?"; Altman, interview.

CHAPTER 7: ARISTOTLE IN YOUR POCKET

121 *Students started referring*: Simone Carter, "CheatGPT: Will Artificial Intelligence Make Students Smarter or Dumber?," *Dallas Observer*, September 13, 2023, https://www.dallasobserver.com/news/cheatgpt-will-artificial-intelligen ce-make-students-smarter-or-dumber-17459509.

121 *"The College Essay Is Dead"*: Stephen Marche, "The College Essay Is Dead," *The Atlantic*, December 6, 2022, https://www.theatlantic.com/technology/ar chive/2022/12/chatgpt-ai-writing-college-student-essays/672371/.

121 *Some school systems*: Dan Rosenzweig-Ziff, "New York City Blocks Use of the ChatGPT Bot in Its Schools," *Washington Post*, January 5, 2023, https://www .washingtonpost.com/education/2023/01/05/nyc-schools-ban-chatgpt/.

121 *In Australia, the country's eight top universities*: Caitlin Cassidy, "Australian Universities to Return to 'Pen and Paper' Exams after Students Caught Using AI to Write Essays," *The Guardian*, January 10, 2023, https://www.theguardian.com /australia-news/2023/jan/10/universities-to-return-to-pen-and-paper-exams -after-students-caught-using-ai-to-write-essays.

121 *It's worth remembering*: Stephen Mihm (Bloomberg), "What a Calculator Can Tell You about ChatGPT," *Washington Post*, September 5, 2023, https://www .washingtonpost.com/business/2023/09/05/chatgpt-is-2023-s-version-of-the -calculator-and-cliffsnotes/716af25a-4bf0-11ee-bfca-04e0ac43f9e4_story.html.

122 *Or that professors have more recently decried*: Ian Bogost, "The First Year of AI College Ends in Ruin," *The Atlantic*, May 16, 2023, https://www.theatlantic.com /technology/archive/2023/05/chatbot-cheating-college-campuses/674073/.

122 *It's a vision of the future that Apple's founder Steve Jobs*: "Steve Jobs in Sweden, 1985 [HQ]," YouTube, 2011, https://youtube/watch?v=2qLuerYx2IA.

122 *"My hope is that in our lifetimes"*: Ibid.

122 *a new revolution based on "free intellectual energy"*: Ibid.

123 *AI detection software*: Bogost, "The First Year."

123 *Chris Gilliard*: Chris Gilliard and Pete Rorabaugh, "You're Not Going to Like How Colleges Respond to That Chatbot That Writes Papers," *Slate*, February 3, 2023, https://slate.com/technology/2023/02/chat-gpt-cheating-college-ai-de tection.html.

124 *Even before AI came along*: A. Marya, "Flipped Classrooms," *British Dental Journal* 232, no. 9 (May 2022): 590.

124 *Modern and Contemporary Poetry*: John Marchese, "Why Are 30,000 People Studying Poetry Online with This Guy?," *Philadelphia Magazine*, June 14, 2023, https://www.phillymag.com/news/2023/06/14/penn-poetry-modpo-online -course/.

125 *Either way, many colleges and universities*: Devan Burris, "Why More and More Colleges Are Closing Down across the U.S," CNBC, June 17, 2023, https:// www.cnbc.com/2023/06/17/why-more-and-more-colleges-are-closing-down -across-the-us.html.

126 *Heather Brantley, a sixth-grade math teacher*: Jocelyn Gecker and the Associated Press, "'It's Coming, Whether We Want It to or Not': Teachers Nationwide Are Using ChatGPT to Prepare Kids for an AI World," *Fortune*, February 14, 2023, https://fortune.com/2023/02/14/chatgpt-school-lessons-cheating-robots -ai-teachers/.

127 *Georgia Tech*: Emily Bobrow, "'A Real Opportunity': How ChatGPT Could Help College Applicants," *The Guardian*, August 27, 2023, https://www.theguardian .com/education/2023/aug/27/chatgpt-ai-disadvantaged-college-applicants-af firmative-action.

127 *At the University of Illinois*: "How ChatGPT Can Be Embraced—Not Feared—in the Classroom," Gies College of Business, accessed October 10, 2023, https:// giesbusiness.illinois.edu/news/2023/02/24/how-chatgpt-can-be-embraced--- not-feared---in-the-classroom.

128 *A mounting body of scientific evidence*: Andre Nickow, Philip Oreopoulos, and Vincent Quan, "The Impressive Effects of Tutoring on PreK–12 Learning: A Systematic Review and Meta-Analysis of the Experimental Evidence," National Bureau of Economic Research, Working Paper 27476, July 2020.

128 *But one-on-one tutoring*: Sal Khan, interview by Jeremy Kahn, July 14, 2023.

128 *Khan, who has computer science*: Ibid.

130 *Khan says educators' current attempts*: Ibid.

130 *Khan predicts that in a decade*: Ibid.

131 *AI software will arm teachers*: Ibid.

131 *History gives little reason for optimism*: Nicol Turner Lee, "Bridging Digital Divides between Schools and Communities," Brookings, March 2, 2020, https://www.brookings.edu/articles/bridging-digital-divides-between-schools-and-communities/; Stuart N. Brotman, "The Real Digital Divide in Educational Technology," Brookings, January 28, 2016, https://www.brookings.edu/articles/the-real-digital-divide-in-educational-technology/.

131 *The impact of this divide*: Hannah Holmes and Gemma Burgess, "Opinion: Coronavirus Has Intensified the UK's Digital Divide," University of Cambridge, May 6, 2020, https://www.cam.ac.uk/stories/digitaldivide; Daphne Leprince-Ringuet, "The Digital Divide Is Only Getting Worse for Those Who Are Left Behind," *ZDNET*, April 28, 2021, https://www.zdnet.com/article/the-digital-divide-is-only-getting-worse-for-those-who-are-left-behind/.

132 *More than previous digital technologies*: Michael Trucano, "AI and the Next Digital Divide in Education," Brookings, July 10, 2023, https://www.brookings.edu/articles/ai-and-the-next-digital-divide-in-education/.

132 *In 2021, only four in ten*: Emily A. Vogels, "Digital Divide Persists Even as Americans with Lower Incomes Make Gains in Tech Adoption," Pew Research Center, June 22, 2021, https://www.pewresearch.org/short-reads/2021/06/22/digital-divide-persists-even-as-americans-with-lower-incomes-make-gains-in-tech-adoption/.

132 *Programs such as*: "E-Rate—Schools & Libraries USF Program," Federal Communications Commission, accessed October 14, 2023, https://www.fcc.gov/general/e-rate-schools-libraries-usf-program.

132 *$475 million for free broadband and laptops*: Makena Kelly, "The Free Laptop Program Built into the Biden Reconciliation Plan," *The Verge*, November 2, 2021, https://www.theverge.com/2021/11/2/22759759/build-back-better-biden-laptop-tablet-low-income-manchin-sinema-broadband.

132 *It charges districts that use the AI*: Rhea Kelly, "Khan Academy Cuts District Price of Khanmigo AI Teaching Assistant, Adds Academic Essay Feature," *THE Journal*, November 16, 2023, https://thejournal.com/articles/2023/11/16/khan-academy-cuts-district-price-of-khanmigo-ai-teaching-assistant.aspx; Natasha Singer, "Tutoring Bots Get a Tryout in Newark Classrooms," *New York Times*, July 13, 2023.

133 *Quizlet also charges*: "Q-Chat: Meet Your New AI Tutor," Quizlet, accessed October 14, 2023, https://quizlet.com/labs/qchat.

133 *In February 2023, the South Korean Ministry of Education*: You-Jin Lee, "Korea to Adopt AI Textbooks for Core Subjects Starting in 2025," *Hankyoreh*, February 24, 2023, https://english.hani.co.kr/arti/english_edition/e_national/1081129.html; Park Jun-hee and Cho Chung-un, "[Herald Interview] Minister Turns to AI Classes to Cool Competition in Education," *The Korea Herald*, June 8, 2023, https://www.koreaherald.com/view.php?ud=20230608000715.

133 *Singapore's "Smart Nation" strategy*: "Tech and Education: How Automation and AI Are Powering Learning in Singapore," GovTech Singapore, February 23, 2023, https://www.tech.gov.sg/media/technews/tech-and-education-how-auto mation-and-ai-is-powering-learning-in-singapore.

134 *The average pupil-teacher ratio*: "Sustainable Development Goals: 4.c.4 Pupil-Qualified Teacher Ratio by Education Level," UNESCO UIS, accessed October 14, 2023, http://data.uis.unesco.org/index.aspx?queryid=3797.

134 *OpenAI's Altman visited Nigeria*: Alexander Onukwue, "Why OpenAI's Sam Altman Was Just in Lagos," *Semafor*, May 24, 2023, https://www.semafor.com /article/05/24/2023/sam-altman-visits-lagos-in-global-ai-push.

134 *He later commented*: Sam Altman, "A Conversation with OpenAI's CEO, Sam Altman | Hosted by UCL," interview by Azeem Azhar, Audio recording of an onstage public fireside chat, May 24, 2023.

134 *Many languages simply don't have enough text*: Anthony Mipawa, "Low Resource Languages vs. Conversational Artificial Intelligence," *NEUROTECH AFRICA*, September 26, 2022, https://blog.neurotech.africa/low-resource-languages-vs -conversational-artificial-intelligence/.

135 *One of them is Berlin-based Lesan*: Andrew Deck, "The AI Start-Up Outperforming Google Translate in Ethiopian Languages," *Rest of World*, July 11, 2023, https://re stofworld.org/2023/3-minutes-with-asmelash-teka-hadgu/; Nana Biamah-Ofosu et al., *Imagining Otherwise with Asmelash Teka Hadgu*, March 2, 2023.

135 *Asmelash Teka Hadgu, Lesan's co-founder*: Biamah-Ofosu et al., *Imagining Otherwise with Asmelash Teka Hadgu*; Asmelash Hadgu, interview by Jeremy Kahn, October 30, 2023.

136 *He is critical of the approach:* Hadgu, interview.

136 *Ghana NLP is a nonprofit*: "About Us," Ghana Natural Language Processing (NLP)—Ghana NLP, accessed October 14, 2023, https://ghananlp.org/about.

136 *"we didn't have to worry about food or clothes"*: Hadgu, interview.

136 *That school had computers*: Ibid.

CHAPTER 8: ART AND ARTIFICE

138 *As the philosopher Walter Benjamin*: Walter Benjamin, "The Work of Art in the Age of Mechanical Reproduction," *Illuminations*, ed. Hannah Arendt, trans. Harry Zohn (1935; repr., New York: Shocken Books, 1969), 2.

140 *In late 2023, OpenAI's Sam Altman*: Sam Altman, "Sam Altman X Feed," July 21, 2023, https://x.com/sama/status/1682493142845763585?s=20; Elizabeth Weil, "Sam Altman Is the Oppenheimer of Our Age," *Intelligencer*, September 25, 2023, https://nymag.com/intelligencer/article/sam-altman-artificial-intelligence -openai-profile.html.

140 *But his basic premise*: Altman, "Sam Altman X Feed."

140 *David Eagleman, the Stanford University neuroscientist*: David Eagleman and

Anthony Brandt, *The Runaway Species: How Human Creativity Remakes the World* (New York: Catapult, 2017).

140 *They also argue*: Ibid., chap. 2.

140 *"Like diamonds, creativity results from"*: Ibid., 36.

140 *Or, as the novelist Michael Chabon*: Jennifer Beamish and Toby Trackman, *The Creative Brain* (United States: Netflix, 2019).

141 *When researchers tested*: Jennifer Haase and Paul H. P. Hanel, "Artificial Muses: Generative Artificial Intelligence Chatbots Have Risen to Human-Level Creativity," arXiv.org, March 21, 2023, http://arxiv.org/abs/2303.12003.

141 *GPT-4 also scored*: Erik E. Guzik, Christian Byrge, and Christian Gilde, "The Originality of Machines: AI Takes the Torrance Test," *Journal of Creativity* 33, no. 3 (December 1, 2023): 100065.

142 *Eagleman and Brandt count synecdoche*: Eagleman and Brandt, *The Runaway Species: How Human Creativity Remakes the World*, 83–86.

142 *To illustrate breaking*: Ibid., 74–75.

143 *DALL-E 3 cannot depict*: Rajeev Raizada, "Surprising Blindspot in ChatGPT+ Image-Creation: Seems Unable to Show a Clean-Shaven Man Painting a Man with a Beard Prompt: Make a Picture of Picasso Painting a Portrait of Leonardo This Pic Is 6th Attempt, after Repeatedly Told Various Ways That the Painter Still Has a Beard!" X, November 26, 2023, https://twitter.com/raj_raizada/status/1728769392731898180.

143 *when researchers prompted Midjourney*: Carmen Drahl, "AI Was Asked to Create Images of Black African Docs Treating White Kids. How'd It Go?," NPR, October 6, 2023, https://www.npr.org/sections/goatsandsoda/2023/10/06/1201 840678/ai-was-asked-to-create-images-of-black-african-docs-treating-white -kids-howd-it-.

143 *researchers from Columbia University*: Tuhin Chakrabarty et al., "Art or Artifice? Large Language Models and the False Promise of Creativity," arXiv.org, September 25, 2023, http://arxiv.org/abs/2309.14556.

144 *Ahmed Elgammal, an Egyptian-born computer scientist*: Ahmed Elgammal et al., "CAN: Creative Adversarial Networks, Generating 'Art' by Learning about Styles and Deviating from Style Norms," arXiv.org, June 21, 2017, http://arxiv .org/abs/1706.07068; Arthur I. Miller, *AI Renaissance Machines: Inside the New World of Machine-Created Art, Literature, and Music* (Cambridge, MA: MIT Press, 2019), 113–18.

144 *Elgammal said that*: Miller, *AI Renaissance Machines: Inside the New World of Machine-Created Art, Literature, and Music*, 116.

144 *an AI that operated in this way*: Julian Schrittwieser et al., "MuZero: Mastering Go, Chess, Shogi and Atari without Rules," Google DeepMind (blog), accessed December 20, 2020, https://deepmind.google/discover/blog/muzero-master ing-go-chess-shogi-and-atari-without-rules/.

145 *Van Gogh sold relatively few works*: "How Many Paintings Did Vincent Sell during His Lifetime?," Van Gogh Museum, accessed March 20, 2024, https://www.vangoghmuseum.nl/en/art-and-stories/vincent-van-gogh-faq /how-many-paintings-did-vincent-sell-during-his-lifetime.

145 *Herman Melville's novel* Moby-Dick *sold*: American Experience, "The Life of Herman Melville," *American Experience*, June 2, 2017, https://www.pbs.org /wgbh/americanexperience/features/whaling-biography-herman-melville/.

145 *A packed room inside Christie's New York*: Eileen Kinsella, "The First AI-Generated Portrait Ever Sold at Auction Shatters Expectations, Fetching $432,500—43 Times Its Estimate," *Artnet News*, October 25, 2018, https:// news.artnet.com/market/first-ever-artificial-intelligence-portrait-painting -sells-at-christies-1379902.

146 *The sale of* Edmond de Belamy: Jonathan Jones, "A Portrait Created by AI Just Sold for $432,000. But Is It Really Art?," *The Guardian*, October 26, 2018, https://www.theguardian.com/artanddesign/shortcuts/2018/oct/26/call-that -art-can-a-computer-be-a-painter.

146 *This is, in fact, what Elgammal discovered*: Miller, *AI Renaissance Machines*, 117–18.

147 *An AI model could create*: Nick Cave, "I Asked Chat GPT to Write a Song in the Style of Nick Cave and This Is What It Produced. What Do You Think?," *The Red Hand Files*, Issue #218, January 2023, https://www.theredhandfiles.com /chat-gpt-what-do-you-think/.

148 *Walter Benjamin, in writing about*: Benjamin, "The Work of Art in the Age of Mechanical Reproduction."

148 *and this remains true even if*: David Smyth, "ABBA Voyage Review: Can This Be Real? I Literally Could Not Believe My Eyes," *Evening Standard*, May 27, 2022, https://www.standard.co.uk/culture/music/abba-voyage-concert-experience -review-london-arena-b1002718.html.

149 *The British crime novelist Ajay Chowdhury*: Ajay Chowdhury, interview by Jeremy Kahn, November 13, 2023.

149 *Silva's technique*: Hannah Silva, interview by Jeremy Kahn, November 14, 2023.

150 *"They've just become much 'better,'"*: Ibid.

150 *In her experience, some of the most*: Ibid.

150 *He used OpenAI's GPT-3*: Andrii Degeler, "Composition Co-Written by AI Performed by Choir and Published as Sheet Music," *The Next Web*, August 14, 2023, https://thenextweb.com/news/composition-cowritten-ai-performed-choir -published-sheet-music.

151 *"One of the biggest benefits"*: Ed Newton-Rex, interview by Jeremy Kahn, July 31, 2023.

151 *Daniel Ambrosi is known for his*: Daniel Ambrosi, interview by Jeremy Kahn and Tristan Bove, November 2, 2023.

151   *DeepDream, which made a big impression*: Alexander Mordvintsev, Christopher
      Olah, and Mike Tyka, "Inceptionism: Going Deeper into Neural Networks,"
      Google Research Blog, June 18, 2015, https://blog.research.google/2015/06
      /inceptionism-going-deeper-into-neural.html; Arthur I. Miller, "DeepDream:
      How Alexander Mordvintsev Excavated the Computer's Hidden Layers,"
      The MIT Press Reader, July 1, 2020, https://thereader.mitpress.mit.edu/deep
      dream-how-alexander-mordvintsev-excavated-the-computers-hidden-layers/;
      "DeepDream," *TensorFlow*, accessed November 10, 2023, https://www.tensor
      flow.org/tutorials/generative/deepdream.

151   *For a series of photographs*: Daniel Ambrosi, interview.

152   *The key here, Ambrosi notes*: Ibid.

152   *he predicts AI's impact*: Ibid.

153   *The American painter Chuck Close*: Roberta Smith, "Chuck Close's Uneasy, In-
      evitable Legacy," *New York Times*, August 20, 2021, https://www.nytimes.com
      /2021/08/20/arts/design/chuck-close-legacy-appraisal-dementia-behavior
      .html.

154   *Meta paid millions to celebrities*: Todd Spangler, "Meta Launches AI Chatbots
      for Snoop Dogg, MrBeast, Tom Brady, Kendall Jenner, Charli D'Amelio and
      More," *Variety*, September 27, 2023, https://variety.com/2023/digital/news/me
      ta-ai-chatbots-snoop-dogg-mrbeast-tom-brady-kendall-jenner-charli-dame
      lio-1235737740/.

154   *The actor James Earl Jones*: Emma Roth, "James Earl Jones Lets AI Take over the
      Voice of Darth Vader," *The Verge*, September 24, 2022, https://www.theverge
      .com/2022/9/24/23370097/darth-vader-james-earl-jones-obi-wan-kenobi-star
      -wars-ai-disney-lucasfilm.

154   *AI helped resurrect John Lennon's voice*: Will Sullivan, "The Beatles Release Their
      Last Song, 'Now and Then,' Featuring A.I.-Extracted Vocals from John Lennon,"
      Smithsonian magazine, November 3, 2023, https://www.smithsonianmag.com
      /smart-news/the-beatles-release-their-last-song-now-and-then-ai-john-len
      non-180983188/.

154   *The musician Grimes*: Sian Cain, "Grimes Invites People to Use Her Voice
      in AI Songs," *The Guardian*, April 26, 2023, https://www.theguardian.com
      /music/2023/apr/26/grimes-invites-people-to-use-her-voice-in-ai-songs.

154   *For celebrities, AI is a brand-extension superpower*: "The Dawn of the Omnistar,"
      The Economist, November 9, 2023, https://www.economist.com/leaders/2023
      /11/09/how-artificial-intelligence-will-transform-fame.

155   *Visual artist Karla Ortiz*: Karla Ortiz, interview by Jeremy Kahn, November 2,
      2023.

155   *"Good artists borrow, great artists steal"*: "Good Artists Copy; Great Artists Steal,"
      Quoteinvestigator.com, March 6, 2013, https://quoteinvestigator.com/2013/03
      /06/artists-steal/.

155 *"The only art I'll ever study is stuff that I can steal from"*: Cameron Crowe, "David Bowie's September 1976 Playboy Interview," *Playboy*, September 1976, https://www.playboy.com/read/playboy-interview-david-bowie.

156 *The exact training set*: Alex Reisner, "Revealed: The Authors Whose Pirated Books Are Powering Generative AI," *The Atlantic*, August 19, 2023, https://www.theatlantic.com/technology/archive/2023/08/books3-ai-meta-llama-pirated-books/675063/.

156 *The LAION 5-B*: Marissa Newman and Aggi Cantrill, "The Future of AI Relies on a High School Teacher's Free Database," Bloomberg, April 24, 2023.

156 *Fair use, as the Harvard legal scholar Benjamin Sobel*: Benjamin Sobel, "Artificial Intelligence's Fair Use Crisis," *Columbia Journal of Law & the Arts*, September 4, 2017, https://papers.ssrn.com/abstract=3032076.

157 *Neil Turkewitz, a former*: Neil Turkewitz, Interviewed on Zoom, interview by Jeremy Kahn, September 28, 2023.

157 *Mark Lemley, the director of*: Mark Lemley, interview for *Fortune* magazine, interview by Jeremy Kahn, May 11, 2023.

157 *Meanwhile, advocates for artists*: Rebecca Klar, "Songwriters to Lobby Congress for Protections from AI," *The Hill*, September 20, 2023, https://thehill.com/policy/technology/4214976-songwriters-to-lobby-congress-for-protections-from-ai/.

157 *Other countries*: ReedSmith LLP, "Entertainment and Media Guide to AI," *Perspectives*, June 20, 2023, https://www.reedsmith.com/en/perspectives/ai-in-entertainment-and-media; Supantha Mukherjee, Foo Yun Chee, Martin Coulter, "EU Proposes New Copyright Rules for Generative AI," Reuters, April 28, 2023, https://www.reuters.com/technology/eu-lawmakers-committee-reaches-deal-artificial-intelligence-act-2023-04-27/.

158 *Japan has gone the furthest*: Andrew Deck, "Japan's New AI Rules Favor Copycats over Artists, Experts Say," *Rest of World*, June 28, 2023, https://restofworld.org/2023/japans-new-ai-rules-favor-copycats-over-artists/.

158 *So far, the U.S. Copyright Office*: Blake Brittain, "US Copyright Office Denies Protection for Another AI-Created Image," Reuters, September 6, 2023, https://www.reuters.com/legal/litigation/us-copyright-office-denies-protection-another-ai-created-image-2023-09-06/.

158 *The Audio Home Recording Act*: Christine C. Carlisle, "The Audio Home Recording Act of 1992," *Journal of Intellectual Property Law* 1, no. 2 (March 1994), https://digitalcommons.law.uga.edu/cgi/viewcontent.cgi?article=1059&context=jipl.

159 *rights holders are busy erecting*: Rachyl Jones, "Major Media Organizations Are Putting Up 'Do Not Enter' Signs for ChatGPT," *Fortune*, August 25, 2023, https://fortune.com/2023/08/25/major-media-organizations-are-blocking-openai-bot-from-scraping-content/; Gintaras Radauskas, "AI and Data Scraping: Websites Scramble to Defend Their Content," *Cybernews*, August 10, 2023, https://cybernews.com/editorial/ai-data-scraping-websites/.

159   *Ben Zhao, a computer science professor:* Shawn Shan et al., "Glaze: Protecting Artists from Style Mimicry by Text-to-Image Models," arXiv.org, February 8, 2023, http://arxiv.org/abs/2302.04222; Ben Zhao, interview by Jeremy Kahn, October 11, 2023.

159   *More recently Zhao has gone further:* Shawn Shan et al., "Prompt-Specific Poisoning Attacks on Text-to-Image Generative Models," arXiv.org, October 20, 2023, http://arxiv.org/abs/2310.13828; Melissa Heikkilä, "This New Data Poisoning Tool Lets Artists Fight Back against Generative AI," *MIT Technology Review*, October 23, 2023, https://www.technologyreview.com/2023/10/23/108 2189/data-poisoning-artists-fight-generative-ai/; Zhao, interview.

160   *Applying Glaze:* Zhao, interview.

160   *Zhao says that art schools:* Ibid.

160   *Zhao has been asked:* Ibid.

CHAPTER 9: A MICROSCOPE FOR DATA

162   *PubMed, a popular repository:* Esther Landhuis, "Scientific Literature: Information Overload," *Nature* 535, no. 7612 (July 21, 2016): 457–58.

162   *Across scientific disciplines:* Karen White, "Publications Output: U.S. Trends and International Comparisons," National Center for Science and Engineering Statistics, October 28, 2021, https://ncses.nsf.gov/pubs/nsb20214/publication -output-by-country-region-or-economy-and-scientific-field.

162   *This disparity between the production of new data:* Michael Park, Erin Leahey, and Russell J. Funk, "Papers and Patents Are Becoming Less Disruptive over Time," *Nature* 613, no. 7942 (January 2023): 138–44.

163   *AI is critical to reversing this trend:* "Is Science Really Getting Less Disruptive— and Does It Matter if It Is?," *Nature* 614, no. 7946 (February 2023): 7–8.

164   *Seoul, South Korea:* Jeremy Kahn, "Know When to Fold 'Em: How a Company Best Known for Playing Games Used A.I. to Solve One of Biology's Greatest Mysteries," *Fortune*, November 30, 2020, https://fortune.com/2020/11/30/deep mind-solved-protein-folding-alphafold/.

164   *Now the two:* Unpublished outtake from the documentary film *AlphaGo* (2017) made available to Kahn courtesy of DeepMind and cited in Ibid.

164   *In the 1960s:* Kahn, "Know When to Fold 'Em."

164   *Proteins are the building blocks:* Kerry Geiler, "Protein Folding: The Good, the Bad, and the Ugly," *Science in the News*, March 1, 2010, https://sitn.hms.harvard .edu/flash/2010/issue65/.

165   *Being able to predict protein structure:* Kahn, "Know When to Fold 'Em."

165   *"Solving" protein folding:* Ibid.

165   *At the time of Hassabis and Silver's:* Mohammed AlQuraishi, "AlphaFold @ CASP13: 'What Just Happened?,'" *Some Thoughts on a Mysterious Universe*

(blog), December 9, 2018, https://moalquraishi.wordpress.com/2018/12/09/al phafold-casp13-what-just-happened/.

165 *Meanwhile, the gold standard*: Kahn, "Know When to Fold 'Em."

166 *Still, in 2016*: "PDB Statistics: Protein-Only Structures Released per Year," Collaboratory for Structural Bioinformatics Protein Data Bank, accessed October 17, 2023, https://www.rcsb.org/stats/growth/growth-protein.

166 *In November 2020*: Kahn, "Know When to Fold 'Em."

166 *it used AlphaFold to produce*: Jeremy Kahn, "A.I. Is Rapidly Transforming Biological Research—with Big Implications for Everything from Drug Discovery to Agriculture to Sustainability," *Fortune*, July 28, 2022, https://fortune.com/2022 /07/28/deepmind-alphafold-every-protein-in-the-universe-structure/.

166 *It's transforming the hunt*: Oana Stroe, "Case Study: AlphaFold Uses Open Data and AI to Discover the 3D Protein Universe," EMBL, February 9, 2023, https:// www.embl.org/news/science/alphafold-using-open-data-and-ai-to-discover -the-3d-protein-universe/.

166 *Paul Nurse, a Nobel laureate*: Jeremy Kahn, "In Giant Leap for Biology, Deep-Mind's A.I. Reveals Secret Building Blocks of Human Life," *Fortune*, July 22, 2021, https://fortune.com/2021/07/22/deepmind-alphafold-human-proteome -database-proteins/.

167 *Experts from Microsoft*: Nathan Baker, "Unlocking a New Era for Scientific Discovery with AI: How Microsoft's AI Screened over 32 Million Candidates to Find a Better Battery," *Microsoft Azure Quantum Blog*, January 9, 2024, https:// cloudblogs.microsoft.com/quantum/2024/01/09/unlocking-a-new-era-for-sci entific-discovery-with-ai-how-microsofts-ai-screened-over-32-million-candi dates-to-find-a-better-battery/.

167 *With help from researchers*: "How Scientists Are Using Artificial Intelligence," *The Economist*, September 13, 2023, https://www.economist.com/science-and -technology/2023/09/13/how-scientists-are-using-artificial-intelligence.

167 *AI is being used to count*: Graeme Green, "Five Ways AI Is Saving Wildlife— from Counting Chimps to Locating Whales," *The Guardian*, February 21, 2022, https://www.theguardian.com/environment/2022/feb/21/five-ways-ai-is-sav ing-wildlife-from-counting-chimps-to-locating-whales-aoe.

167 *It is being used by astronomers*: Aaron McDade, "Artificial Intelligence May Have Just Given Astronomers a Better Idea of What Black Holes Really Look Like," *Business Insider*, April 14, 2023, https://www.businessinsider.com/astronomers -use-ai-to-generate-clearer-picture-of-black-hole-2023-4.

167 *It is helping archaeologists*: Nabil Bachagha et al., "The Use of Machine Learning and Satellite Imagery to Detect Roman Fortified Sites: The Case Study of Blad Talh (Tunisia Section)," *NATO Advanced Science Institutes Series E: Applied Sciences* 13, no. 4 (February 17, 2023): 2613.

167 *helping classicists decipher ancient texts*: Yannis Assael et al., "Predicting the Past with Ithaca," Google DeepMind (blog), March 9, 2022, https://deepmind .google/discover/blog/predicting-the-past-with-ithaca/.

168 *"reading" scrolls*: Jo Marchant, "AI Reads Text from Ancient Herculaneum Scroll for the First Time," *Nature*, October 12, 2023, doi:10.1038/d41586-023-03212-1.

168 *And it is helping us unlock*: Jeremy Kahn and Jonathan Vanian, "Inside Neuralink, Elon Musk's Mysterious Brain Chip Start-up: A Culture of Blame, Impossible Deadlines, and a Missing CEO," *Fortune*, January 27, 2022, https://fortune .com/longform/neuralink-brain-computer-interface-chip-implant-elon-musk/; Jose Antonio Lanz, "Meta Has an AI That Can Read Your Mind and Draw Your Thoughts," *Decrypt*, October 18, 2023, https://decrypt.co/202258/meta-has-an -ai-that-can-read-your-mind-and-draw-your-thoughts; Jonathan Vanian, "The Next Generation of Brain-Computing Interfaces Could Be Supercharged by Artificial Intelligence," *Fortune*, February 24, 2022, https://fortune.com/2022/02/24 /artificial-intelligence-artificial-neural-networks-brain-computing-neuralink/.

168 *John Jumper, the DeepMind senior researcher*: John Jumper and Pushmeet Kohli, interview by Jeremy Kahn, August 23, 2023.

168 *Jumper says that one of the biggest limitations*: Ibid.

168 *But AI itself will help*: Ibid.

168 *A free LLM-based search tool called Elicit*: "How Scientists Are Using Artificial Intelligence," *The Economist*.

169 *AI can analyze*: Igor Grossmann et al., "AI and the Transformation of Social Science Research," *Science* 380, no. 6650 (June 16, 2023): 1108–9.

169 *Academics in Singapore*: Haocong Rao, Cyril Leung, and Chunyan Miao, "Can ChatGPT Assess Human Personalities? A General Evaluation Framework," arXiv.org, March 1, 2023, http://arxiv.org/abs/2303.01248.

169 *Igor Grossmann, a psychologist*: Alexander Stavropoulos, Damien Crone, and Igor Grossmann, "Shadows of Wisdom: Classifying Meta-Cognitive and Morally-Grounded Narrative Content via Large Language Models," PsyArXiv Preprints, September 12, 2023, doi:10.31234/osf.io/x2f4a; Grossmann et al., "AI and the Transformation of Social Science Research."

169 *Academics in Qatar and Finland*: Bernard J. Jansen, Soon-Gyo Jung, and Joni Salminen, "Employing Large Language Models in Survey Research," *Natural Language Processing Journal* 4 (September 1, 2023): 100020.

169 *LLMs could also simulate human behavior*: Grossmann et al., "AI and the Transformation of Social Science Research."

169 *Recognizing this danger, the U.S. government*: Steve Lohr, "Universities and Tech Giants Back National Cloud Computing Project," *New York Times*, June 30, 2020, https://www.nytimes.com/2020/06/30/technology/national-cloud-com puting-project.html.

170 *This shifts us firmly away*: Chris Anderson, "The End of Theory: The Data Deluge

Makes the Scientific Method Obsolete," *Wired*, June 23, 2008, https://www.wired .com/2008/06/pb-theory/; Laura Spinney, "Are We Witnessing the Dawn of Post-Theory Science?," *The Guardian*, January 9, 2022, https://www.theguardian.com /technology/2022/jan/09/are-we-witnessing-the-dawn-of-post-theory-science.

170 *Sumit Chopra, an AI researcher*: Spinney, "Are We Witnessing the Dawn of Post-Theory Science?"

171 *We've been using it for the better part*: Ed Cara, "Scientists Just Learned Something New about How Aspirin Works," *Gizmodo*, March 28, 2023, https://giz modo.com/how-aspirin-works-inflammation-1850274046.

171 *Instrumentalists believe*: Paul K. Feyerabend, *Realism, Rationalism and Scientific Method: Volume 1: Philosophical Papers* (Cambridge, UK: Cambridge University Press, 1981).

171 *"What is the core of science?"*: Jumper and Kohli, interview.

171 *Scientific realists, on the other hand*: Feyerabend, *Realism, Rationalism and Scientific Method: Volume 1: Philosophical Papers*.

171 *He once criticized purely statistical predictions*: Chomsky quoted in Peter Norvig, "Colorless Green Ideas Learn Furiously," *Significance (Oxford, England)* 9, no. 4 (August 1, 2012): 30–33.

171 *The professor Jonathan Zittrain*: Jonathan Zittrain, "The Hidden Costs of Automated Thinking," *The New Yorker*, July 23, 2019, https://www.newyorker.com /tech/annals-of-technology/the-hidden-costs-of-automated-thinking.

172 *In December 2021*: "Machine Learning Helps Mathematicians Make New Connections," University of Oxford, accessed February 5, 2024, https://www.ox.ac .uk/news/2021-12-01-machine-learning-helps-mathematicians-make-new -connections-0.

172 *Pushmeet Kohli, the head*: Jumper and Kohli, interview.

173 *In the basement of a former art museum*: Ali Madani, interview by Jeremy Kahn, July 19, 2023.

174 *Along with collaborators from Salesforce*: Ali Madani et al., "Large Language Models Generate Functional Protein Sequences across Diverse Families," *Nature Biotechnology* 41, no. 8 (August 2023): 1099–1106.

174 *Eventually, Madani hopes*: Madani, interview.

174 *Traditional protein design methods*: Tian Zhu et al., "Hit Identification and Optimization in Virtual Screening: Practical Recommendations Based on a Critical Literature Analysis," *Journal of Medicinal Chemistry* 56, no. 17 (September 12, 2013): 6560–72.

175 *Madani says that Profluent's AI selection process*: Madani, interview.

175 *Right now, it takes*: Olivier J. Wouters, Martin McKee, and Jeroen Luyten, "Estimated Research and Development Investment Needed to Bring a New Medicine to Market, 2009–2018," *JAMA: The Journal of the American Medical Association* 323, no. 9 (March 3, 2020): 844–53.

175 *LabGenius is a London-based start-up*: James Field, founder and CEO of LabGenius, interview by Jeremy Kahn, June 22, 2023; LabGenius, "LabGenius Debuts T-Cell Engager Optimisation Capability That Yields Molecules with >400-Fold Tumour Killing Selectivity versus Clinical Benchmark," LabGenius, May 15, 2023, https://labgeni.us/news-1/pegsboston2023.

175 *AI can help us combat*: "How Scientists Are Using Artificial Intelligence," *The Economist*.

176 *The technology is already helping radiologists*: Steven Schalekamp, Willemijn M. Klein, and Kicky G. van Leeuwen, "Current and Emerging Artificial Intelligence Applications in Chest Imaging: A Pediatric Perspective," *Pediatric Radiology* 52, no. 11 (October 2022): 2120–30; Hwa-Yen Chiu, Heng-Sheng Chao, and Yuh-Min Chen, "Application of Artificial Intelligence in Lung Cancer," *Cancers* 14, no. 6 (March 8, 2022), doi:10.3390/cancers14061370; Judith Becker et al., "Artificial Intelligence-Based Detection of Pneumonia in Chest Radiographs," *Diagnostics (Basel, Switzerland)* 12, no. 6 (June 14, 2022), doi:10.3390/diagnostics12061465.

176 *At Johns Hopkins Hospital*: Laura Cech, "AI to Detect Sepsis," *John Hopkins Magazine*, December 16, 2022, https://hub.jhu.edu/magazine/2022/winter/ai-technology-to-detect-sepsis/.

176 *At Moorfields Eye Hospital*: UCL, "World-First AI Foundation Model for Eye Care to Supercharge Global Efforts to Prevent Blindness," *UCL News*, September 13, 2023, https://www.ucl.ac.uk/news/2023/sep/world-first-ai-foundation-model-eye-care-supercharge-global-efforts-prevent-blindness.

176 *AI is also helping surgeons*: Jim McCartney, "AI Is Poised to 'Revolutionize' Surgery," American College of Surgeons (ACS), accessed October 26, 2023, https://www.facs.org/for-medical-professionals/news-publications/news-and-articles/bulletin/2023/june-2023-volume-108-issue-6/ai-is-poised-to-revolutionize-surgery/.

176 *And medical-specific LLMs*: Karan Singhal et al., "Large Language Models Encode Clinical Knowledge," *Nature* 620, no. 7972 (August 2023): 172–80; Kyle Wiggers, "Hippocratic Is Building a Large Language Model for Healthcare," *TechCrunch*, May 16, 2023, https://techcrunch.com/2023/05/16/hippocratic-is-building-a-large-language-model-for-healthcare/; Suehyun Lee and Hun-Sung Kim, "Prospect of Artificial Intelligence Based on Electronic Medical Record," *Journal of Lipid and Atherosclerosis* 10, no. 3 (September 2021): 282–90; Thomas Davenport and Ravi Kalakota, "The Potential for Artificial Intelligence in Healthcare," *Future Healthcare Journal* 6, no. 2 (June 2019): 94–98.

176 *When combined with widely available genome sequencing*: Joshua C. Denny and Francis S. Collins, "Precision Medicine in 2030—Seven Ways to Transform Healthcare," *Cell* 184, no. 6 (March 18, 2021): 1415–19.

177 *For instance, an algorithm that researchers*: Karandeep Singh, "An AI Model

Predicting Acute Kidney Injury Works, but Not without Some Tweaking," Institute for Healthcare Policy & Innovation, January 20, 2023, https://ihpi.umich.edu/news/ai-model-predicting-acute-kidney-injury-works-not-without-some-tweaking.

177 *One major study*: Laure Wynants et al., "Prediction Models for Diagnosis and Prognosis of Covid-19: Systematic Review and Critical Appraisal," *BMJ* 369 (April 7, 2020): m1328; Will Douglas Heaven, "Hundreds of AI Tools Have Been Built to Catch Covid. None of Them Helped," *MIT Technology Review*, July 30, 2021, https://www.technologyreview.com/2021/07/30/1030329/machine-learning-ai-failed-covid-hospital-diagnosis-pandemic/.

177 *Another that looked at 415 published tools*: Michael Roberts et al., "Common Pitfalls and Recommendations for Using Machine Learning to Detect and Prognosticate for COVID-19 Using Chest Radiographs and CT Scans," *Nature Machine Intelligence* 3, no. 3 (March 15, 2021): 199–217; Heaven, "Hundreds of AI Tools Have Been Built to Catch Covid. None of Them Helped."

178 *Meanwhile, fewer than 3 percent*: Denny and Collins, "Precision Medicine in 2030—Seven Ways to Transform Healthcare."

178 *Right now, AI software companies*: Liz Szabo and Kaiser Health News, "Artificial Intelligence Is Rushing Into Patient Care—and Could Raise Risks," *Scientific American*, accessed October 26, 2023, https://www.scientificamerican.com/article/artificial-intelligence-is-rushing-into-patient-care-and-could-raise-risks/.

178 *In many cases, AI models*: Andreas Heindl, "The Step-by-Step Guide to Getting Your AI Models through FDA Approval," Encord (blog), May 16, 2023, https://encord.com/blog/ai-algorithm-fda-approval/; Eric Wu et al., "How Medical AI Devices Are Evaluated: Limitations and Recommendations from an Analysis of FDA Approvals," *Nature Medicine* 27, no. 4 (April 2021): 582–84.

178 *As of December 2023*: Andrea Koncz, "The Current State of FDA-Approved AI-Enabled Medical Devices," *The Medical Futurist*, December 12, 2023, https://medicalfuturist.com/the-current-state-of-fda-approved-ai-based-medical-devices/.

178 *Also, we know that Black*: Casey Ross, "A Research Team Airs the Messy Truth about AI in Medicine—and Gives Hospitals a Guide to Fix It," *STAT*, April 27, 2023, https://www.statnews.com/2023/04/27/hospitals-health-artificial-intelligence-ai/; Wu et al., "How Medical AI Devices Are Evaluated: Limitations and Recommendations from an Analysis of FDA Approvals."

178 *This has left many doctors*: Christina Jewett, "Doctors Wrestle With A.I. in Patient Care, Citing Lax Oversight," *New York Times*, October 30, 2023, https://www.nytimes.com/2023/10/30/health/doctors-ai-technology-health-care.html.

178 *But some hospital systems are hiring*: Ross, "A Research Team Airs the Messy Truth about AI in Medicine."

179 *be used to engineer novel bioweapons*: Kate Charlet, "The New Killer Pathogens,"

Foreign Affairs, April 16, 2018, https://www.foreignaffairs.com/world/new-killer-pathogens; Christopher Mouton, Caleb Lucas, and Ella Guest, "The Operational Risks of AI in Large-Scale Biological Attacks," RAND Corporation Research Reports, October 16, 2023, https://doi.org/10.7249/RRA2977-1; Mustafa Suleyman, *The Coming Wave: Technology, Power, and the Twenty-First Century's Greatest Dilemma* (New York: Crown, 2023), 12–13, 173–77, 273–74.

179 *The sale and export of*: Suleyman, *The Coming Wave*.

179 *One small consolation*: Yolanda Botti-Lodovico et al., "The Origins and Future of Sentinel: An Early-Warning System for Pandemic Preemption and Response," *Viruses* 13, no. 8 (August 13, 2021), doi:10.3390/v13081605; Simar Bajaj and Abdullahi Tsanni, "Meet the Scientists Trying to Stop the Next Global Pandemic from Starting in Africa," *STAT*, August 9, 2023, https://www.statnews.com/2023/08/09/happi-sabeti-sentinel-geneticists-global-pandemic-africa/; Hannah Kuchler and Sarah Neville, "Bill Gates Calls for Global Surveillance Team to Spot Pandemic Threats," *Financial Times*, May 1, 2022, https://www.ft.com/content/c8896c10-35da-46aa-957f-cf2b4e18cfce.

CHAPTER 10: MORE HEAT THAN LIGHT

182 *"solve climate change"*: Hamid Maher et al., "AI Is Essential for Solving the Climate Crisis," BCG Global, July 7, 2022, https://www.bcg.com/publications/2022/how-ai-can-help-climate-change.

183 *The DeepMind project*: Carl Elkin and Sims Witherspoon, "Machine Learning Can Boost the Value of Wind Energy," Google DeepMind (blog), February 26, 2019, https://deepmind.google/discover/blog/machine-learning-can-boost-the-value-of-wind-energy/.

183 *Kelly wanted to do much more*: Jack Kelly, "Starting a Non-Profit Research Lab to Help Fix Climate Change ASAP," Open Climate Fix (blog), January 7, 2019, https://openclimatefix.org/post/starting-a-non-profit-research-lab-to-help-fix-climate-change-asap.

183 *Kelly's first project at the new lab*: Jack Kelly, interview by Jeremy Kahn, September 27, 2023.

184 *Google's Project Green Light*: Yossi Matias, "Project Green Light's Work to Reduce Urban Emissions Using AI," Google, October 10, 2023, https://blog.google/outreach-initiatives/sustainability/google-ai-reduce-greenhouse-emissions-project-greenlight/.

184 *A start-up called DroneDeploy*: "Solar Construction AI Reports," DroneDeploy, accessed November 8, 2023, https://www.dronedeploy.com/lp/solar-construction-ai-reports.

185 *Silicon Valley start-up Aionics*: Casey Crownhart, "How AI Could Supercharge Battery Research," *MIT Technology Review*, October 12, 2023, https://www.technologyreview.com/2023/10/12/1081502/ai-battery-research/.

185 *researchers at labs*: Jonas Degrave et al., "Magnetic Control of Tokamak Plasmas through Deep Reinforcement Learning," *Nature* 602, no. 7897 (February 2022): 414–19; Pulsar Team and Swiss Plasma Center, "Accelerating Fusion Science through Learned Plasma Control," Google DeepMind (blog), February 16, 2022, https://deepmind.google/discover/blog/accelerating-fusion-science-through-learned-plasma-control/; Luke Auburn, "Could Artificial Intelligence Power the Future of Fusion?," University of Rochester News Center, September 5, 2023, https://www.rochester.edu/newscenter/could-artificial-intelligence-power-er-the-future-of-fusion-565252/; Cynthia Dillon, "U.S. Department of Energy Selects Team to Advance Fusion Research," *UC San Diego Today*, September 1, 2023, https://today.ucsd.edu/story/u.s-department-of-energy-selects-team-to-advance-fusion-research.

185 *Right now, the power that fusion reactors produce*: Breanna Bishop, "Lawrence Livermore National Laboratory Achieves Fusion Ignition," Lawrence Livermore National Laboratory (blog), December 14, 2022, https://www.llnl.gov/archive/news/lawrence-livermore-national-laboratory-achieves-fusion-ignition.

185 *adapt to a changing environment*: Dylan Walsh, "Tackling Climate Change with Machine Learning," MIT Sloan, October 24, 2023, https://mitsloan.mit.edu/ideas-made-to-matter/tackling-climate-change-machine-learning; Michelle Ma and Nadia Lopez, "AI Is Giving the Climate Forecast for Supply Chains a Makeover," Bloomberg News, September 12, 2023, https://www.bloomberg.com/news/articles/2023-09-12/artificial-intelligence-climate-forecast-could-help-supply-chain-management; Andrew J. Hawkins, "Google Wants to Be at the Center of All Your Climate Change Decisions," *The Verge*, October 10, 2023, https://www.theverge.com/2023/10/10/23906496/google-ai-transportation-ev-heat-pump-flood-wildfire.

185 *Moore's law*: Robert R. Schaller, "Moore's Law: Past, Present and Future," *IEEE Spectrum* 34, no. 6 (June 1997): 52–59.

185 *Climate researcher Jonathan Koomey*: "A Deeper Law than Moore's?," *The Economist*, October 10, 2011, https://www.economist.com/graphic-detail/2011/10/10/a-deeper-law-than-moores.

186 *Since 2000*: Jonathan Koomey, "Moore's Law Might Be Slowing Down, but Not Energy Efficiency," *IEEE Spectrum*, March 31, 2015, https://spectrum.ieee.org/moores-law-might-be-slowing-down-but-not-energy-efficiency.

186 *typically consumes more power*: Martín Puig et al., "Are GPUs Non-Green Computing Devices?" *Journal of Computer Science and Technology* 18, no. 2 (October 2018).

186 *One assessment of the carbon footprint*: Katyanna Quach, "AI Me to the Moon . . . Carbon Footprint for 'Training GPT-3' Same as Driving to Our Natural Satellite and Back," *The Register*, November 4, 2020, https://www.theregister.com/2020/11/04/gpt3_carbon_footprint_estimate/.

186   *AI, the authors of that study*: Lasse F. Wolff Anthony, Benjamin Kanding, and Raghavendra Selvan, "Carbontracker: Tracking and Predicting the Carbon Footprint of Training Deep Learning Models," arXiv.org, July 6, 2020, http://arxiv.org/abs/2007.03051.

186   *Researchers at the AI company Hugging Face*: Melissa Heikkilä, "We're Getting a Better Idea of AI's True Carbon Footprint," *MIT Technology Review*, November 14, 2022, https://www.technologyreview.com/2022/11/14/1063192/were-getting-a-better-idea-of-ais-true-carbon-footprint/.

186   *But BLOOM*: "Bigscience/Bloom · Hugging Face," Bloom Model Card, July 6, 2022, https://huggingface.co/bigscience/bloom; Dylan Patel and Gerald Wong, "GPT-4 Architecture, Infrastructure, Training Dataset, Costs, Vision, MoE," *SemiAnalysis*, July 10, 2023, https://www.semianalysis.com/p/gpt-4-architecture-infrastructure?.

186   *Throughout the past decade*: OpenAI, "AI and Compute," Research, May 16, 2018, https://openai.com/research/ai-and-compute.

186   *It helps that Hugging Face trained BLOOM in France*: Heikkilä, "We're Getting a Better Idea of AI's True Carbon Footprint."

186   *What's more, the vast majority of the energy*: David Patterson et al., "Carbon Emissions and Large Neural Network Training," arXiv.org, April 21, 2021, http://arxiv.org/abs/2104.10350.

187   *Some AI experts have estimated*: Chris Stokel-Walker, "The Generative AI Race Has a Dirty Secret," *Wired*, February 10, 2023, https://www.wired.com/story/the-generative-ai-search-race-has-a-dirty-secret/.

187   *in the decade between 2010 and 2020*: Eric Masanet et al., "Recalibrating Global Data Center Energy-Use Estimates," *Science* 367, no. 6481 (February 28, 2020): 984–86.

187   *And some analyses have shown*: Katie Arcieri, "Path to Net-Zero: Datacenter Demands Push Amazon, Big Tech toward Renewables," December 12, 2022, https://www.spglobal.com/marketintelligence/en/news-insights/latest-news-headlines/path-to-net-zero-datacenter-demands-push-amazon-big-tech-toward-renewables-72752727.

187   *Microsoft, for example, has recently proposed*: Jennifer Hiller, "Microsoft Targets Nuclear to Power AI Operations," *Wall Street Journal*, December 12, 2023, https://www.wsj.com/tech/ai/microsoft-targets-nuclear-to-power-ai-operations-e10ff798.

187   *AI constituted between 10 percent and 15 percent*: Patterson et al., "Carbon Emissions and Large Neural Network Training."

187   *Microsoft, Google, and Amazon collectively invested*: Camilla Hodgson, "Tech Giants Pour Billions into Cloud Capacity in AI Push," *Financial Times*, November 5, 2023, https://www.ft.com/content/f01529ad-88ca-456e-ad41-d6b7d449a409.

187 *One study estimates*: Zoe Kleinman and Chris Vallance, "Warning AI Industry Could Use as Much Energy as the Netherlands," BBC, October 10, 2023, https://www.bbc.co.uk/news/technology-67053139.

188 *Local communities have accused*: Nikitha Sattiraju, "The Secret Cost of Google's Data Centers: Billions of Gallons of Water to Cool Servers," *Time*, April 2, 2020, https://time.com/5814276/google-data-centers-water/; Matt O'Brien and Hannah Fingerhut, "Artificial Intelligence Technology behind ChatGPT Was Built in Iowa — with a Lot of Water," *AP News*, September 9, 2023, https://apnews.com/article/chatgpt-gpt4-iowa-ai-water-consumption-microsoft-f551fde98083d17a7e8d904f8be822c4.

188 *Microsoft reported that between*: O'Brien and Fingerhut, "Artificial Intelligence Technology behind ChatGPT Was Built in Iowa."

188 *Microsoft's five vast data centers*: Ibid.

188 *But the Raccoon*: "Raccoon River Named among America's Most Endangered Rivers," American Rivers, April 13, 2021, https://www.americanrivers.org/media-item/raccoon-river-named-among-americas-most-endangered-rivers/.

188 *Shaolei Ren, a researcher*: Pengfei Li et al., "Making AI Less 'Thirsty': Uncovering and Addressing the Secret Water Footprint of AI Models," arXiv.org, April 6, 2023, http://arxiv.org/abs/2304.03271.

189 *Google's on-site water consumption*: Victor Tangermann, "Google Is Using a Flabbergasting Amount of Water on AI," *Futurism*, July 28, 2023, https://futurism.com/the-byte/google-water-ai.

189 *A study jointly conducted*: Md Abu Bakar Siddik, Arman Shehabi, and Landon Marston, "The Environmental Footprint of Data Centers in the United States," *Environmental Research Letters: ERL [Website]* 16, no. 6 (May 21, 2021): 064017.

189 *Rare earths and many of these other minerals*: Jaya Nayar, "Not So 'Green' Technology: The Complicated Legacy of Rare Earth Mining," *Harvard International Review*, August 12, 2021, https://hir.harvard.edu/not-so-green-technology-the-complicated-legacy-of-rare-earth-mining/.

190 *Taiwan Semiconductor Manufacturing Corporation*: "Press Center—Top Ten Semiconductor Foundries Report a 1.1% Quarterly Revenue Decline in 2Q23, Anticipated to Rebound in 3Q23, Says TrendForce," TrendForce, accessed November 8, 2023, https://www.trendforce.com/presscenter/news/20230905-11827.html.

190 *produces AI-specific chips for Google and Microsoft*: Rob Toews, "The Geopolitics of AI Chips Will Define the Future of AI," *Forbesco*, May 7, 2023, https://www.forbes.com/sites/robtoews/2023/05/07/the-geopolitics-of-ai-chips-will-define-the-future-of-ai/.

190 *TSMC uses more than 6 percent*: Eugene Chausovsky, "Energy Is Taiwan's Achilles' Heel," *Foreign Policy*, July 31, 2023, https://foreignpolicy.com/2023/07/31/energy-taiwan-semiconductor-chips-china-tsmc/.

190   *It produced 11.6 million metric tons*: "TSMC 2022 Corporate Sustainability Report," June 30, 2023, 228.

190   *That's three to four times higher*: Exerica LTD, "Ford Motor," Exerica, accessed November 6, 2023, https://esg.exerica.com/Company?Name=Ford%20Motor; Exerica LTD, "General Motors Company," Exerica, accessed November 6, 2023, https://esg.exerica.com/Company?Name=General%20Motors%20Company.

190   *It has committed to sourcing 100 percent*: Pádraig Belton, "The Computer Chip Industry Has a Dirty Climate Secret," *The Guardian*, September 18, 2021, https://www.theguardian.com/environment/2021/sep/18/semiconductor-silicon-chips-carbon-footprint-climate#:~:text=But%20chip%20manufacturing%20also%20contributes,day%20%E2%80%93%20and%20creates%20hazardous%20waste.

190   *In 2022, TSMC said renewables*: "TSMC 2022 Corporate Sustainability Report," 228.

191   *TSMC's Taiwan fabs consumed*: Ibid., 229.

191   *In recent years Taiwan has experienced droughts*: Belton, "The Computer Chip Industry Has a Dirty Climate Secret."

191   *PFAS (per- and polyfluoroalkyl substances)*: Ian Bott and Cheng Ting-Fang, "The Crackdown on Risky Chemicals That Could Derail the Chip Industry," *Financial Times*, May 22, 2023, https://www.ft.com/content/76979768-59c0-436f-b731-40ba329a7544.

191   *Currently, there are no substitutes for PFAS*: Ibid.

191   *Silicon Valley, the birthplace of America's semiconductor industry*: Tatiana Schlossberg, "Silicon Valley Is One of the Most Polluted Places in the Country," *The Atlantic*, September 22, 2019, https://www.theatlantic.com/technology/archive/2019/09/silicon-valley-full-superfund-sites/598531/; Cam Simpson, "American Chipmakers Had a Toxic Problem. Then They Outsourced It," Bloomberg News, June 15, 2017, https://www.bloomberg.com/news/features/2017-06-15/american-chipmakers-had-a-toxic-problem-so-they-outsourced-it; Jane Horton, "I Live next to Google—and on Top of a Toxic Site. Don't Let Polluters Be Evil," *The Guardian*, March 19, 2014, https://www.theguardian.com/commentisfree/2014/mar/19/google-mountain-view-toxic-waste.

191   *With TSMC and other semiconductor makers*: Catherine Thorbecke, "The US Is Spending Billions to Boost Chip Manufacturing. Will It Be Enough?," CNN, October 18, 2022, https://www.cnn.com/2022/10/18/tech/us-chip-manufacturing-semiconductors/index.html.

192   *By some estimates, the human brain uses*: "Emulating the Energy Efficiency of the Brain," Mohamed Bin Zayed University of Artificial Intelligence (MBZUAI), December 27, 2023, https://mbzuai.ac.ae/news/emulating-the-energy-efficiency-of-the-brain/.

CHAPTER II: THE TRUST BOMB

196 *An algorithm that was widely sold*: Jeff Larson et al., "How We Analyzed the COMPAS Recidivism Algorithm," *ProPublica* (5 2016) 9, no. 1 (2016): 3–13.

196 *Tools that claim to be able to help police*: Will Douglas Heaven, "Predictive Policing Algorithms Are Racist. They Need to Be Dismantled," *MIT Technology Review*, July 17, 2020, https://www.technologyreview.com/2020/07/17/1005396/predictive-policing-algorithms-racist-dismantled-machine-learning-bias-criminal-justice/.

196 *And that data reflects systemic biases in policing*: William Terrill and Michael D. Reisig, "Neighborhood Context and Police Use of Force," *Journal of Research in Crime and Delinquency* 40, no. 3 (August 1, 2003): 291–321; Sharad Goel, Justin M. Rao, and Ravi Shroff, "Precinct or Prejudice? Understanding Racial Disparities in New York City's Stop-and-Frisk Policy," *The Annals of Applied Statistics* 10, no. 1 (March 2016): 365–94.

196 *Using arrest data*: Heaven, "Predictive Policing Algorithms are Racist."

196 *The use of facial-recognition software by police*: Joy Buolamwini and Timnit Gebru, "Gender Shades: Intersectional Accuracy Disparities in Commercial Gender Classification," in *Proceedings of the 1st Conference on Fairness, Accountability and Transparency*, ed. Sorelle A. Friedler and Christo Wilson, vol. 81, Proceedings of Machine Learning Research (PMLR, 23–24 Feb 2018), 77–91.

196 *The controversial facial-recognition app*: James Clayton and Ben Derico, "Clearview AI Used Nearly 1m Times by US Police, It Tells the BBC," BBC, March 27, 2023, https://www.bbc.co.uk/news/technology-65057011.

196 *Relying on data analytics*: Heaven, "Predictive Policing Algorithms are Racist."

197 *This means, in essence*: Ibid.

197 *The European Union in its AI Act*: "AI Act: A Step Closer to the First Rules on Artificial Intelligence," European Parliament, November 5, 2023, https://www.europarl.europa.eu/news/en/press-room/20230505IPR84904/ai-act-a-step-closer-to-the-first-rules-on-artificial-intelligence.

197 *An American Civil Liberties Union study*: Heaven, "Predictive Policing Algorithms Are Racist. They Need to Be Dismantled."

197 *In Kentucky, for example*: Ibid.

198 *In 2019, a landmark study demonstrated*: Ziad Obermeyer et al., "Dissecting Racial Bias in an Algorithm Used to Manage the Health of Populations," *Science* 366, no. 6464 (October 25, 2019): 447–53.

198 *Black patients, for instance*: Patrick Boyle, "Clinical Trials Seek to Fix Their Lack of Racial Mix," Association of American Medical Colleges, August 19, 2021, https://www.aamc.org/news/clinical-trials-seek-fix-their-lack-racial-mix.

198 *Doctors and nurses*: Kelly M. Hoffman et al., "Racial Bias in Pain Assessment and Treatment Recommendations, and False Beliefs about Biological Differences between Blacks and Whites," *Proceedings of the National Academy of*

Sciences of the United States of America 113, no. 16 (April 19, 2016): 4296–4301; Carrie Arnold, "How Biased Data and Algorithms Can Harm Health," *Hopkins Bloomberg Public Health* magazine, accessed November 1, 2023, https://maga zine.jhsph.edu/2022/how-biased-data-and-algorithms-can-harm-health.

199   *One European study*: Aaron Klein, "Credit Denial in the Age of AI," Brookings, April 11, 2019, https://www.brookings.edu/articles/credit-denial-in-the-age-of -ai/.

199   *This makes it too easy*: Jeremy Kahn, "Can an A.I. Algorithm Help End Unfair Lending? This Company Says Yes," *Fortune*, October 20, 2020, https://fortune .com/2020/10/20/artificial-intelligence-unfair-lending/; Jeremy Kahn, "A.I. and Tackling the Risk of 'Digital Redlining,'" *Fortune*, February 11, 2020, https:// fortune.com/2020/02/11/a-i-fairness-eye-on-a-i/.

199   *VyStar Credit Union*: Kahn, "Can an A.I. Algorithm Help End Unfair Lending?"

200   *Give an LLM a sentence*: Hadas Kotek, Rikker Dockum, and David Q. Sun, "Gen-der Bias in LLMs," arXiv.org, August 28, 2023, https://arxiv.org/abs/2308.14921.

200   *if you prompt the image-generating AI software Midjourney*: Arsenii Alenichev, Patricia Kingori, and Koen Peeters Grietens, "Reflections before the Storm: The AI Reproduction of Biased Imagery in Global Health Visuals," *The Lancet Global Health* 11, no. 10 (October 2023): E1496–E1498, https://doi.org/10.1016 /S2214-109X(23)00329-7.

200   *Another study found text-to-image generators tend to depict*: Leonardo Nicoletti and Dina Bass, "Generative AI Takes Stereotypes and Bias From Bad to Worse," Bloomberg, June 8, 2023, https://www.bloomberg.com/graphics/2023-genera tive-ai-bias/?sref=b0SdE1lu.

200   *There are ways to solve this bias*: Dylan Baker, interview by Jeremy Kahn, No-vember 1, 2023.

201   *Smaller AI models*: Ibid.

202   *Already fraudsters are using voice cloning*: Pranshu Verma, "They Thought Loved Ones Were Calling for Help. It Was an AI Scam," *Washington Post*, March 5, 2023, https://www.washingtonpost.com/technology/2023/03/05/ai-voice-scam/.

202   *To make it more likely that one victim would pay*: Siddharth Venkataramakrishnan, "AI Heralds the Next Generation of Financial Scams," *Financial Times*, January 19, 2024, https://www.ft.com/content/beea7f8a-2fa9-4b63-a542-88be231b0266.

202   *Voice clones are also being used to impersonate*: Thomas Brewster, "Fraudsters Cloned Company Director's Voice in $35 Million Heist, Police Find," *Forbes*, October 14, 2021, https://www.forbes.com/sites/thomasbrewster/2021/10/14 /huge-bank-fraud-uses-deep-fake-voice-tech-to-steal-millions/.

202   *One company appears to have been swindled*: Heather Chen and Kathleen Ma-gramo, "Finance Worker Pays out $25 Million after Video Call with Deepfake 'Chief Financial Officer,'" CNN, February 4, 2024, https://www.cnn.com/2024 /02/04/asia/deepfake-cfo-scam-hong-kong-intl-hnk/index.html.

202 *The cybersecurity firm Check Point*: Jeremy Kahn, "ChatGPT Lets Scammers Craft Emails That Are so Convincing They Can Get Cash from Victims without Even Relying on Malware," *Fortune*, February 4, 2023, https://fortune.com /2023/02/03/chatgpt-cyberattacks-cybersecurity-social-engineering-darktrace -abnormal/; Maya Horowitz, interview by Jeremy Kahn, November 2, 2023.

202 *Microsoft and OpenAI said in early 2024*: Tom Warren, "Microsoft and OpenAI Say Hackers Are Using ChatGPT to Improve Cyberattacks," *The Verge*, February 14, 2024, https://www.theverge.com/2024/2/14/24072706/microsoft -openai-cyberattack-tools-ai-chatgpt.

202 *On the dark web*: "Exploring the Realm of Malicious Generative AI: A New Digital Security Challenge," *The Hacker News*, October 17, 2023, https://thehack ernews.com/2023/10/exploring-realm-of-malicious-generative.html.

202 *Even before AI chatbots came along*: Jonny Ball, "Malware: On Sale for the Price of a Pint on Dark Web," *New Statesman*, July 22, 2022, https://www.newstates man.com/spotlight/2022/07/malware-on-sale-price-pint-dark-web.

203 *Google has trained*: Sunil Potti, "How Google Cloud Plans to Supercharge Security with Generative AI," Google Cloud (blog), April 24, 2023, https://cloud .google.com/blog/products/identity-security/rsa-google-cloud-security-ai -workbench-generative-ai.

203 *And there are already AI-enabled cybersecurity programs*: Nicole Kobie, "Darktrace's AI Is Now Automatically Responding to Hacks—and Stopping Them," *WIRED UK*, April 4, 2017, https://www.wired.co.uk/article/darktrace-machine -learning-security.

203 *As Evan Reiser*: Anne Sraders, "Abnormal Security's CEO Explains How 'Defensive A.I.' Will Someday Defeat Cyber Attacks," *Fortune*, August 16, 2023, https:// fortune.com/2023/08/16/abnormal-security-ceo-defensive-ai-cyber-attacks/.

203 *Maya Horowitz, vice president of research at Check Point*: Horowitz, interview.

203 *Chatbot AI systems are vulnerable*: Jeremy Kahn, "Researchers Find a Way to Easily Bypass Guardrails on OpenAI's ChatGPT and All Other A.I. Chatbots," *Fortune*, July 28, 2023, https://fortune.com/2023/07/28/openai-chatgpt-mi crosoft-bing-google-bard-anthropic-claude-meta-llama-guardrails-easily-by passed-carnegie-mellon-research-finds-eye-on-a-i/; Thomas Claburn, "How Prompt Injection Attacks Hijack Today's Top-End AI—and It's Tough to Fix," *The Register*, April 26, 2023, https://www.theregister.com/2023/04/26/simon _willison_prompt_injection/.

204 *Horowitz is particularly concerned*: Horowitz, interview.

204 *Researchers have shown*: Abigail Bealle, "Visual Trick Fools AI into Thinking a Turtle Is Really a Rifle," *New Scientist*, November 3, 2017, https://www.new scientist.com/article/2152331-visual-trick-fools-ai-into-thinking-a-turtle-is -really-a-rifle/.

204 *Horowitz says the fact*: Horowitz, interview.

205   *sponsored red-teaming exercises*: Benj Edwards, "White House Challenges Hackers to Break Top AI Models at DEF CON 31," *Ars Technica*, May 8, 2023, https://arstechnica.com/information-technology/2023/05/white-house-challenges-hackers-to-break-top-ai-models-at-def-con-31/.

205   *The federal government is developing*: The White House, "FACT SHEET: President Biden Issues Executive Order on Safe, Secure, and Trustworthy Artificial Intelligence," The White House, October 30, 2023, https://www.whitehouse.gov/briefing-room/statements-releases/2023/10/30/fact-sheet-president-biden-issues-executive-order-on-safe-secure-and-trustworthy-artificial-intelligence/.

205   *Gary Gensler, the head of the U.S. Securities and Exchange Commission*: Patrick Jenkins and Stefania Palma, "Gary Gensler Urges Regulators to Tame AI Risks to Financial Stability," *Financial Times*, October 15, 2023, https://www.ft.com/content/8227636f-e819-443a-aeba-c8237f0ec1ac.

205   *In 2017, the first examples*: Laura Payne, "Deepfake," in *Encyclopedia Britannica*, October 5, 2023, https://www.britannica.com/technology/deepfake.

205   *researchers at the University of Washington*: "Incident 39: Deepfake Obama Introduction of Deepfakes," AI Incident Database, accessed October 28, 2023, https://incidentdatabase.ai/cite/39/.

206   *At the time, deepfakes depended*: Jeremy Kahn, "Here's Who Created Those Viral Tom Cruise Deepfake Videos," *Fortune*, March 2, 2021, https://fortune.com/2021/03/02/tom-cruise-deepfake-videos-tik-tok-chris-ume/.

206   *Viral fake images*: Ashley Belanger, "AI Platform Allegedly Bans Journalist over Fake Trump Arrest Images," *Ars Technica*, March 22, 2023, https://arstechnica.com/tech-policy/2023/03/ai-platform-allegedly-bans-journalist-over-fake-trump-arrest-images/; Christiaan Hetzner, "What Is Midjourney? The A.I. Image Generator Used to Create the Viral Image of the Pope in a Puffer Jacket," *Fortune*, March 28, 2023, https://fortune.com/2023/03/28/pope-francis-balenciaga-puffer-jacket-midjourney-ai-deepfake-image-generator-openai-dalle/.

206   *Meanwhile, video generation software from the start-up Runway*: Cade Metz, "Instant Videos Could Represent the Next Leap in A.I. Technology," *New York Times*, April 4, 2023, https://www.nytimes.com/2023/04/04/technology/runway-ai-videos.html.

206   *And the start-up ElevenLabs*: "ElevenLabs - Generative AI Text to Speech & Voice Cloning," ElevenLabs, accessed October 1, 2023; "Free AI Text to Speech Online," https://elevenlabs.io/text-to-speech; "AI Voice Cloning: Clone Your Voice in Minutes," https://elevenlabs.io/voice-cloning.

206   *In India, during the Delhi mayoral election*: Kim Lyons, "An Indian Politician Used AI to Translate His Speech into Other Languages," *The Verge*, February 18, 2020, https://www.theverge.com/2020/2/18/21142782/india-politician-deepfakes-ai-elections.

206 *In the U.S., the Republican Party:* James Vincent, "Republicans Respond to Biden Reelection Announcement with AI-Generated Attack Ad," *The Verge*, April 25, 2023, https://www.theverge.com/2023/4/25/23697328/biden-reelection-rnc-ai -generated-attack-ad-deepfake.

207 *In 2016, Russia waged:* Sarah Kreps and Doug Kriner, "How AI Threatens Democracy," *Journal of Democracy* 34, no. 4 (2023): 122–31.

208 *Deepfake audio is particularly difficult:* Jeremy Kahn, "Advanced A.I. like ChatGPT, DALL-E, and Voice-Cloning Tech Is Already Raising Big Fears for the 2024 Election," *Fortune*, April 8, 2023, https://fortune.com/2023/04/08/ai-chat gpt-dalle-voice-cloning-2024-us-presidential-election-misinformation/.

208 *In Slovakia, an audio deepfake:* Morgan Meaker, "Slovakia's Election Deepfakes Show AI Is a Danger to Democracy," *WIRED UK*, October 3, 2023, https://www .wired.co.uk/article/slovakia-election-deepfakes.

208 *outcomes of U.S. presidential elections:* "Cook Political Report Initial 2024 Electoral College Race Ratings," 270toWin, July 28, 2023, https://www.270towin .com/news/2023/07/28/cook-political-report-initial-2024-electoral-college -race-ratings_1512.html.

208 *That said, studies of disinformation:* Ullrich K. H. Ecker et al., "The Psychological Drivers of Misinformation Belief and Its Resistance to Correction," *Nature Reviews Psychology* 1, no. 1 (January 12, 2022): 13–29.

208 *Russia subscribes to:* Christopher Paul and Miriam Matthews, *The Russian "Firehose of Falsehood" Propaganda Model: Why It Might Work and Options to Counter It* (Santa Monica, CA: RAND Corporation, 2016).

209 *A prevalence of deepfake misinformation:* Kaylyn Jackson Schiff, Daniel Schiff, and Natália S. Bueno, "The Liar's Dividend: Can Politicians Claim Misinformation to Evade Accountability?" SocArXiv Papers, October 19, 2023, https://files .osf.io/v1/resources/x43ph/providers/osfstorage/64d228b4a2be6b59fa314730.

209 *Samsung, for example:* Brady Snyder, "Unlike Google, Samsung Will Digitally Watermark Wallpapers and Images Made with AI," *Yahoo News*, January 19, 2024, https://news.yahoo.com/unlike-google-samsung-digitally-watermark-07 1117152.html.

209 *Watermarks, in any case, are not a foolproof solution:* Zhengyuan Jiang, Jinghuai Zhang, and Neil Zhenqiang Gong, "Evading Watermark Based Detection of AI-Generated Content," arXiv, May 5, 2023, http://arxiv.org/abs/2305.03807.

209 *In some cases, it's even easier than that:* Kyle Barr, "Samsung's Galaxy S24 Can Remove Its Own AI Watermarks Meant to Show an Image Is Fake," *Gizmodo*, January 19, 2024, https://gizmodo.com/galaxy-s24-ai-removes-ai-watermark -phones-photos-1851180966.

210 *Adobe, Microsoft, and others:* Ina Fried, "The Fight against Deepfakes Expands to Hardware," *Axios*, October 26, 2023, https://www.axios.com/2023/10/26 /deepfakes-content-credentials-hardware-software.

210 *The Biden administration:* The White House, "FACT SHEET: President Biden Issues Executive Order on Safe, Secure, and Trustworthy Artificial Intelligence."

210 *France passed a law in 2018*: Daniel Funke and Daniela Flamini, "A Guide to Anti-Misinformation Actions around the World," *Poynter*, April 9, 2019, https://www.poynter.org/ifcn/anti-misinformation-actions/.

210 *The EU's sweeping new Digital Services Act*: Robert Freedman and Lyle Moran, "Sweeping EU Digital Misinformation Law Takes Effect," *Legal Dive*, August 23, 2023, https://www.legaldive.com/news/digital-services-act-dsa-eu-misinformation-law-propaganda-compliance-facebook-gdpr/691657/; "Press Corner: Questions and Answers: Digital Services Act," European Commission, April 25, 2003, https://ec.europa.eu/commission/presscorner/detail/en/qanda_20_2348.

211 *In 2017, when the Federal Communications Commission*: Sarah Kreps and Doug Kriner, "How AI Threatens Democracy," *Journal of Democracy* 34, no. 4 (October 2023): 122–31.

211 *without having to depend on polls*: Courtney Kennedy, "Does Public Opinion Polling about Issues Still Work?," Pew Research Center, September 21, 2022, https://www.pewresearch.org/short-reads/2022/09/21/does-public-opinion-polling-about-issues-still-work/.

211 *This was the vision of Noam Slonim*: Jeremy Kahn, "IBM's A.I. Can Now Mine People's Collective Thoughts. Will Businesses Use This Data Thoughtfully?," *Fortune*, December 12, 2019, https://fortune.com/2019/12/12/ibm-ai-artificial-intelligence-business-survey-polling-speech-by-crowd/; Jeremy Kahn, "IBM Showcases A.I. That Can Parse Arguments in Cambridge Union Debate," *Fortune*, November 22, 2019, https://fortune.com/2019/11/22/ibm-ai-debate-arguments-cambridge-union/; Noam Slonim et al., "An Autonomous Debating System," *Nature* 591, no. 7850 (March 2021): 379–84.

CHAPTER 12: WAR AT MACHINE SPEED

213 *Confederate forces in the U.S. Civil War*: Lorraine Boissoneault, "The Historic Innovation of Land Mines—and Why We've Struggled to Get Rid of Them," *Smithsonian* magazine, February 24, 2017, https://www.smithsonianmag.com/innovation/historic-innovation-land-minesand-why-weve-struggled-get-rid-them-180962276/.

215 *This is the dream of those building AI-equipped weapons*: Brandon Tseng, interview by Jeremy Kahn, August 23, 2023.

215 *The military historian John Keegan*: John Keegan, *The Face of Battle: A Study of Agincourt, Waterloo, and the Somme* (New York: Penguin, 1983).

216 *Facial-recognition AI*: Sudhin Thanawala, "Facial Recognition Technology Jailed a Man for Days. His Lawsuit Joins Others from Black Plaintiffs," *AP News*, September 25, 2023, https://apnews.com/article/mistaken-arrests-fa

cial-recognition-technology-lawsuits-b613161c56472459df683f54320d08a7; Innocence Project, "When Artificial Intelligence Gets It Wrong," Innocence Project, September 19, 2023, https://innocenceproject.org/when-artificial-in telligence-gets-it-wrong/.

216 *Self-driving cars*: The Tesla Team, "A Tragic Loss," Tesla (blog), June 30, 2016, https://www.tesla.com/blog/tragic-loss.

217 *"There is no silver bullet here"*: Mary Wareham, interview by Jeremy Kahn, November 16, 2023.

217 *the Ukrainian technology company Saker*: David Hambling, "Ukraine's AI Drones Seek and Attack Russian Forces Without Human Oversight," *Forbes*, October 17, 2023, https://www.forbes.com/sites/davidhambling/2023/10/17/uk raines-ai-drones-seek-and-attack-russian-forces-without-human-oversight/.

217 *International humanitarian law*: Neil Davison, "A Legal Perspective: Autonomous Weapon Systems under International Humanitarian Law," in *Perspectives on Lethal Autonomous Weapon Systems*, vol. 30, UNODA Occassional Papers, United Nations, 2018, 5–18.

218 *A human with highly honed reflexes*: Zachary Kallenborn, "Applying Arms-Control Frameworks to Autonomous Weapons," Brookings, October 5, 2021, https://www.brookings.edu/articles/applying-arms-control-frameworks-to-au tonomous-weapons/.

218 *Noel Sharkey, a British roboticist*: Noel Sharkey, interview by Jeremy Kahn, December 2020.

218 *There will inevitably be situations*: Ibid.

218 *The philosopher Paul W. Kahn*: Paul W. Kahn, "The Paradox of Riskless Warfare," in *War after September 11*, ed. Verna V. Gehring (Lanham, MD: Rowman & Littlefield, 2002), 37–49.

219 *Michael Walzer, a philosopher*: Paul Scharre, *Army of None: Autonomous Weapons and the Future of War* (New York: W. W. Norton, 2018).

219 *Some military officers*: Ibid.

220 *Zachary Kallenborn, an international relations scholar*: Zachary Kallenborn, interview by Jeremy Kahn, November 17, 2023.

220 *Some of the Reaper drones*: Rob Blackhurst, "The Air Force Men Who Fly Drones in Afghanistan by Remote Control," *Daily Telegraph*, September 24, 2012, https://www.telegraph.co.uk/news/uknews/defence/9552547/The-air-force -men-who-fly-drones-in-Afghanistan-by-remote-control.html.

220 *U.S. commanders warned their drone pilots*: Peter Warren Singer, *Wired for War: The Robotics Revolution and Conflict in the Twenty-First Century* (New York: Penguin, 2009), 386.

220 *Kallenborn notes that in the war in Ukraine*: Kallenborn, interview.

221 *The UN's Convention on Certain Conventional Weapons*: Kelley M. Sayler, "International Discussions Concerning Lethal Autonomous Weapon Systems

(IF11294)," Congressional Research Service, February 14, 2023, https://crsre ports.congress.gov/product/pdf/IF/IF11294.

221 *The U.S., whose military*: Kelley M. Sayler, "Defense Primer: U.S. Policy on Lethal Autonomous Weapon Systems (IF11150)," Congressional Research Service, May 15, 2023, https://crsreports.congress.gov/product/pdf/IF/IF11150.

221 *But that wording*: Mary Wareham, interview by Jeremy Kahn, November 16, 2023; Sharkey, interview.

221 *Meanwhile, Russia, Israel, Turkey, and India*: Mary Wareham, "Stopping Killer Robots," Human Rights Watch, August 10, 2020, https://www.hrw.org/report /2020/08/10/stopping-killer-robots/country-positions-banning-fully-autono mous-weapons-and.

221 *In both cases*: Wareham, interview.

222 *Wareham and others*: Ibid.; Toby Walsh, interview by Jeremy Kahn, November 20, 2023.

222 *Dozens of countries*: Kelley M. Sayler, "International Discussions Concerning Lethal Autonomous Weapon Systems (IF11294)," Congressional Research Service, February 14, 2023.

222 *seventy have said*: Ousman Noor, "70 States Deliver Joint Statement on Autonomous Weapons Systems at UN General Assembly," Stop Killer Robots, October 21, 2022, https://www.stopkillerrobots.org/news/70-states-deliver-joint -statement-on-autonomous-weapons-systems-at-un-general-assembly/.

222 *In October 2023, UN secretary general*: "UN and Red Cross Call for Restrictions on Autonomous Weapon Systems to Protect Humanity," UN News, October 5, 2023, https://news.un.org/en/story/2023/10/1141922.

222 *Advocates were also buoyed*: "First Committee Approves New Resolution on Lethal Autonomous Weapons, as Speaker Warns 'an Algorithm Must Not Be in Full Control of Decisions Involving Killing,'" United Nations Media Coverage and Press Releases, November 1, 2023, https://press.un.org/en/2023/gadis3731 .doc.htm.

222 *Paul Scharre, a former U.S. Army Ranger*: Scharre, *Army of None*, 351.

223 *Bans have generally worked*: Ibid., 331–44; Robert F. Trager, "Deliberating Autonomous Weapons," *Issues in Science and Technology* XXXVIII, no. 4 (July 12, 2022), https://issues.org/autonomous-weapons-russell-forum/.

223 *Countries were willing to ban chemical weapons*: Scharre, *Army of None*, 340.

223 *They were willing to ban biological weapons*: Trager, "Deliberating Autonomous Weapons."

223 *Even the landmine and cluster munitions treaties*: "Anti-Personnel Landmines: Friend or Foe? A Study of the Military Use and Effectiveness of Anti-Personnel Mines," International Committee of the Red Cross, June 9, 2020, https://www .icrc.org/en/publication/0654-anti-personnel-landmines-friend-or-foe-study

-military-use-and-effectiveness-anti. Although military opinion on the effectiveness of land mines may be shifting in light of the role land mines seem to have played in aiding defensive positions of both Ukrainian and Russian forces in the Ukraine war. See: David E. Johnson, "Is the Virtue in the Weapon or the Cause?" (*Lawfire*, August 5, 2022), https://www.rand.org/pubs/commentary/2022/08/is-the-virtue-in-the-weapon-or-the-cause.html.

223 *For instance, the 1899 and 1907 Hague Declarations*: Scharre, *Army of None*, 334–44; Walsh, interview.

223 *Experts in international relations think*: Zachary Kallenborn, interview; Kallenborn, "Applying Arms-Control."

223 *The Future of Life Institute*: Sharkey, interview.

224 *Palantir, which has worked extensively*: Reinhardt Krause, "Palantir Wins $250M U.S. Army Services Contract for AI," *Investor's Business Daily*, September 27, 2023, https://www.investors.com/news/technology/pltr-stock-palantir-wins-250-million-army-ai-services-contract/.

224 *NATO militaries have also been captivated*: Lieutenant Colonel Thomas Doll et al., "From the Game Map to the Battlefield—Using DeepMind's Advanced Alphastar Techniques to Support Military Decision-Makers," *Towards Training and Decision Support for Complex Multi-Domain Operations, NATO Modelling and Simulation Group (NMSG)*, Symposium Held on 21–22 Ocotober 2021, in Amsterdam, the Netherlands, 2021, 14–11.

224 *is investing almost $1 billion*: Sherrill Lee Lingel et al., *Joint All-Domain Command and Control for Modern Warfare: An Analytic Framework for Identifying and Developing Artificial Intelligence Applications* (RAND, 2020); Colin Demarest, "Siemens, 29 Others Added to Air Force's $950 Million JADC2 Contract," *C4ISRNet*, September 23, 2022, https://www.c4isrnet.com/industry/2022/09/23/siemens-29-others-added-to-air-forces-950-million-jadc2-contract/.

224 *Meanwhile, Palantir, as well as competitors*: Katrina Manson, "The US Military Is Taking Generative AI Out for a Spin," *Bloomberg News*, July 5, 2023, https://www.bloomberg.com/news/newsletters/2023-07-05/the-us-military-is-taking-generative-ai-out-for-a-spin.

224 *But during Israel's war in Gaza in 2024, newspaper reports emerged*: Yuval Abraham, "'Lavender': The AI Machine Directing Israel's Bombing Spree in Gaza," *+972 Magazine*, April 3, 2024, https://www.972mag.com/lavender-ai-israeli-army-gaza/; Harry Davies, Bethan McKernan, and Dan Sabbagh, "'The Gospel': How Israel Uses AI to Select Bombing Targets in Gaza," *The Guardian*, December 1, 2023, https://www.theguardian.com/world/2023/dec/01/the-gospel-how-israel-uses-ai-to-select-bombing-targets.

225 *When researchers from a number of universities*: Hera Rizwan, "AI In Warfare: Study Finds LLM Models Escalate Violence In War Simulations," *BOOM*,

February 12, 2024, https://www.boomlive.in/news/ai-in-warfare-study-finds -llm-models-escalate-violence-in-war-simulations-24334.

225   *Current U.S. policy*: Olivier Knox, "A.I. and Nuclear Decisions Shouldn't Mix, U.S. Says Ahead of Biden-Xi Summit," *Washington Post*, November 9, 2023, https://www.washingtonpost.com/politics/2023/11/09/ai-nuclear-decisions -shouldnt-mix-us-says-ahead-biden-xi-summit/.

225   *even Lieutenant General John Shanahan*: Ross Andersen, "Never Give Artifi- cial Intelligence the Nuclear Codes," *The Atlantic*, May 2, 2023, https://www .theatlantic.com/magazine/archive/2023/06/ai-warfare-nuclear-weapons-strike /673780/.

225   *Stanley Kubrick's Cold War classic*: *Dr. Strangelove or: How I Learned to Stop Worrying and Love the Bomb*, directed by Stanley Kubrick (Columbia Pictures, 1964).

225   *It was called "Perimeter"*: Andersen, "Never Give Artificial."

226   *Adam Lowther and Curtis McGiffin*: Ibid.; Susan D'Agostino, "Biden Should End the Launch-on-Warning Option," *Bulletin of the Atomic Scientists*, June 22, 2021, https://thebulletin.org/2021/06/biden-should-end-the-launch-on-warning-op tion/; Adam Lowther and Curtis McGiffin, "America Needs a 'Dead Hand,'" Max- well Air Force Base, Air Force Institute of Technology, August 23, 2019, https:// www.maxwell.af.mil/News/Commentaries/Display/Article/1942374/america -needs-a-dead-hand/.

226   *most famously in 1983*: Andersen, "Never Give Artificial"; Wikipedia contrib- utors, "1983 Soviet Nuclear False Alarm Incident," *Wikipedia*, September 26, 2023, https://en.wikipedia.org/w/index.php?title=1983_Soviet_nuclear_false _alarm_incident&oldid=1177249343.

226   *as those fatal self-driving car accidents attest*: Phil McCausland, "Self-Driving Uber Car That Hit and Killed Woman Did Not Recognize That Pedestrians Jaywalk," NBC News, November 9, 2019, https://www.nbcnews.com/tech/tech -news/self-driving-uber-car-hit-killed-woman-did-not-recognize-n1079281; "11 More People Killed in Crashes Involving Automated-Tech Vehicles," CBS News, October 19, 2022, https://www.cbsnews.com/news/self-driving-vehicles -crash-deaths-elon-musk-tesla-nhtsa-2022/.

226   *This raises the prospect*: Michael T. Klare, "'Skynet' Revisited: The Dangerous Allure of Nuclear Command Automation," *Arms Control Today*, April 2020, https://www.armscontrol.org/act/2020-04/features/skynet-revisited-danger ous-allure-nuclear-command-automation.

226   *Imagine an erroneous signal*: Andersen, "Never Give Artificial."

227   *Biden and Chinese president Xi Jinping*: Trevor Hunnicutt and Jeff Mason, "TAKEAWAYS—Biden and Xi Meeting: Taiwan, Iran, Fentanyl and AI," Re- uters, November 16, 2023, https://www.reuters.com/world/takeaways-biden-xi -meeting-taiwan-iran-fentanyl-ai-2023-11-16/.

227 *Russian president Vladimir Putin*: James Vincent, "Putin Says the Nation That Leads in AI 'Will Be the Ruler of the World,'" *The Verge*, September 4, 2017, https://www.theverge.com/2017/9/4/16251226/russia-ai-putin-rule-the-world.

227 *The country's national AI strategy*: "Full Translation: China's 'New Generation Artificial Intelligence Development Plan' (2017)," *DigiChina*, August 1, 2017, https://digichina.stanford.edu/work/full-translation-chinas-new-generation -artificial-intelligence-development-plan-2017/.

228 *the U.S. has tried to constrain*: Will Henshall, "What to Know about the U.S. Curbs on AI Chip Exports to China," *Time*, October 17, 2023, https://time.com /6324619/us-biden-ai-chips-china/.

228 *China has retaliated*: Dominique Patton and Amy Lv, "China Exported No Germanium, Gallium in August after Export Curbs," Reuters, September 20, 2023, https://www.reuters.com/world/china/china-exported-no-germanium-gal lium-aug-due-export-curbs-2023-09-20/.

229 *U.S. government officials have said*: Phil Stewart et al., "Chinese Blockade of Taiwan Would Likely Fail, Pentagon Official Says," Reuters, September 19, 2023, https://www.reuters.com/world/asia-pacific/chinese-blockade-taiwan-would -likely-fail-pentagon-official-says-2023-09-19/.

229 *the Taiwan Semiconductor Manufacturing Company*: Rob Toews, "The Geopolitics of AI Chips Will Define the Future of AI," *Forbes*, May 7, 2023, https:// www.forbes.com/sites/robtoews/2023/05/07/the-geopolitics-of-ai-chips-will -define-the-future-of-ai/?sh=4abdae0e5c5c.

229 *Aware of the vulnerability*: Makena Kelly, "President Joe Biden's $39 Billion Semiconductor Project Is Open for Business," *The Verge*, February 28, 2023, https://www.theverge.com/2023/2/28/23618885/semiconductor-chip-manu facturing-commerce-biden-white-house.

CHAPTER 13: LIGHTS OUT FOR ALL OF US

230 *This is the danger that*: Matt McFarland, "Elon Musk: 'With Artificial Intelligence We Are Summoning the Demon,'" *Washington Post*, October 24, 2014, https://www.washingtonpost.com/news/innovations/wp/2014/10/24/elon -musk-with-artificial-intelligence-we-are-summoning-the-demon/.

230 *It is also what motivates*: Jeremy Kahn, "The Inside Story of ChatGPT: How OpenAI Founder Sam Altman Built the World's Hottest Technology with Billions from Microsoft," *Fortune*, January 25, 2023, https://fortune.com/long form/chatgpt-openai-sam-altman-microsoft/.

231 *Geoff Hinton, the deep learning pioneer*: Will Douglas Heaven, "Geoffrey Hinton Tells Us Why He's Now Scared of the Tech He Helped Build," *MIT Technology Review*, May 2, 2023, https://www.technologyreview.com/2023/05/02/1072528 /geoffrey-hinton-google-why-scared-ai/.

232 *But the idea began to receive*: Irving John Good, "Speculations Concerning

the First Ultraintelligent Machine," in *Advances in Computers, Volume 6*, ed. Franz L. Alt and Morris Rubinoff (Amsterdam: Elsevier, 1966), 31–88.

232 *Good focused mostly on the benefits*: Ibid.

232 *That proviso and the potentially catastrophic consequences*: Vernor Vinge, "The Coming Technological Singularity: How to Survive in the Post-Human Era," (conference paper, NASA, Lewis Research Center, *Vision 21: Interdisciplinary Science and Engineering in the Era of Cyberspace*, December 1, 1993), https://ntrs.nasa.gov/citations/19940022856.

233 *popularized by the futurist and inventor Ray Kurzweil*: Ray Kurzweil, *The Singularity Is Near: When Humans Transcend Biology* (London: Gerald Duckworth & Co., 2006).

233 *Kurzweil's writing on superintelligence*: Shane Legg, interview by Jeremy Kahn, August 22, 2023; Dario Amodei, interview by Jeremy Kahn, July 17, 2023.

233 *He sees superintelligence*: Kurzweil, *The Singularity Is Near*; Ray Kurzweil, "Spiritual Machines: The Merging of Man and Machine," *The Futurist*, vol. 33, November 1999, 16–21.

233 *Bostrom, who collected his thoughts on ASI*: Nick Bostrom, *Superintelligence: Paths, Dangers, Strategies* (Oxford, UK: Oxford University Press, 2014).

234 *AI researcher Ilya Sutskever*: Noah Payne-Frank et al., "Ilya: The AI Scientist Shaping the World," online video, *The Guardian*, 2023, https://www.theguardian.com/technology/video/2023/nov/02/ilya-the-ai-scientist-shaping-the-world.

235 *Algorithms that drive people to extreme and partisan*: Alexander Pan, Kush Bhatia, and Jacob Steinhardt, "The Effects of Reward Misspecification: Mapping and Mitigating Misaligned Models," arXiv.org, January 10, 2022, http://arxiv.org/abs/2201.03544.

235 *In* Superintelligence: Bostrom, *Superintelligence*.

236 *This is what AI safety experts*: Marius Hobbhahn, "Understanding Strategic Deception and Deceptive Alignment," Apollo Research, September 25, 2023, https://www.apolloresearch.ai/blog/understanding-da-and-sd.

236 *When OpenAI was testing GPT-4*: OpenAI, "GPT-4 Technical Report," arXiv, March 15, 2023, 55–6, http://arxiv.org/abs/2303.08774.

237 *OpenAI has promised*: Jan Leike and Ilya Sutskever, "Introducing Superalignment," OpenAI (blog), July 5, 2023, https://openai.com/blog/introducing-superalignment.

237 *While at OpenAI*: Amodei, interview.

238 *Called* constitutional AI: Yuntao Bai et al., "Constitutional AI: Harmlessness from AI Feedback," arXiv, December 15, 2022, http://arxiv.org/abs/2212.08073.

238 *Independent tests have shown*: Patrick Chao et al., "Jailbreaking Black Box Large Language Models in Twenty Queries," arXiv, October 12, 2023, http://arxiv.org/abs/2310.08419; Andy Zou et al., "Universal and Transferable Adversarial

Attacks on Aligned Language Models," arXiv, July 27, 2023, http://arxiv.org/abs/2307.15043.

238 *But the fact that Claude 2 can still be jailbroken*: Zico Kolter and Matt Fredrikson, interview by Jeremy Kahn, July 27, 2023; Dario Amodei, interview.

238 *In October 2023*: P. B. C. Anthropic, "Collective Constitutional AI: Aligning a Language Model with Public Input," Anthropic, October 17, 2023, https://www.anthropic.com/index/collective-constitutional-ai-aligning-a-language-model-with-public-input.

239 *Elon Musk has criticized*: Maxwell Zeff, "Elon Musk's 'Anti-Woke' AI Is Here, Snowflakes Need Not Apply," *Gizmodo*, December 7, 2023, https://gizmodo.com/elon-musk-x-grok-ai-chatbot-is-here-1851081047; James Vincent, "As Conservatives Criticize 'Woke AI,' Here Are ChatGPT's Rules for Answering Culture War Queries," *The Verge*, February 17, 2023, https://www.theverge.com/2023/2/17/23603906/openai-chatgpt-woke-criticism-culture-war-rules.

239 *Grok has a "spicy mode"*: Lance Whitney, "I Tried X's 'Anti-Woke' Grok AI Chatbot. The Results Were the Opposite of What I Expected," *ZDNET*, December 21, 2023, https://www.zdnet.com/article/i-tried-xs-anti-woke-grok-ai-chatbot-the-results-were-the-opposite-of-what-i-expected/.

239 *For example, CoinRun*: Stuart Armstrong et al., "CoinRun: Solving Goal Misgeneralisation," arXiv, September 28, 2023, http://arxiv.org/abs/2309.16166; Matija Franklin et al., "Concept Extrapolation: A Conceptual Primer," arXiv, June 19, 2023, http://arxiv.org/abs/2306.10999.

240 *On a test of content moderation skills*: Jeremy Kahn, "Some Small Start-ups Making Headway on Generative A.I.'s Biggest Challenges," *Fortune*, May 23, 2023, https://fortune.com/2023/05/23/small-startups-making-headway-on-generative-a-i-s-biggest-challenges-xayn-aligned-ai-eye-on-ai/.

241 *"To build the safe thing"*: Amodei, interview.

241 *J. Robert Oppenheimer's explanation*: U.S. Atomic Energy Commission, "In the matter of J. Robert Oppenheimer: transcript of hearing before Personnel Security Board, Washington, D.C.," April 12, 1954 through May 5, 1954, U.S. Government Printing Office, 81.

241 *But the weakness of relying*: Rachel Metz and Shirin Ghaffary, "OpenAI's Sam Altman Returns to Board After Probe Clears Him," Bloomberg News, March 8, 2024, https://www.bloomberg.com/news/articles/2024-03-08/openai-s-altman-returns-to-board-after-probe-clears-him.

242 *But as Helen Toner and Tasha McCauley*: Helen Toner (@hlntnr), "A statement from Helen Toner and Tasha McCauley," statement on release of WilmerHale Report on investigation into Sam Altman's firing, X (formerly Twitter), March 9, 2024, https://x.com/hlntnr/status/1766269137628590185?s=20.

242 *The Biden administration persuaded a handful of leading*: The White House, "FACT SHEET: President Biden Issues Executive Order on Safe, Secure, and

Trustworthy Artificial Intelligence," October 30, 2023, https://www.white house.gov/briefing-room/statements-releases/2023/10/30/fact-sheet-president -biden-issues-executive-order-on-safe-secure-and-trustworthy-artificial-intel ligence/.

243 *AI Act, finalized*: European Council, "Artificial Intelligence Act: Council and Parliament Strike a Deal on the First Rules for AI in the World," European Council News, December 9, 2023, https://www.consilium.europa.eu/en/press /press-releases/2023/12/09/artificial-intelligence-act-council-and-parliament -strike-a-deal-on-the-first-worldwide-rules-for-ai/.

244 *At the first international AI Safety Summit*: "The Bletchley Declaration by Countries Attending the AI Safety Summit, 1–2 November 2023," GOV.UK, November 1, 2023, https://www.gov.uk/government/publications/ai-safety-sum mit-2023-the-bletchley-declaration/the-bletchley-declaration-by-countries -attending-the-ai-safety-summit-1-2-november-2023.

244 *Eighteen of these countries*: Dashveenjit Kaur, "First-of-Its-Kind International Agreement on AI Safety Introduced by the US and Allies," *Tech Wire Asia*, November 28, 2023, https://techwireasia.com/11/2023/what-agreement-on-inter national-agreement-on-ai-safety-has-been-reached-by-the-us-and-allies/.

244 *The International Atomic Energy Agency offers*: Robert Trager et al., "International Governance of Civilian AI: A Jurisdictional Certification Approach," Social Science Research Network, August 31, 2023, https://papers.ssrn.com/sol3 /papers.cfm?abstract_id=4579899.

INDEX

ABOUT THE AUTHOR

JEREMY KAHN is an award-winning journalist for *Fortune* magazine, where he covers artificial intelligence and other emerging technologies. He supervises a team of reporters who cover AI for the publication. He also writes *Fortune*'s weekly *Eye on AI* newsletter and cochairs its Brainstorm AI technology conferences. Previously, he wrote about technology, including AI, for Bloomberg. His writing on a range of subjects has appeared in *The New York Times*, *Newsweek*, *The Atlantic*, *Smithsonian* magazine, *The Boston Globe*, *The New Republic*, and *Slate*. He lived in and reported from India between 2007 and 2011. He has reported from Nepal, Sri Lanka, the Ivory Coast, Iraq, Venezuela, and most countries in Western Europe. He is a former managing editor of *The New Republic*. He holds degrees from the University of Pennsylvania and the London School of Economics. A native of Cleveland, Ohio, he now lives with his family in Oxford, England.